Processes of Urban
Stone Decay

Processes of Urban Stone Decay

Proceedings of **SWAPNET '95**
Stone Weathering and Atmospheric Pollution
Network Conference held in Belfast,
19–20 May 1995

EDITED BY

BERNARD J. SMITH and PATRICIA A. WARKE
School of Geosciences
The Queen's University of Belfast

© Donhead Publishing Ltd 1996

All rights reserved.
No part of this book may be reproduced or transmitted in
any form or by any means electronic, mechanical or
otherwise without prior permission from the publisher,
Donhead Publishing.

First published in the United Kingdom 1996 by
Donhead Publishing Ltd
28 Southdean Gardens
Wimbledon
London SW19 6NU
Tel: 0181-789 0138

ISBN 1 873394 20 9

A CIP catalogue record for this book is available from the
British Library.

Printed in Great Britain by SRP Ltd, Exeter

This book is produced using camera copy
provided by the editors and contributors.

Contents

(B) Physical Breakdown

SECTION THREE – ANALYSIS AND APPLICATION

(A) Analytical Methods

(B) Conservation Practice

Acknowledgements

The editors are indebted to The Queen's University of Belfast Publications Fund for a grant towards the publication costs of these proceedings. John Wiley & Sons Ltd kindly gave permission for the reproduction of Figure 1.5, The Building Research Establishment for Figure 15.3, English Heritage for Chapter 19, the Department of the Environment (NI) for Figures 22.1 and 22.3 and Faber & Faber for the quote from Coniston Flag by Norman Nicholson. Production of the volume in a coherent fashion would not have been possible without the assistance of Gill Alexander and Maura Pringle of the Cartographic Unit of the School of Geosciences at Queen's. More than anyone, however, we must thank Emer Carlin for her tireless efforts in preparing the manuscript and maintaining a sense of order and calm when the editors were approaching panic. Finally, special mention should be made of Jill Pearce and the editorial staff at Donhead Publishing, both for their technical input into this book and their long-term support of stone decay research and the interdisciplinary approach to building conservation.

Contributors

P.A.M. Basheer	School of the Built Environment, The Queen's University of Belfast, BT7 1NN, UK.
J. Beggan	School of the Built Environment, The Queen's University of Belfast, BT7 1NN, UK.
E. Bell	Willis Corroon Hinton, 80 Harcourt Street, Dublin 2, Ireland.
E. Brechet	School of Applied Sciences, The Robert Gordon University, St Andrew Street, Aberdeen, AB1 1HG, UK.
R. Butlin	Building Research Establishment, Garston, Watford, WD2 7JR, UK.
S. Caro Calatayud	University of La Rioja, Obispo Bustamante 3, 26001, Logroño, La Rioja, Spain.
T.P. Cooper	Director of Buildings, West Chapel, Trinity College, Dublin 2, Ireland.
S.J. Dews	School of Construction, Engineering and Technology, University of Wolverhampton, Wulfruna Street, Wolverhampton, WV1 1SB, UK.

P. Dowding	Botany Department, Trinity College, Dublin 2, Ireland.
A.P. Duffy	Carrig Conservation Engineering Ltd, 32 Westland Square, Pearse Street, Dublin 2, Ireland.
J. Fidler	English Heritage, 429 Oxford Street, London, W1R 2HD, UK.
G. Forsyth	School of Applied Sciences, The Robert Gordon University, St Andrew Street, Aberdeen, AB1 1HG, UK.
M.F. Fry	Environment Service, Historic Monuments and Buildings, Department of the Environment (NI), 5–33 Hill Street, Belfast, BT1 2LA, UK.
D.P. Halsey	School of Construction, Engineering and Technology, University of Wolverhampton, Wulfruna Street, Wolverhampton, WV1 1SB, UK.
F.C. Harris	School of Construction, Engineering and Technology, University of Wolverhampton, Wulfruna Street, Wolverhampton, WV1 1SB, UK.
R.J. Inkpen	Department of Geography, University of Portsmouth, Buckingham Building, Lion Terrace, Portsmouth, PO1 3HE, UK.
M.S. Jones	School of Surveying, The Robert Gordon University, Garthdee Road, Aberdeen, AB9 2QB, UK.
A.E. Long	School of the Built Environment, The Queen's University of Belfast, BT7 1NN, UK.
A. Martin	Environment Service, Historic Monuments and Buildings, Department of the Environment (NI), 5–33 Hill Street, Belfast, BT1 2LA, UK.
D.J. Mitchell	School of Construction, Engineering and Technology, University of Wolverhampton, Wulfruna Street, Wolverhampton, WV1 1SB, UK.
C.A. Moses	The Geography Laboratory, Arts Building, University of Sussex, Falmer, Brighton, BN1 9QN, UK.
W. Murphy	Department of Geology, University of Portsmouth, The Burnaby Building, Burnaby Road, Portsmouth, PO1 3QL, UK.
J.J. McAlister	School of Geosciences, The Queen's University of Belfast, BT7 1NN, UK.
J. MacDonald	School of Applied Sciences, The Robert Gordon University, St Andrew Street, Aberdeen, AB1 1HG, UK.
J.P. McGreevy	Conservation Laboratory, Ulster Museum, Botanic Gardens, Belfast, BT9 5AB, UK
D. McStay	School of Applied Sciences, The Robert Gordon University, St Andrew Street, Aberdeen, AB1 1HG, UK.

A. Nandiwada	Institute of Archaeology, University College London, 31–34 Gordon Square, London, WC1H 0PY, UK.
H.L. Neill	School of Geosciences, The Queen's University of Belfast, BT7 1NN, UK.
K.A. Nicholson	School of Applied Sciences, The Robert Gordon University, St Andrew Street, Aberdeen, AB1 1HG, UK.
P. O'Brien	Carrig Conservation Engineering Ltd, 32 Westland Square, Pearse Street, Dublin 2, Ireland.
S. Pavia Santamaria	Director of Buildings' Office, West Chapel, Trinity College, Dublin 2, Ireland.
D. Payne	Department of Geography, University of Portsmouth, Buckingham Building, Lion Terrace, Portsmouth, PO1 3HE, UK.
C.A. Price	Institute of Archaeology, University College London, 31–34 Gordon Square, London, WC1H 0PY, UK.
D.A. Robinson	School of African and Asian Studies, University of Sussex, Falmer, Brighton, BN1 9QN, UK.
A. Shelford	Department of Geography, University of Portsmouth, Buckingham Building, Lion Terrace, Portsmouth, PO1 3HE, UK.
B.J. Smith	School of Geosciences, The Queen's University of Belfast, BT7 1NN, UK.
J. Smith	Department of Geology, University of Portsmouth, The Burnaby Building, Burnaby Road, Portsmouth, PO1 3QL, UK.
A.V. Turkington	School of Geosciences, The Queen's University of Belfast, BT7 1NN, UK.
D.C.M. Urquhart	Faculty of Design, The Robert Gordon University, St Andrew Street, Aberdeen, AB1 1HG, UK.
R.D. Wakefield	School of Applied Sciences, The Robert Gordon University, St Andrew Street, AB1 1HG, UK.
P.A. Warke	School of Geosciences, The Queen's University of Belfast, BT7 1NN, UK
R.B.G. Williams	School of African and Asian Studies, University of Sussex, Falmer, Brighton, BN1 9QN, UK.
T. Yates	Building Research Establishment, Garston, Watford, WD2 7JR, UK.
M.E. Young	School of Surveying, The Robert Gordon University, Garthdee Road, Aberdeen, AB9 2QB, UK.

Foreword

It has taken quite some time for those interested in natural rock weathering and urban stone decay in the British Isles to come together to explore the benefits of interdisciplinary research. At an international level, there have been many meetings of conservators, architects and chemists, but only recently have geologists and geomorphologists begun to introduce a longer-term dimension into discussions. With the inception of the Stone Weathering and Atmospheric Pollution Network (SWAPNET) this integrative approach reached the UK. Initially, the stimulus for the group was provided by Professor Ron Cooke at University College London, where the first meetings of SWAPNET were held. These occasional meetings provided a forum for discussion and groups of people, generally unused to conversing outside of their own specialisms, began to talk and work together. Right from the very beginning it was clear that there was much to be learned from each other, and that on the topic of conservation of cultural heritage there was a common purpose. The International Conference on Stone Cleaning, held in Edinburgh in 1992, saw the first fruits of this collaborative work and a wide variety of specialists were able to present their work in a multidisciplinary setting (1).

Despite the increasing problems of group members finding the time to attend conferences, SWAPNET has continued to meet regularly and to provide a focus for the conservation of the built heritage of these Islands. Meetings have now moved out of London and, following excursions to Oxford and Portsmouth, the first 'overseas' visit was planned for Belfast in May of 1995. This move coincided with a feeling that a more formal element should be introduced to the gatherings, in the shape of short paper presentations, and that every effort should be made to broaden the appeal of the group even further. We were very pleased therefore, to welcome to Belfast not only colleagues from previous SWAPNET meetings, but also many new faces, particularly from Scotland and Ireland. In all, some forty participants attended the two days of papers, posters and field visits and they clearly demonstrated the growing interest in all aspects of stone decay. This breadth of interest is reflected in the contents of this book and the backgrounds of its contributors who range from geologists and engineers to conservators and architects. In bringing these people and their ideas together in one volume, it is hoped to expose the wider reaches of each discipline to the benefits of information exchange, especially between the academic and professional communities.

The central theme of the book investigates the underlying mechanisms and processes of stone decay. These have been a particular concern of geomorphologists and the first section on 'Theoretical Frameworks' highlights the difficulties of determining the long-term decay of structures from short-term studies of small areas of stonework. This is often because of the non-linear behaviour of stone when placed under stress (Chapter 1), confusion over the stone properties that constitute durability (Chapter 2) and/or the influence of past conditions on future decay through the so-called 'memory effect' (Chapter 3). These theoretical considerations are followed by a number of specific investigations into decay mechanisms. The papers can be conveniently grouped into two categories; those (including biological mechanisms) which deal predominantly with surface modification and those which, in conjunction with salts, operate below the surface to bring about physical disruption. None of these investigations would be possible without the availability of a comprehensive corpus of analytical methods. The third section therefore presents papers which cover techniques that range from ultrasonic testing of stone to direct measurements of permeability and surface roughness. Included in this section is an extensive review of chemical methods, which emphasises the importance of sample preparation and the need to understand fully the requirements of procedures before samples are collected. The final group of papers deals with conservation in practice, either as specific cases or investigations of the philosophies behind treatment. What is clear from both practical and theoretical considerations is that the only succesful conservation procedures will be those that are informed by an understanding of the decay processes that operate, their causes and controls. We trust that this book will show how interdisciplinary studies can advance this understanding.

(1) Webster, R.G.M. (ed.) (1992) *Stone cleaning and the nature, soiling and decay mechanisms of stone*. Donhead Publishing, London.

Brian Whalley,
Director,
School of Geosciences,
The Queen's University of Belfast

SECTION ONE

THEORETICAL FRAMEWORKS

*'Time sharpens its teeth for
everything – it devours body and
soul and stone.'*

Andrei Bely, Petersberg, (1916)

1 Scale problems in the interpretation of urban stone decay

B.J. SMITH

ABSTRACT

Many studies of stone decay are based upon experiments using small stone blocks and/or observations over a relatively short time period. This paper identifies the difficulties of extrapolating small scale, short-term data to the performance of large, complex structures over their design life. Problems arise because of the inherent complexity of stone decay systems and their indeterminate behaviour, the variable sensitivity to decay of the same stone types, random and systematic variations in external environmental controls and the different stress histories of individual stone blocks – the so-called 'memory effect'. It is proposed that this complexity is best understood within an open-systems framework allied to the recognition of decay as an inherently episodic phenomenon triggered by the crossing of stress/resistance thresholds. Application of these concepts permits construction of conceptual models of stone behaviour tailored to specific environmental conditions, stone properties and building morphologies.

INTRODUCTION

Research into stone decay in polluted urban environments is invariably restricted to studies of 2–3 years duration or less. Occasionally dated stonework can be used to synthesise behaviour over longer periods, but such studies have little control over factors that have contributed to decay and frequently little is known of environmental conditions over the complete life of a structure. Because of these difficulties much reliance is placed upon short-

Processes of Urban Stone Decay. Edited by B.J. Smith and P.A. Warke. © 1996 Donhead Publishing Ltd.

term field and laboratory studies under controlled conditions. Results from these studies must then be extrapolated to produce, for example, long-term estimates of decay rates or decay patterns. Coincident with the use of short-term studies, researchers have frequently used small samples(dimensions in cm) in their experiments. Results from these must then be expanded to characterise weathering features on complete buildings. These approaches have been formalised in standard durability procedures such as the 'sodium sulphate' test, where small cubes of stone are exposed to severe salt weathering conditions that frequently result in complete disintegration after only a few heating/moisture cycles.

The difficulties of extrapolating short-term, small-area data over long periods to cover large surfaces have long been recognised by earth scientists. Similar problems are encountered when, for example, landscapes have to be interpreted on the basis of short-term studies of individual landforms. Because of this, earth scientists have had to learn caution, both when assessing long-term rates of surface change and when ascribing patterns of change to particular processes (Smith, *et al.*, 1992). Before this can be done it is necessary to understand the nature of weathering and erosion systems, how they operate and the factors that control them.

THE NATURE OF STONE DECAY SYSTEMS

Stone decay is the product of interactions within a system which links together four variables.

1. Material

This includes chemical properties such as solubility and susceptibility to other weathering processes, physical properties such as strength (shear, compressive and tensional), porosity and permeability, and thermal properties including specific heat capacity, thermal conductivity and albedo. All of these influence the occurrence and rate of weathering processes but also vary themselves as weathering progresses.

2. Form

This refers to the surface morphology of the stone and ranges from surface roughness at a granular scale to weathering phenomena such as honeycombs and architectural detail. Changes in surface form can be created by weathering, but form can also control which weathering processes operate by, for example, sheltering areas from rainwash, creating shade or influencing airflow.

3. Process

Weathering processes provide the key to understanding stone decay, they are the instigators of change and the agents by which change is accomplished. In general the range of possible processes is controlled by environmental factors, but those which are effective are dictated by material properties. The situation is further complicated by the operation of positive and negative feedback mechanisms. Surface morphology, for example, can influence micro-environment which may in turn permit new processes to operate, and accelerate or curtail those already in action. Distinction must be made between processes and the mechanisms through which these operate. For example, the distinction has to be made between salt weathering as a process and crystal wedging as a mechanism.

4. Environment

This can be either independent or dependent upon the other three variables related to the scale of the investigation. The urban 'weathering environment' is a combination of meteorological variables (temperature and moisture regimes) and natural atmospheric constituents which include marine salts and anthropogenic contributions of atmospheric pollutants. This environment exists at the interface between stone and atmosphere and is therefore controlled by factors such as surface pore characteristics and morphology, albedo and other thermal properties. However, this micro-environment is constrained within limits set by local and regional climate.

Interactions between these variables are illustrated in Figure 1.1. This shows how change in one variable can influence another, either directly or through one or both of the other variables. The recognition of this system, its characteristics and interactions is essential for the understanding of stone decay. In reality, however, observation and measurement of all system components is unrealistic. In particular, the dynamics of weathering processes make them extremely difficult to study. Because of this it is common, especially in field sciences, for processes and mechanisms to be inferred from studies of form, materials and environment.

CONTROLS ON THE PREDICTION OF LONG-TERM STONE BEHAVIOUR

When attempting to predict long-term behaviour from short-term, small scale observations of stone decay there are seductive arguments for employing a strict uniformitarian approach. Within this it is assumed that the same processes will continue to operate at the same rate and that change will be gradual, uniform and progressive. This concept has lain at the heart of geological reasoning since the work of Hutton in the eighteenth century (see Thorn, 1988) and has the advantage that long-term change is the simple

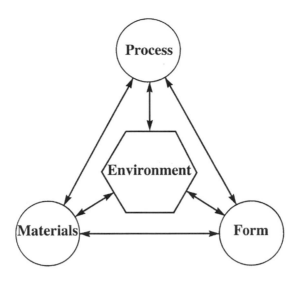

Figure 1.1 The stone decay system.

addition of short-term changes. Equally, large areas of stone would be assumed to weather at the same rate as small areas measured in field or laboratory trials. Common sense dictates, however, that these are unlikely scenarios as they assume a temporal and spatial uniformity at odds with environmental and material variability. Yet, it is common for natural processes to be considered in this way, be they soil erosion rates calculated from small 'erosion plots', evaporation rates inferred from small pans or weathering rates predicted from point data (Trudgill, *et al.*, 1989).

What follows is an attempt to identify reasons why the uniformitarian extrapolation of small scale studies can be inappropriate for studies of stone decay. Possible complicating factors are listed below.

Inherent complexity

Stone decay systems are inherently complex, with several processes and numerous mechanisms acting in parallel and/or sequence. There are multiple interactions, with frequent positive and negative feedbacks. Small changes in one variable often trigger complex responses within the system as a whole.

Indeterminacy

The principle of indeterminacy (e.g. Cooke and Doornkamp, 1990) holds for stone decay. Changing inputs into stone decay systems are accommodated or responded to in a variety of ways by adjustments between different sets of interdependent variables. The precise nature of the adjustment will vary from location to location. 'Any individual case, therefore, cannot be forecast or specified except in a statistical sense. The result of an individual case is indeterminate' (Leopold and Langbein, 1963, p. 189).

External variability

External conditions do not remain constant. Long-term pollution levels have varied and pollution constituents have changed as power sources are superseded and legislation curtails the use of certain fuels. There is also the possibility that climate as a whole will vary over the lifetime of a building and that local climate will change as surrounding buildings are constructed or demolished.

Uniqueness

Each stone decay system is a unique combination of specific stone properties, spatial geometry and the micro-environmental conditions it creates. Because of this, buildings, parts of buildings or even sections of the same wall exhibit a 'Variable Sensitivity to Change'. This concept was explored for natural geomorphic systems by Brunsden and Thornes (1979), who characterized sensitivity as a product of the spatial and temporal distribution of characteristic 'disturbing' and 'resisting' forces. The ratio of disturbing to resisting forces determines sensitivity to change; if this is > 1 the system is inherently unstable. If the ratio is < 1 the system is inherently stable and able to resist or absorb most impulses of change. This ratio can change as, for example, resistance is lowered through chemical alteration, or stress increases within stonework as salts accumulate. Eventually, therefore the 'threshold of change' can be breached, either by a gradual change in the ratio or triggered by an extreme stress as the ratio approaches unity. Variability in this ratio can be readily seen on any wall where individual stone blocks weather at different rates and via different mechanisms or where architectural detail creates a range of micro-climates and different stone responses.

Variable response

Responses of stone decay systems to a particular stress are not consistent. Certain responses may also be conditioned by a precise sequence of events. Stone may, for example, only become susceptible to salt weathering once solution has modified its pore size characteristics. Within this context it is important to note that all building stone carries an inheritance of chemical changes and physical stresses. This has been termed by some the 'Memory Effect'. Current rates of stone decay in many cities do not reflect present-

7

day pollution levels. This is illustrated by the failure of decay rates to dramatically decrease following introduction of clean-air legislation. This is frequently explained by invocation of a pollution legacy of interstitial salts that continue to facilitate decay. Similar effects are noted with solution loss. This could be because solution is predominantly controlled by factors such as rainfall amount, frequency or duration rather than high levels of atmospheric pollution. Alternatively, susceptibility to solution could in some way have been enhanced through previous weathering. Such effects also extend to prior physical weakening of the stone and/or chemical alteration. It is therefore possible to envisage a variety of 'inheritance-effects', some of which derive from pre-emplacement conditions while others may be related to post-emplacement conditions on the building face itself. These effects are investigated in detail in Chapter 3 of this book.

Small test blocks

In addition to time constraints upon stone decay experiments, spatial constraints frequently result in a reliance upon small test blocks. Dimensional disparity between these, building stones and ultimately buildings creates many problems of interpretation. These problems find parallels in natural weathering systems where they can be likened to differences between studies of how rock debris behaves as compared with, for example, the retreat of a cliff face. Extrapolation between these scales can never be a simple procedure because as scale boundaries are crossed the nature of variables changes. Those which at the scale of small blocks can be considered as independent, for example, the weathering environment, can assume a degree of dependence on large scale structures. The question of scale boundaries in natural systems was considered in a seminal paper by Schumm and Lichty (1965) and in the context of stone decay studies there are a number of specific problems that can be identified (Table 1.1).

Magnitude and frequency

Monitoring and sampling over short time periods cannot take into account the range of magnitudes and frequencies over which decay processes operate. Stonework is subject to a hierarchy of stresses from long-term changes to infrequent but potentially very damaging extreme events (Table 1.2). To truly understand long-term stone behaviour all of these effects should be accommodated. The significance of this is examined in the next section.

MAGNITUDE AND FREQUENCY IN STONE DECAY SYSTEMS

Most experimental studies of stone decay encompass the periodic time frame, with an emphasis upon diurnal cycling. Thus long-term trends and/or

- Small samples accentuate edge effects which, during temperature/moisture cycling, influence internal temperature and moisture regimes, salt distribution and, through these, patterns of chemical alteration and internal stress.

- Small blocks cannot replicate the confining pressures to which building stones are subject.

- Unless set into a larger surface, small blocks will alter air-flow around them which can influence, for example, particulate deposition.

- The thermal response of small blocks, because of heat storage capacity, must differ from large stone surfaces.

- Many studies, including standard durability tests, use free-standing blocks and ignore the fact that environmental cycling on most stonework takes place through one exposed face.

- Many decay features seen on buildings, for example, contour scales, have dimensions greater than those of test blocks. This is particularly applicable to mechanical breakdown, but solution rates are also influenced by the length of stone surface over which runoff flows.

Table 1.1 Scale problems encountered by the use of small test blocks in experiments and durability tests.

Secular (long-term variations)	• Climatic change • Pollution trends • Gradual chemical alteration • Gradual accumulation of pollutants • Biological colonisation
Periodic	• Seasonal rainfall and temperature variations. • Diurnal temperature and humidity variations • Seasonal pollution variations • Diurnal pollution variations • Seasonal biological growth/decline
Effectively random	• Weather systems • Rain within weather systems • Short-term temperature variations (for example, cloud cover variability)
Catastrophic	• Severe frosts • Stone cleaning • Clean-air legislation

Table 1.2 Examples of temporal variations in factors that can influence stone decay.

effectively random events of differing magnitudes have tended to be ignored. The cumulative effects of these stresses is to produce natural patterns of decay that are characterised by periods of quiescence interspersed with episodes of relatively rapid and possibly catastrophic change. Quiescence may be characterised by short-term variability but no long-term change (Figure 1.2A) or, more characteristically, there will be an underlying trend of stone loss or pollution accumulation about which conditions oscillate (Figure 1.2B). Quiescence is interrupted when a threshold of change is breached disrupting the previous equilibrium between the chemical and/or physical strength of the stone and the stresses to which it is subject. This is represented in Figure 1.3, which illustrates the situations under which thresholds can be breached within the context of the variations listed in Table 1.2. Change on a stone surface is a response to either an external (exogenetic) trigger or the breaching of an internal threshold by the gradual accumulation of stress, the repetition of small magnitude stress events leading to fatigue failure or simply by the gradual reduction in material strength (Schumm, 1979). Incorporation of threshold concepts into decay models creates possibilities for alternative equilibrium conditions within stone decay systems (Figure 1.2C, D and E). Some systems characteristically experience static equilibrium in which any abnormal stress triggers a dramatic change to a new static equilibrium (1.2C). More commonly, breaching of thresholds will mark the transition between steady states (1.2D) or dynamic equilibrium conditions (1.2E).

The episodic change concept particularly applies to mechanical disruption of stone by salt weathering. It can, however, also be applied to solution loss. Solution is episodic, in that it occurs in response to rainfall and is interspersed with periods of surface alteration/sulphation in response to dry or occult deposition which might enhance solution during the next storm. Gradual solution may also remove calcareous cements which can lead to episodic removal of individual grains or crystals.

System responses to increased stress may not be immediate and stonework may absorb change before it eventually reacts. This period, between the stimulus for change and system response, is the 'reaction time' (Figure 1.4) and is followed by a period ('relaxation time') during which morphology and materials adjust to changed conditions. Brunsden (1980) referred to this as 'Transient Form Time'. Within the life of a building stone, transient forms may occupy a relatively short period compared to characteristic forms associated with conditions of dynamic equilibrium. At any one time, therefore, few individual stones in a wall may exhibit transient (active) characteristics, while most are in dynamic equilibrium. Because of this it is tempting to concentrate upon examination of dynamic equilibrium conditions when studying stone decay, at the expense of transient conditions that are rare, but during which most decay may be accomplished. Exceptions to this balance between transient and characteristic forms occur when positive feedback is initiated during rapid change. Examples include already mentioned situations where weathering creates a surface morphology which in turn creates conditions conducive to further decay (Figure 1.4). Negative

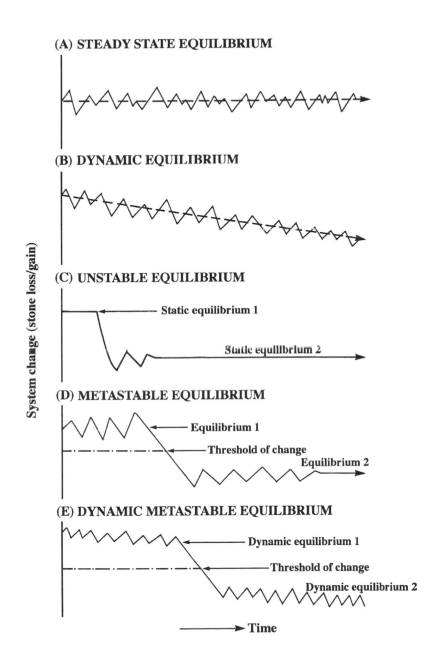

Figure 1.2 Equilibrium conditions experienced by stone decay systems (adapted from Chorley and Kennedy (1971) and White, *et al.*, (1993)).

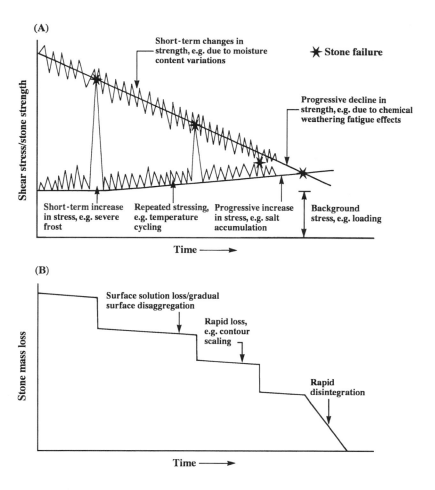

Figure 1.3 (A) Stone strength/stress relationships during decay and conditions when decay thresholds are breached. (B) Mass loss from stonework during decay (Smith, *et al.*, 1992).

feedback whereby, for example, removal of a weakened surface exposes previously unweathered substrate, will encourage stabilisation and a return to dynamic equilibrium.

DISCUSSION: THE APPLICATION OF THRESHOLD CONCEPTS TO STONE DECAY

Prediction of stone decay is extremely difficult, as it depends upon innumerable combinations between environmental conditions, human impacts

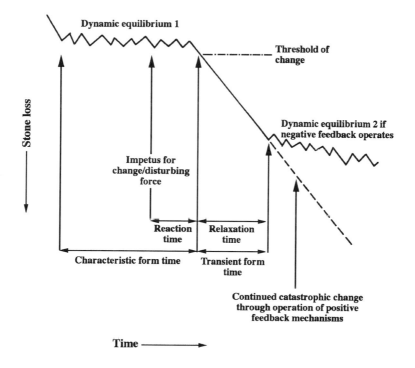

Figure 1.4 Episodic change in a stone decay system showing how, once rapid change is triggered by crossing of stress/strength thresholds it can resume a dynamic equilibrium or continue rapid decay.

and original and modified stone characteristics. From initial conditions of 'fresh stone' (which will already contain inherited characteristics) numerous subsequent decay routes can be envisaged. It is extremely unlikely that rates and patterns of decay will remain constant over the lifetime of stonework. Initial surface morphologies will be succeeded by others, sometimes unrelated to each other, but frequently as stages within preconditioned sequences. Elucidation of these sequences can be approached in a number of ways. Firstly, through laboratory simulations. This can be difficult because of scale problems, but also very useful because of the control that can be exerted over causative factors. Secondly, mathematical/statistical simulations may be used. These hold great potential, but are constrained by a poor knowledge of process and feedback and hampered by the variety of site/environmental conditions. Thirdly, ergodic principles may be applied, in which decay phenomena from different locations of different age are examined and arranged into possible decay sequences. Lastly, conceptual models of decay sequences could be formulated related to possible environmental conditions, stone properties and decay processes.

Clearly, these strategies are interrelated, for example, information on actual decay phenomena can be used in the design and confirmation of experiments and models. Of the four approaches the last is clearly the most subjective, but equally, with careful consideration of the factors involved it could produce a more profound understanding of stone decay. It is axiomatic that experienced stone masons are invariably the best predictors of stone durability and behaviour. What is proposed is in effect a systematic equivalent of this process. To illustrate this approach a number of hypothetical decay sequences are presented. Figure 1.5 shows possible pathways for a non-calcareous sandstone in a polluted environment taken from Smith *et al.* (1994). The time scale is neither uniform nor directly comparable between stone types, but it does show how different routes can be related to concepts of thresholds, equilibrium and feedback described in preceding sections. For this particular stone type the role of surface alteration is emphasised in the creation of case-hardened layers and black, depositional crusts. These can lead to long periods of apparent stability, but often at the expense of an internal weakening of the stone that leads to rapid, progressive decay once protective layers are breached or removed during cleaning. Such projections are not restricted to non-calcareous stone and Figure 1.6 presents sequences for a porous limestone such as Portland Stone in which solution processes play an important part. For these stones periods of apparent inactivity are better described as dynamic equilibrium during which there is a gradual, though episodic, loss of material by solution. Equilibrium can, however, still be disrupted by catastrophic failure due to blistering and scaling under suitable conditions of porosity and salt availability that are not unique to calcareous materials. In Figure 1.6 a distinction is drawn between exposed stonework and that sheltered from rainwash. This is based upon the observation that salt retention and the significance of dry and occult deposition in sheltered areas must contrast with the predominance of solution loss on exposed surfaces. This is not to say that salts and other pollutants cannot accumulate upon exposed surfaces. Pollution retention or removal depends upon the balance between input and output through, for example, rainwash. In highly polluted environments therefore it is possible to see complete buildings covered in black crusts or scabs (Smith, *et al.*, 1993). If the rate of presentation of pollutants to the stone surface decreases or if rainwash increases it is possible that crusts would be gradually removed from exposed surfaces. In this way effective clean air legislation could result in the selective self-cleaning of buildings.

The sequences shown are not prescriptive, as, for example, surface solution loss need not be a precursor to salt-induced decay. Similarly, patterns of decay can be repeated many times and for individual stones thresholds of rapid decay may never be breached during the lifetime of a structure as a whole. Within individual decay patterns, however, there may, as previously noted be essential pre-requisites. In non-calcareous sandstones, for example, gypsum can migrate into stonework beneath a black crust (Smith, *et al.*, 1994). If the black crust is breached, environmental cycling of this interstitial salt can lead to rapid decay through granular disaggregation and/or multiple flaking. Similarly, changes in pore characteristics conse-

14

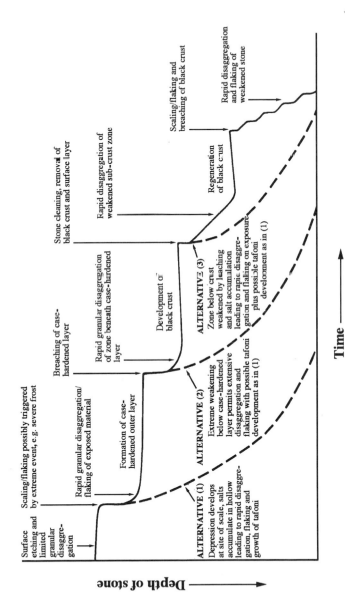

Figure 1.5 Hypothetical decay sequences observed on non-calcareous quartz sandstones (Smith, *et al.*, 1994), reproduced with permission of J. Wiley & Sons Ltd.

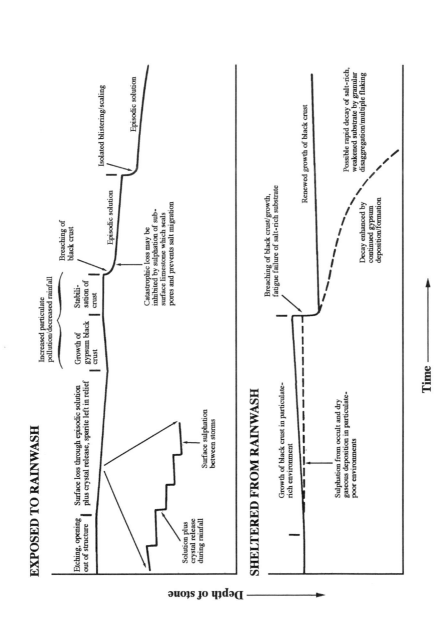

Figure 1.6 Hypothetical decay patterns on porous limestones in a polluted environment.

quent upon solution and redeposition (for example, an increase in microporosity) may increase susceptibility to salt weathering in stones such as Portland limestone.

CONCLUSIONS

The hypothetical decay sequences shown illustrate the dangers of a simple extrapolation of decay rates measured over short periods to explain long-term stone behaviour. Measurements taken during a period of dynamic or steady state equilibrium could result in considerable overestimates of durability. Observations during episodes of rapid change, or based upon extreme durability tests, could conversely underestimate durability. Especially, in the latter case, if threshold conditions are rarely if ever breached under natural conditions or if, as with stones such as marble, a lack of porosity severely limits susceptibility to salt-induced decay. Recognition that decay can proceed episodically in response to a range of external stimuli or through the crossing of internal thresholds must also question the commonly made assumption that accelerated decay has to be due to increased atmospheric pollution. Conversely, a failure to detect any overt sign of surface change cannot be taken as evidence that no damage in the form of internal modification or stress accumulation has taken place.

The need to be more circumspect in the prediction of long-term change in a particular stone block is paralleled by problems in extrapolating the behaviour of a small area or block of stone over, for example, the complex façade of a building. In particular, Table 1.1 has identified specific problems associated with the use of small test blocks in durability tests. These range from an accentuation of edge effects and an absence of confining pressures to the inability to replicate decay features found on buildings that are larger than the test blocks. The question of durability and durability testing is examined in detail in the following chapter.

Acknowledgements

Research for this chapter was carried out as part of a Science, Technology and Environmental Protection project for the European Community – Number CT90 0107 on the Conservation of Historic Buildings, Monuments and associated Cultural Heritage.

References

Brunsden, D. (1980) Applicable models of long-term landform evolution. *Zeitschrift für Geomorphologie Suppl.* **36**: 16–26.
Brunsden, D. and Thornes, J.B. (1979) Landscape sensitivity and change: a review. *Transactions, Institute of British Geographers* **4**: 463–484.

Chorley, R.J. and Kennedy, B.A. (1974) *Physical Geography, a systems approach.* Prentice Hall, London.

Cooke, R.U. and Doornkamp, J.C. (1990) *Geomorphology in Environmental Management* (2nd edn). OUP, Oxford.

Leopold, L.B. and Langbein, W.B. (1963) Association and indeterminacy in geomorphology. In C.C. Albritton (ed.) *The Fabric of Geology.* Addison-Wesley, Reading, pp. 184–192.

Schumm, S.A. (1979) Geomorphic thresholds, the concept and its applications. *Transactions, Institute of British Geographers* **4**: 485–515.

Schumm, S.A. and Lichty, R.W. (1965) Time space and causality in geomorphology. *American Journal of Science* **263**: 110–119.

Smith, B.J., Magee, R.W. and Whalley, W.B. (1993) Decay of granite in a polluted environment: Budapest. In M.A.V. Hernández, *et al.*, (ed.) *Alteración de Granitas y Rocas Afinas.* C.S.I.S., Salamanca, pp. 159–162.

Smith, B.J., Magee, R.W. and Whalley, W.B. (1994) Breakdown patterns of quartz sandstone in a polluted urban environment: Belfast, N. Ireland. In D.A. Robinson, and R.B.G. Williams (eds) *Rock Weathering and Landform Evolution.* J. Wiley & Sons, Chichester, pp. 131–150.

Smith, B.J., Whalley, W.B. and Magee, R.W. (1992) Assessment of building stone decay: a geomorphological approach. In R.G.M. Webster (ed.) *Stone Cleaning.* Donhead Publishing, London, pp. 249–257.

Thorn, C.E. (1988) *Introduction to Theoretical Geomorphology.* Unwin Hyman, London.

Trudgill, S.T., Viles, H.A., Inkpen, R.J. and Cooke, R.U. (1989) Remeasurement of weathering rates, St Paul's Cathedral, London. *Earth Surface Processes and Landforms* **14**: 175–198.

White, I.D., Mottershead, D.N. and Harrison, S.J. (1992) *Environmental Systems* (2nd edn). Chapman & Hall, London.

Contact address
School of Geosciences
The Queen's University Belfast
Belfast
BT7 1NN
United Kingdom

2 Stone durability

A.V. TURKINGTON

ABSTRACT

'Durability' is a vague and ambiguous term which has been allocated diverse definitions from research workers in different fields. Assessment of durability is a major contemporary issue, as increasing numbers of stone structures, valued for historical or cultural importance, are under conservation or preservation orders. To improve understanding of stone durability there must first be a more rigorous and universal definition of the term. It is suggested that a systems approach provides a framework for studies of stone durability. Deterioration of stone is a function of environmental conditions, weathering processes and material properties of the stone. Thus, the weathering system as a whole dictates the rate and nature of stone decay. This holistic approach may be the key to improved prediction of stone durability.

INTRODUCTION

Weathering is a natural phenomenon that has occurred since stone was formed and will continue as long as stone exists. Change through ageing is inevitable, but deterioration is defined as those changes that are regarded as undesirable. The rate and nature of this deterioration is in turn a function of the 'durability' of the stone. Although natural weathering has long been acknowledged the decay of building stone has only recently become a major issue. This is a consequence of the recognition by the construction and scientific communities of the threats which face many structures, due to the acceleration of stone decay in recent decades (Fitzner, 1990). This is despite the fact that atmospheric pollutants, acid rain and stone decay are phenom-

Processes of Urban Stone Decay. Edited by B.J. Smith and P.A. Warke. © 1996 Donhead Publishing Ltd.

ena that have been documented since the seventeenth century (Camuffo, 1992).

Building stone decay, unlike weathering of natural rock outcrops and debris, has a variety of cultural and financial implications, although the processes of deterioration are broadly similar. Natural stone has always been widely used as a construction material and much of our knowledge of civilisation from ancient through historic times is based on artifacts which have been written on, sculpted from or built of stone. Not only is stone the material of buildings, it also comprises many important works of art; Rodrigues (1989) emphasises the social significance of building stone, describing it as a 'culture-bearing material'. For historical, social, aesthetic or scientific reasons, stone structures judged to be heritage are kept intact for as long as possible. Yet such artifacts are inevitably marked by age and decay. This can have positive as well as negative implications. Visible marks of time may make buildings evocative (Lowenthal, 1994), but the benefits of decay diminish over time and, beyond some critical point, stone decay becomes disfiguring and may threaten the existence of the entire structure.

To minimise the rates of deterioration, a prerequisite must be the ability to predict the durability of different materials. The apparently changeable durability of stone monuments must be documented and the weathering damage evaluated in order to determine the causal factors involved in deterioration, and apply this knowledge to the implementation of successful preservation measures. The problem of defining stone durability is also relevant to the contemporary building industry since resistance to weathering has become an important criterion for selecting stone in conjunction with architectural, construction, workability, financial and artistic requirements. Because builders and designers are faced with a bewildering choice of materials there is a need, therefore, to clarify the concept of durability, which the Building Research Establishment (1989) describes as 'difficult to define and even more difficult to measure'.

CONCEPTS OF DURABILITY

Stone durability is inextricably bound up with weathering processes and products and could be considered to represent the degree of resistance of stone to weathering or deterioration. Rodrigues (1989) distinguishes between natural rock weathering studies and studies of building stone decay, suggesting that the latter is a particular application of the more general idea of rock weathering to the specific conditions of man-made constructions. The extension of studies of natural weathering processes to studies of their effects on building stone, combined with pollution-related degradation, has been a logical progression of many geomorphologists towards a more practical application of their work. However, geomorphologists are not the only group interested in stone durability in urban environments. Engineers and researchers involved in the building industry are also concerned with weathering processes that tarnish or destroy natural and artificial building materials and with predicting the durability of materials and preventing their decay (Cooke and Doornkamp, 1990). Cross-fertilisation of ideas between the interested groups is surprisingly limited and there is clearly scope for collaboration between disciplines to improve studies of stone durability, not least in defining the term which has been allotted a diverse assortment of meanings.

'Durability' is an entrenched term, which Thorn (1988) describes as 'inadequately defined', embracing an uncertain number of individual weathering processes and stone properties. This uncertainty has persisted until the idea of durability embodies many separate ideas, making lucid definition and precise scientific study difficult. The term durability derives from the Latin word 'durabilis', which translates to mean 'lasting'; hence stone durability indicates the resistance of the material to weakening or deterioration over time. Consequently, the concept of durability could be considered to be synonymous with the nature and rate of the weathering processes on exposed rock, the alteration of the material and the creation of secondary weathering products. Thus, in attempting to define the factors involved in determining durability, the causal factors of the weathering system must be understood.

The consensus among workers in the building industry is that durability of natural stone is influenced mainly by the physical and chemical properties of the stone, exemplified by the claim of the Building Research Establishment (1984) that the internal structure of the stone, together with the nature of the cementing material, dictates durability. In 1967, Richardson suggested that the durability of building stones depends on their porosity, or rather the relationship between the porosity and the true microporosity, a ratio which he named the 'durability factor'. This school of thought postulates that the resistance of any stone to weathering processes, instigated by environmental and pollution-related stresses, is dictated solely by the inherent properties of the rock. More recent work on the decay of building materials (Ashurst, 1988; Knöfel, 1991) continues to support this argument, in spite of widespread knowledge of the fact that stones with closely similar structural and mineralogical characteristics can exhibit a diversity of behaviour under different environmental regimes (Frohnsdorff and Masters, 1980; Tombach, 1982). Although it is indisputable that the nature of the environment, particularly climatic and anthropogenic influences, has a major effect on the decay of building stone, many building research workers still shy away from this aspect, perhaps because of its complexity. Cooke and Doornkamp (1990) argue that only at a local scale is it possible to study precisely the unique relationships between the complex of variables that determine specific weathering phenomena. This is particularly the case for microscale features which are most likely to respond to contemporary conditions and processes. Indeed, on buildings the dominance of local variables can be seen very clearly, where architectural detail creates a range of microclimates and where individual stone blocks invariably weather at different rates and by different processes. Lacy (1977) concedes that no index of cli-

21

mate can be devised that will serve as an effective measure of the behaviour of complex structures such as buildings.

While largely ignoring the role played by environmental conditions and their variability, some engineers and building research workers have concentrated on a third major factor included in the concept of durability: the requirements the stone must meet. The length of time during which the stone fulfils these requirements is symptomatic of its durability. Carruthers (1980) uses the term 'performance with time' to convey this notion, which is defined as the ability of a building component to maintain its initial performance to an acceptable extent at an acceptable cost. Durability is viewed as one influence on performance with time, and is considered to be a constant property representing cumulatively the intrinsic properties of the stone. Alternatively, Nireki (1980) rejects the narrower definition of durability, suggesting that it cannot be a single property or quality. Durability testing, Nireki (1980) suggests, should be conducted as 'performance evaluation', which identifies the performance over time of an object, and compares this to performance requirements.

One engineer who encompassed a range of aspects of building stone durability in his examination is Garden (1980), who states that no material is of itself durable or non-durable, but that it is the interaction of environment and materials that determines durability. Garden (1980) also states, more specifically, that durability of a material cannot be considered rationally except in the context of that material in service and of the environment in which it must function. Since the position of the stone in the building determines durability, the idea of the use of stone could be extended, as not only does the situation of stone in a building influence its durability (through variations in microclimate), but the employment of stone dictates the performance requirements initially designated by the designer or construction worker. For example, the degree of weathering or deterioration which may be tolerated on an ashlar wall is very different from that on intricately sculpted ornamental stone. Equally, some buildings or monuments may have greater importance placed on them for historical, cultural, social or artistic reasons, so their deterioration is of much greater consequence. Therefore, durability can only be defined in the light of the perception of what the performance requirements should be. This perception may be very subjective, particularly with respect to aesthetic and artistic considerations, but even simple service life requirements are based on society's ideals of economic and financial returns. The value of stone may be defined on many different bases, so durability of building stone cannot be considered as merely the product of physical, chemical and biological processes.

A GEOMORPHOLOGICAL DIMENSION

Workers in the building industry use natural stone as their raw material; it is a resource which must be put to optimum use in order to achieve maximum returns, be they financial, cultural, social, artistic or otherwise, and a resource which must also be preserved for the same reasons. Thus, their interest in stone durability is fuelled by those considerations.

Geomorphologists, however, are concerned with less practical objectives, seeking primarily for a fuller understanding of processes and the evolution of landforms, from macro- to micro-scales. However, groups interested in stone decay and rock weathering converge in the aim of predicting the rate and nature of deterioration of any material in any location (Boyd, 1980). Not surprisingly, therefore, broadly similar themes emerge when the definitions of durability within construction and geomorphological works are compared.

Rodrigues (1989) suggested that stone durability depends on the mineral components of rock, particularly their dimensions and mechanical properties. This limited definition misrepresents an understanding of the generally accepted theory of rock weathering, namely that mechanisms and rates of decay are dependent on both intrinsic and extrinsic factors. Rodrigues (1989) may have chosen to use the term durability to be synonymous with rock properties, but does contend that stone decay is a 'continuous and inexorable process. . . that varies between stones and between environments'. Mirwald and Zaumaizig (1986) suggest that such a limited approach to stone durability still exists among much geomorphological work, labelling it the 'genetic view', which proposes that intrinsic stone properties can be used to estimate durability. However, durability is more usefully defined as 'weatherability', which includes climatic and pollution related factors. Rock weathering is influenced by lithological and mineralogical rock properties and environmental factors; this theory is concisely explained by Dibb, *et al.* (1983), who consider the overall durability of a rock type to be the combination of two opposed forces: the disruptive forces of the decay processes, and the cohesive forces of the rock. Geomorphologists who have concentrated on building stone have also incorporated the notion of the application of the stone playing an important role. Fitzner (1990), in a discussion of his classification of weathering forms, emphasises that assessment of weathering damage depends on the type of building element that has been affected, according to its use. Given the great variation in decay over small spatial scales, and the knowledge that weathering *in situ* can never be absolutely defined or replicated, a more appropriate view may be that offered by Litvan (1980), who advocates that a statement of durability is only meaningful in the context of specific geographical areas and particular applications.

Due to the wide scope of weathering studies, the majority of work published on this subject is concerned with specific weathering forms or specific weathering processes in action; it is relatively uncommon for geomorphologists in this field to provide an integrated study of all aspects of durability. This reductionist approach to weathering studies, while failing to clarify the concept of durability, has undoubtedly been fertile and instructive in the search for a more complete understanding of the effects of weathering processes in a range of environments. Trofimov and Phillips (1992) stated that the ultimate goal of geomorphology is prediction. The prediction of the behaviour of weathering systems is not, however, only of scientific value;

the application of prognosis to practical problems of stone decay is also important. Unfortunately, prediction of stone response to environmental stresses, the foretelling of future evolution and outcomes, is rarely possible; rather it is more feasible to attempt to forecast stone response, by estimating or calculating possible, likely or desired outcomes.

Within this context, weathering processes are perceived as degenerative, or as giving rise to cumulative degenerative effects on stone structures, but the exact nature and rate of degradation is highly variable. Thus, durability could be indicated by comparing rates of overall deterioration against time, under real or standard conditions. Figure 2.1 illustrates possible variations in degradation rates. Difficulties arise in forecasting these curves because stone decay is frequently the result of interactions between environmental factors. Line 1 represents no deterioration over time, whereas line 2 represents a regular decrease in durability, which allows the forecast of the time at which 'performance' of the stone will fall below acceptable levels. Line 3 indicates the quality of stone decreasing asymptomatically,

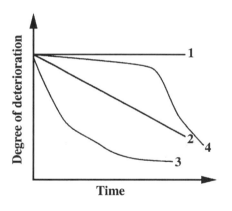

Figure 2.1 Possible patterns in stone decay rates (modified from Orna, *et al.*,1994).

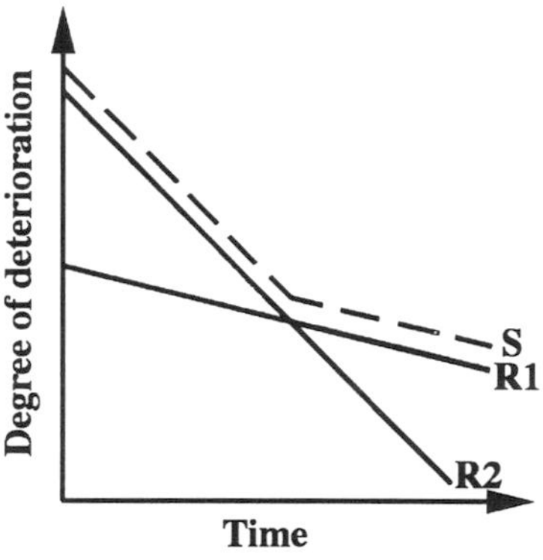

Figure 2.2 The overall decay rate for stone (S) under two environmental stresses (R1 & R2) acting simultaneously (from an idea by Brimblecombe, 1994).

but line 4 presents the thorniest problem for durability prediction, where it is essential to know when the sudden and rapid deterioration will occur. Figure 2.2 depicts the influence on total stone response of the effect of two environmental stresses acting simultaneously.

These graphs demonstrate the danger of assuming uniformitarianism in stone decay, as the durability scale of stone is not a simple linear time-related process. As demonstrated in Chapter 1 of this book (Figure 1.1), recognition of the components of the 'weathering system' with their many negative and positive feedbacks, has lead to the adoption of a systems-oriented approach to many geomorphological studies. This emphasises interactions between landscape elements, particularly the dynamic behaviour of phenomena, and the mutual adjustment of landforms, materials, processes and environmental controls (Brunsden and Thornes, 1979).

Prediction of stone response to environmental conditions depends on an almost infinite number of combinations of stone characteristics, uses and locations, environmental conditions and human impacts; indeed it could be argued that each geomorphological system is unique. No geomorphologist would deny the uniqueness of specific places, or the dependence on time and space of specific landscape phenomena, but there can be no science of singularities. The study of systems at least implicitly presupposes some level of universality, and accepts that there are some universal, or widely applicable, laws or principles which govern the behaviour of classes of systems independently of space and time. Conceptual models, then, comprise the basis for functional geomorphic prediction, but methodologies for assessment of durability have not yet been conducted within the framework of a systems approach.

STRATEGIES FOR PREDICTING DURABILITY

Methods of predicting durability employed by engineers and those working within the building industry have remained somewhat entrenched over the past few decades. Since the first salt crystallisation test performed by Brard (1828) and subsequently modified by Schaffer (1932), assessment of durability has focused almost exclusively on materials testing but also include laboratory-based weathering simulation studies, field exposure trials and the characterisation and classification of existing weathering features.

Materials testing

There exists a wide selection of tests for stone materials; the most commonly used methods are discussed by Ashurst and Dimes (1977). Tests, such as the strength of stone, often used by engineers, give no indication of potential resistance to weathering; similarly, examination of chemical composition may be uninformative in the context of durability assessment. The most acceptable test for assessing the weathering resistance of stone is viewed to be, among those involved in materials testing, the sodium sulphate crystallisation test. In spite of its widespread use, there are problems in the interpretation of the results of this test as they depend on the concentration of the saline solution, the temperature of the solution, drying conditions and the duration of the immersion of the specimen in the salt solution (Price, 1978). A lack of standardisation in methodology between those practising the test throws doubt on the validity of even comparative as well as quantitative results; seemingly minor variations of the test can completely reverse the ranking order of stones in terms of their durability (Bell, 1990).

Weathering simulation studies

Within geomorphological studies of weathering, much of our knowledge about processes, particularly the operation of processes in hostile environments, is derived from an experimental approach based on laboratory simulation of weathering. These simulation experiments are also a type of accelerated ageing test. Whereas the methods of materials testing employed by engineers evaluate durability under artificial conditions, regardless of the relationship between the ageing conditions and in-use conditions, simulation experiments give consideration to this relationship, aiming for close correlations between environmental and controlled laboratory conditions, particularly through the use of environmental chambers. Meteorological data cannot represent conditions on all exposed rock outcrops or buildings; for example, local variations in altitude, aspect, orientation and cloud cover control actual rock temperatures, as do intrinsic rock properties such as albedo, specific heat capacity and thermal conductivity (McGreevy, 1985).

Although the environmental regimes used in the experiments are intended to correlate with those measured in natural and urban environments, the 'rate determining step' (Johnson, *et al.*, 1990), the ratio of periods of time that result in the same level of degradation between natural and laboratory conditions, may be altered through the acceleration of weathering processes. A further problem in attempting to predict stone durability on the basis of an experimental approach lies in the inheritance of stress by exposed stone, which is extremely difficult to estimate, measure or recreate artificially (Warke and Smith, 1994). Weathering features on rock in natural environments result from the cumulative effects of weathering processes often over long periods, and may be products of processes no longer active. Building stone can also inherit weaknesses or susceptibilities to particular degradation processes from previous exposure conditions, and pre-emplacement treatment, for example, the quarrying methods used (see Chapter 3).

Exposure trials

Natural exposure tests offer an alternative method of assessing rock durability by subjecting 'fresh' or weathered stone specimens to real exposure conditions. This allows monitoring of short-term change as 'fresh' stone decays under present-day environmental conditions and could promote a better understanding of the nature and rates of the weathering processes (Smith, *et al.*, 1994). Varying results are obtained, related to the height, aspect and orientation of specimens, and variations in the material properties of individual blocks (Nireki, 1980). However, by taking account of such variations in their design, exposure tests can reveal the effects of dissimilarities in microclimatic regime on the operation of weathering processes. Interpretation of exposure trials can present problems similar to those encountered in interpreting the results of laboratory-based simulation experiments. Not least is the problem of scale and questions of how weathering features on small-scale specimens can be related to features on large buildings and the micro-environments these features create (McGreevy and Smith, 1982). Nevertheless, an examination of the combined effects of weathering mechanisms within complex urban and natural environments is crucial to an accurate assessment of stone durability. Exposure trials could therefore have a significant role to play in bridging the gap between laboratory-based and building-based studies.

Characterisation and classification of weathering features

In addition to field- and laboratory-based trials, relative rock durability has frequently been ascertained by geomorphologists using traditional methods of field surveying. This comprises the recognition, measurement, characterisation and classification of weathering features and products on natural rock outcrops and, more recently, on building stone. Examination of weathering features in different locations and on material of different ages can help to discern the rate and nature of past weathering processes on the basis of ergodic principles. This may then be used in an attempt to forecast the future course of rock deterioration within contemporary weathering environments (Turkington, 1993). There exists, however, a wide disparity between the range of weathering features observed by workers in the field and the nature of rock breakdown achieved in laboratory simulation experiments or materials testing, which predominantly result in granular disintegration.

CONCLUSIONS

Stone durability is essentially the resistance of stone to deterioration and weakening by weathering processes over a period of time. Attempts to predict stone durability predominantly rely on short-term, small-scale studies; clearly uniformitarian extrapolation of such studies is inappropriate. These 'special case forecasts', which are common in geomorphology and in weathering studies, are specific to particular locations, areas and phenomena, and therefore incorporate space-specific and time-specific conditions. Such studies have limited applicability to other locations and situations, so it is necessary to adjust them to achieve acceptable reliability. One way to accomplish this could be through adoption of a systems-oriented approach. The range of approaches to studies of stone durability which have been outlined must be integrated in order to achieve a more complete understanding of the nature and assessment of the durability of natural stone. This integration should be at a number of levels.

1. The effects of combinations of processes, and the interactions between them, must be investigated – physical, chemical and biological – as stone durability is a response to weathering in its entirety.

2. The influence of regional environmental parameters must be integrated with the effects of variations in micro-environmental regimes.

3. The action of contemporary weathering processes should be combined with inherited weaknesses or alteration of stone derived from past processes (see Chapter 3).

4. The results of simulation experiments, exposure trials and field studies must be compared to ensure their representativeness.

5. Work on stone durability by geomorphologists, workers in the building industry and engineers must be integrated to allow cross-fertilisation of ideas, promotion of a more complete understanding of decay processes, and a rationalisation of durability studies.

6. In order to forecast rates and nature of stone deterioration, the weathering system must be examined in its entirety, because the features of the system derive from both the characteristics of individual elements and the relations between them. This holistic approach is essential if stone durability is ever to be successfully predicted for the enormous variety of stone available to builders and the array of situations into which these stones are placed.

Acknowledgements

Thanks must go to Dr B.J. Smith for advice concerning this research, and Prof. R.W. Young for helpful comments on an early draft of this paper. This research is funded by the Department of Education, Northern Ireland.

References

Ashurst, J. (1988) Conserving stone. *Architecture Journal Renovation Supplement*, pp. 36–37.

Ashurst, J. and Dimes, F.G. (1977) *Stone in Building*. Architectural Press, London.

Bell, A. (1990) The durability of natural sandstone: Scrabo sandstone. Unpublished seminar paper, School of Geosciences, The Queen's University of Belfast.

Boyd, D. W. (1980) Weather and the deterioration of building materials. In P.J. Sereda and G.G. Litvan (eds) *Durability of Building Materials and*

Components. ASTM STP 691, pp. 145–156.

Brard, — (1828) On the method proposed by Mr Brard for the immediate detection of stones unable to resist the action of frost. Héricart de Thury, *Annales de Chimie et de Physique* **38**: 160–192.

BRE (1984) *Decay and conservation of stone masonry.* BRE Digest 177.

BRE (1989) *The selection of natural building stone.* BRE Digest 269.

Brimblecombe, P. (1994) The balance of environmental factors attacking artifacts. In W.E. Krumbein, P. Brimblecombe, D.E. Cosgrove and S. Staniforth (eds) *Durability and Change: The science, responsibility and cost of sustaining cultural heritage.* J. Wiley & Sons, Chichester, pp. 67–79.

Brunsden, D. and Thornes, J.B. (1979) Landscape sensitivity and change. *Transactions, Institute of British Geographers* **4**: 463–484.

Camuffo, D. (1992) Acid rain and the deterioration of monuments: how old is the phenomenon? *Atmospheric Environment* **26B**: 241–247.

Carruthers, J.F.S. (1980) The performance with time of components. In P.J. Sereda and G.G. Litvan (eds) *Durability of Building Materials and Components.* ASTM STP 691.

Cooke, R.U. and Doornkamp, J.C. (1990) *Geomorphology in Environmental Management.* (2nd edn). Oxford University Press, Oxford.

Dibb, T.E., Hughes, D.W. and Poole, A.B. (1983) The identification of critical factors affecting rock durability in marine environments. *Quaternary Journal of Engineering Geology* **16**: 149–161.

Fitzner, B. (1990) *Mapping of natural stone monuments – Documentation of lithotypes and weathering forms.* Advanced Workshop on Analytical Methodologies for the Investigation of Damaged Stone, Pavia, 14–21 September.

Frohnsdroff, G. and Masters, L.W. (1980) The meaning of durability and durability prediction. In P.J. Sereda and G.G. Litvan (eds), *Durability of Building Materials and Components* ASTM STP 691, pp. 17–30.

Garden, G.K. (1980) Design determines durability. In P.J. Sereda and G.G. Litvan (eds), *Durability of Building Materials and Components.* ASTM STP 691, pp. 31–37.

Johnson, J.B., Haneef, S.J., Hepburn, B.J., Hutchinson, A.J., Thompson, G.E. and Wood, G.C. (1990) Laboratory exposure systems to simulate atmospheric degradation of building stone under dry and wet deposition conditions. *Atmospheric Environment* **24A**: 2585–2592.

Knöfel, D. (1991) Causes, mechanisms and measurement of damage in cultural heritage materials: the state of the art: concrete structure. In N.S. Baer, C. Sabboni and A.I. Sors (eds) *Science, Technology and European Cultural Heritage*, Proceedings of European Symposium, Bologna, Italy 13–16 June 1989, pp. 138–147. Butterworth–Heinemann.

Lacy, R.E. (1977) *Climate and building in Britain.* BRE Report.

Litvan, G.G. (1980) Freeze–thaw durability of porous building materials. In P.J. Sereda and G.G. Litvan (eds) *Durability of Building Materials and Components.* ASTM STP 691.

Lowenthal, D. (1994) The value of age and decay. In W. E. Krumbein, P. Brimblecombe, D.E. Cosgrove and S. Staniforth (eds) *Durability and Change: The science, responsibility and cost of sustaining cultural heritage.* J. Wiley & Sons, Chichester, pp. 39–49.

McGreevy, J.P. (1985) Thermal properties as controls on rock surface temperatures maxima, and possible implications for rock weathering. *Earth Surface Processes and Landforms* **10**: 125–136.

McGreevy, J.P. and Smith, B.J. (1982) Salt weathering in hot deserts: observations on the design of simulation experiments. *Geografiska Annaler* **64A**: 161–170.

Mirwald, P.W. and Zaumaizig, J. (1986) The influence of air pollution on natural stone. I, *Goldschmidt informiert. . . a survey of the activities of the Goldschmidt AG 1/86*, No. 64, pp. 10–19.

Nireki, T. (1980) Examination of durability test methods for building materials based on performance evaluation. In P.J. Sereda and G.G. Litvan (eds) *Durability of Building Materials and Components.* ASTM STP 691, pp. 119–130.

Orna, M.V., Anderson, R., Bender, B., Cramer, F., De Witte, E., Drever, J.I., Ehling, A., Heckl, W.M., Lowenthal, D., Madsen, H.B., Melnick, R.Z., Samuel, D. and Westheimer, F.H. (1994) Group report: What is durability in artifacts and what inherent factors determine it? In W.E. Krumbein, P. Brimblecombe, D.E. Cosgrove and S. Staniforth (eds) *Durability and Change: The science, responsibility and cost of sustaining cultural heritage.* J. Wiley & Sons, Chichester, pp. 51–66.

Price, C. (1978) The use of sodium sulphate crystallisation test for determining the weathering resistance of untreated stone. *Proceedings of the International Sumposium on Deterioration and Protection of Stone Monuments*, pp. 1–9.

Richardson, B.A. (1967) Selecting porous building stone. *Stone Industries* September/October.

Rodrigues, J.D. (1989) Causes, mechanisms and measurement of damage in stone monuments. *Pub. of Laboratorio Nacional de Engenharia Civil*, Memoria No. 774: 1–20.

Schaffer, R.R. (1932) *The weathering of natural building stones.* BRE Special Report, No. 18. HMSO, London.

Smith, B.J., Whalley, W.B., Wright, J. and Fassina, V. (1994) Short-term surface modification of limestone test samples: examples from Venice and the surrounding area. In V. Fassina, H. Ott and F. Zezza (eds) *Proceedings of the 3rd International Symposium on the Conservation of Monuments in the Mediterranean Basin.* Venice, 22–25 June, pp. 217–226.

Thorn, C.E. (1988) *Introduction to Theoretical Geomorphology.* Unwin Hyman, London.

Tombach, I. (1982) Measurement of local climatological and air pollution factors affecting stone decay. In *Proceedings of the National Academy of Science*, Conference on Conservation of Historic Stone Buildings and Monuments. Washington DC, 2–4 February, pp. 197–210.

Trofimov, A.M. and Phillips, J.D. (1992) Theoretical and methodological premises of geomorphological forecasting. *Geomorphology* **5**: 203–211.

Turkington, A. (1993) *How is superficial debris weathered in a hot desert environment? An ergodic study of an alluvial fan in Death Valley.* B.A. Hons. Thesis, The Queen's University of Belfast (unpub.).

Warke, P.A. and Smith, B.J. (1994) Inheritance effects on the efficacy of salt weathering mechanisms in thermally cycled granite blocks under laboratory and field conditions. In E. Bell and T.P. Cooper (eds) *Granite weathering and conservation.* Trinity College, Dublin, pp. 19–27.

Contact address
School of Geosciences
The Queen's University Belfast
Belfast
BT7 1NN
United Kingdom

3 Inheritance effects in building stone decay

P.A. WARKE

ABSTRACT

Urban stone decay is the product of complex interactions between components of the weathering system and is determined by durability characteristics of stone, the extent and severity of current environmental conditions and the weathering/exposure history or inheritance of the stone. Current rates and patterns of decay reflect the effects of spatially and temporally variable weathering and may also be related to the cumulative effects of former weathering events, environmental conditions and treatment of stone prior to emplacement. Consequently, an inheritance of structural and mineralogical weaknesses can profoundly influence stone response to contemporary conditions and must therefore be included as a factor in any attempt to predict the efficacy of conservation procedures and their effect on future rates and patterns of decay.

INTRODUCTION

Building stones in urban areas are natural materials exposed to, what can best be described as, unnatural conditions. In addition to environmental stresses experienced by natural stone outcrops, for example, wetting/drying, insolation, frost action, salt and biological activity, extra variables are introduced. These include high general levels of environmental acidity and a wide assortment of particulate matter derived primarily from combustion of fossil fuels, but also including salt, dust, pollen and other forms of organic and inorganic detritus. Urban stone is therefore, frequently exposed to con-

Processes of Urban Stone Decay. Edited by B.J. Smith and P.A. Warke. © 1996 Donhead Publishing Ltd.

ditions more severe than those encountered in natural environments.

Urban stone decay cannot, therefore, be explained by simple analysis of the individual components of the weathering system described in Chapter 1 (Figure 1.1), but is the product of complex interactions between these components. Further complexity is introduced through the temporal dimen-sion of this system whereby past conditions and processes can profoundly influence stone response to contemporary environmental conditions through an often complex inheritance of structural and mineralogical weaknesses. These may increase stone susceptibility to weathering and thereby lessen durability. In many instances current patterns and rates of stone decay may be more accurately attributed to former, more polluted conditions and possibly to treatment of the stone prior to emplacement. Consequently, contemporary environmental conditions may merely complement decay initiated or predetermined in the past. Decay is thus determined by a combination of the durability characteristics of the stone, the extent and severity of current environmental stresses and finally, its weathering/exposure history (inheritance).

In this chapter stone durability and environmental stresses are considered first as a background to an appreciation of the nature of inheritance effects and how they operate to influence stone behaviour and confuse attempts to relate observed rates and patterns of decay to current environmental conditions.

STONE DURABILITY AND CHANGE

Stone durability concepts are extensively discussed in Chapter 2, where the difficulty of ascribing a fixed value/measure to a material in which physical change is inherent, is highlighted. Despite this, stone continues to be widely perceived as a highly durable and virtually unchanging material. Stone, like all natural material once removed from its formative conditions will, however, change over time. These changes may begin long before emplacement in buildings and prior to exposure at the earth's surface. Because stone invariably forms under conditions of great heat and/or pressure, ascent to the earth's surface and exposure to low temperature/low pressure subaerial conditions initiates structural and mineralogical change. For example, in stones such as granite and sandstone, dilatation, arising from stress release through removal of overburden by erosion or quarrying, may result in fracture initiation and growth. This is a form of structural alteration which occurs independently of subaerial processes and which could be described as predetermined change. Once exposed to subaerial conditions various chemical, physical and biological weathering processes may cause mineralogical alteration and extend and widen these predetermined fractures and lines of weakness. The effects of changes initiated prior to exposure and those incurred subsequently through the action of subaerial processes are not easily isolated. Dilatation, for example, facilitates the ingress of salt and/or moisture, enhancing their weathering effectiveness (see Chapter 10, Neill and Smith).

33

While change is an inherent characteristic of stone, the rate and extent of structural and mineralogical deterioration and the associated decline in durability is determined by the reactivity of constituent minerals with prevailing environmental conditions (Drever, 1994). The topography of a building creates a range of micro-environmental conditions which contribute to the spatial variability of rates and patterns of decay. Conditions in one location may facilitate accelerated decay through, for example, retention of moisture and accumulation of salts, while elsewhere on the same building where micro-environmental conditions are less detrimental the same stone type may exhibit comparatively minor evidence of deterioration (see Chapter 2 – Figure 2.1).

In addition to spatially variable rates and patterns of decay, alteration of stone does not proceed uniformly over the lifetime of a building. Instead, it tends to progress episodically in response to changing environmental conditions and/or changes in the structural and mineralogical properties of the stone itself (see Chapter 1 – Figures 1.5 and 1.6).

THE NATURE OF ENVIRONMENTAL STRESS

Under subaerial conditions stone is exposed to a wide range of weathering mechanisms operating in combination with infrastructural components such as loading. Environmental stress may be exerted by, for example, repeated heating and cooling of stone surfaces and intergranular salt crystallisation. Such mechanisms rarely, if ever, act in isolation but through their cumulative and sequential effects ultimately lead to stone deterioration. In addition, some weathering mechanisms exhibit synergistic relationships where their combined effects are greater than the sum of their individual actions. Consequently, stone exposed simultaneously to different mechanisms may be more severely stressed over time than indicated by environmental conditions. The effectiveness of individual environmental stresses such as frost action and salt crystallisation is determined by several factors, for example, the magnitude and frequency of the stress event, its scope of impact and the presence of conducive environmental conditions.

Magnitude and frequency

Sudden, high magnitude increases in stress burden may result in breakdown of stone fabric – breakdown which may not have occurred if the stress had been applied more gradually. For example, Lautridou and Ozouf (1982) emphasise the importance of freezing rate in determining efficacy of frost weathering. Rapid freezing of moisture within rock fabric reduces losses through evaporation and 'cryosuction' increasing the potential energy available for shattering. This is related to the threshold concept described in Chapter 1 where, if the critical threshold of material strength is greater than the stress applied then no apparent change will occur. The absence of obvious visual damage can, however, be misleading as it implies that the stone is unaltered when microscopic external and internal changes may have occurred, an accumulation of which may eventually reduce cohesive strength and lead to 'fatigue' failure. Similarly, the efficacy of extreme heating and high rates of surface temperature change (thermal shock) are clearly demonstrated in the natural environment during bushfires, with widespread splitting and spalling of natural rock outcrops (Bierman and Gillespie, 1991; Dragovich, 1993) as critical thresholds of strength are exceeded. The deleterious effect of thermal shock on building materials such as glass has also been shown, where rapid changes in temperature conditions create high stress conditions and fracturing (Mai and Jacob, 1980).

Depending on the nature of the environmental stress, prolonged and continuous stressing of stone may be less destructive or not so obviously destructive as repeated short-term events. For example, in the case of frost weathering, the number of oscillations across freezing point are of greater significance than the intensity or duration of individual freezing events (Potts, 1970). Although the magnitude and frequency of stress events are important, material characteristics must also be considered. For example, prolonged exposure to acid rainfall will have serious implications for calcareous stone leading to a gradual loss of material and architectural detail. It may also alter stone surface characteristics such as pore dimensions, where enlargement facilitates penetration of salt, moisture and biota.

Scope of impact

Localised application of stress may have only a very limited impact on overall material integrity. Conversely, localised stressing, if applied to a particularly sensitive area weakened by previous stress events, may trigger failure disproportionate to the magnitude of the stress applied. For example, localised and repetitive weathering of a load bearing structure may have serious implications for the remainder of the building.

Environmental conditions conducive to decay

The presence of recognised weathering agents such as salt and/or moisture does not necessarily imply their effective action, only their potential. For example, salt and moisture, although present in abundance within buried rock, remain relatively ineffective with regard to rock breakdown until exposed to the temperature/humidity fluctuations associated with subaerial conditions (Goudie, 1977; Warke, 1994). A stone façade, while possessing the potential for accelerated decay could, therefore, remain relatively stable until exposure conditions are altered through, for example, demolition or construction of neighbouring structures. The resulting changes in factors such as shade, airflow and moisture receipt may trigger hitherto inactive processes or accelerate existing ones. In addition, a factor often overlooked in decay studies is that salts can also have a binding effect with no release of material until subsequent wetting and dissolution. So, for example, in some instances a heavy rainfall event may be required to release individual grains and flakes held in place by crystallised salt.

In summary, from initial exposure at the quarry face, environmental factors impose a variety of stresses on stone. Stress episodes may be localised or widespread and of variable magnitude and frequency. The ability of stone to resolve these stresses will primarily be determined by its structural and mineralogical characteristics. If these have been altered during previous weathering activity the stone will carry an inheritance of structural and mineralogical weaknesses which may increase its susceptibility to subsequent stress events.

INHERITANCE EFFECTS IN BUILDING STONE DECAY

Many studies of building stone decay have sought to explain patterns and rates of breakdown in terms of prevailing environmental conditions. However, as preceding sections illustrate, change is an inherent characteristic of stone and over the lifetime of any building, stone is exposed to a range of spatially and temporally variable weathering processes and environmental conditions.

As stone progresses from the quarry face to emplacement in a building and thence through various stages of decay, it is probable that it accumulates an inheritance of previous conditions and treatments. These can include structural and mineralogical weaknesses incurred during quarrying and processing (e.g. dressing of stone) prior to emplacement and subsequently as a result of exposure to subaerial conditions, pollutants and conservation treatments. This inheritance gradually reduces the ability of stone to resolve stress arising from, for example, common weathering events such as repeated heating and cooling, freezing of moisture in pore spaces and interstitial salt crystallisation (Figure 3.1).

Decay depends upon the physical and chemical characteristics of the stone. Any factor that alters these properties will therefore influence subsequent rates of decay. These changes may result from contemporary weathering processes. However, many changes may be cumulative, each reflecting a set of environmental conditions and/or processes that acted in the past. Indeed, the significance of inheritance effects lies in the fact that frequently they are unrelated to contemporary environmental conditions but were incurred under former conditions. For example, in many urban areas within the British Isles air quality control measures introduced during the latter half of this century have improved atmospheric conditions, especially with regard to particulate emissions. In many instances, however, these 'cleaner' conditions have not been matched by a decline in rates of stone decay. Despite the reduction in certain pollutants many building stones carry within their fabric a legacy of salt deposits and structural damage inherited from former more polluted conditions and these continue to cause breakdown

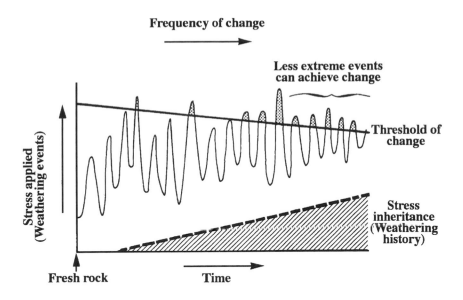

Figure 3.1 Schematic representation of inheritance effects on stone susceptibility to weathering (adapted from Rose (1985)).

(BERG 1989).

Table 3.1 shows the range of factors that can give rise to structural and mineralogical changes in stone which can subsequently affect rates and patterns of decay. A general examination of structural and chemical inheritance effects and those arising from intervention measures such as cleaning will illustrate the complexity of urban stone decay. They may also help to explain certain anomalies where, for example, stone of the same lithology responds quite differently to similar micro-environmental conditions on the face of a building.

Structural effects

Micro-scale structural discontinuities within stone facilitate weathering and breakdown. The most important structural discontinuities are firstly, microfractures formed by endogenetic processes which are present within stone before it is exposed at the earth's surface; secondly, microfractures that result from quarry blasting; thirdly, mineralogical concentrations which form potential weathering lines and lines of fracture development and, finally, microfractures extended by subaerial processes. This final group may only develop from the other three but despite this, studies of building stone decay tend to emphasise this particular group neglecting the weaknesses ini-

CAUSATIVE FACTORS	INHERITANCE EFFECTS
PRE-EMPLACEMENT FACTORS	
•Dilatation effects	Removal of overburden leads to compressional stress release in stone causing gradual opening of joint systems and microfracturing.
•Microfracturing caused by quarrying	Quarry blasting can initiate microfracture development and/or propagate existing fracture lines.
•Cutting and dressing of stone	May cause roughening of stone surfaces creating potential sites for subsequent accumulation of moisture, salts, organic matter.
POST-EMPLACEMENT FACTORS	
•Thermally induced microfracturing	Differential thermal expansion and contraction of surface mineral grains and interstitial salt deposits in response to long- and short-term temperature fluctuations may eventually lead to microfracture development.
•Frost induced microfracturing	Repeated freezing of moisture in pore spaces and microfractures may eventually lead to shattering of stone and loss of material.
•Chemical dissolution	Dissolution of stone fabric alters surface pore dimensions and may facilitate the subsequent ingress of salt and moisture.
•Soiling of stone surface	Soiling of stone surface by particulate deposition changes albedo, increasing absorption of solar radiation and hence surface/subsurface temperature conditions.
•Surface crust development	Crusts act as salt reservoirs and can contribute to a decrease in substrate strength as material is leached out.
•Salt accumulation and deposition	Interstitial deposition of salt contributes to stone decay through the mechanisms of intergranular crystallisation, hydration/ dehydration and thermal expansion/contraction.
•Changes in surface morphology	Prolonged exposure to weathering processes leads to increased stone surface roughening allowing accumulation of moisture, salts and general particulate material which facilitate surface weathering processes.
•Cleaning	Removal of crusts may expose a weakened substrate to attack by weathering mechanisms resulting in accelerated decay. Additionally, high pressure washing may drive salts deep into the stone fabric and application of biocides may damage individual grain structure and/or intergranular bonds.
•Conservation treatments	Application of stone consolidants and other surface preparations alter surface characteristics and may influence stone response to weathering processes.

Table 3.1 Inheritance effects and causative factors.

tiated prior to exposure and/or during quarrying.

Endogenetic processes affect stone before it is exposed at the earth's surface creating different scales of structural weakness from fracturing of individual mineral grains to macro-scale fracturing of the rock mass. Fracture development may be caused, for example, by non-hydrostatic stress and differential expansion/contraction of mineral grains because of changes in temperature and pressure (Simmons and Cooper, 1978).

Ascent to the surface through gradual removal of overburden and the resulting release of compressional stress causes dilatation during which new fractures are initiated and pre-existing fracture planes are opened. The process of dilatation is closely associated with stone such as granite formed under conditions of great heat and pressure but can also affect other relatively homogeneous stone like sandstone (Bradley, 1963) and marble. The process of quarrying itself can also cause microfracturing, identified as shock induced cracking (Simmons and Richter, 1976).

In addition to the deleterious effects of endogenetic processes and, in some instances quarrying, on the structural integrity of stone, other structural anomalies may also influence rates and patterns of breakdown. Certain mineralogical concentrations may create potential weathering lines (McGreevy, 1982; McGreevy and Smith, 1984) which remain intact until exposure. The existence, for example, of clay-rich inclusions which may be preferentially weathered by subaerial processes can act as major controls on patterns and rates of decay.

From initial exposure at the quarry face stone is subjected to a wide range of subaerial processes, most are exploitative (e.g. salt, frost and moisture) entering and extending pre-existing lines of weakness. Other processes such as insolation weathering are non-exploitative, directly initiating micro-fracture development through their own action and indirectly by enhancing the effectiveness of exploitative weathering agents and chemical phenomena.

Often the weathering processes directly associated with observed patterns of building stone decay are assumed to be solely responsible for their formation. Such assumptions, however, exclude the role of past events and environmental conditions – the history of the material.

Chemical effects

Chemical inheritance comprises three main categories. Firstly, mineral alteration which degrades the primary mineral components of the stone; secondly, changes in pore dimensions through removal of material primarily by dissolution and, finally, surface crust development.

Alteration of primary minerals by chemical weathering can create areas of less resistant material more susceptible to physical weathering processes such as salt weathering, frost action and biological activity. Mineral alteration may also change other important stone properties such as porosity and permeability thereby facilitating the ingress of salt and/or moisture.

Changes in pore dimensions can deleteriously affect stone durability. Increases in pore size resulting from chemical dissolution may alter stone response to mechanical weathering processes such as frost action by enhancing moisture penetration (Honeybourne and Harris, 1958). Consequently, stone may only become susceptible to the action of a particular weathering process once dissolution has modified its superficial pore characteristics.

Surface soiling and black crust development mostly affects areas sheltered from direct rain wash. Crusts can provide an indication of the degree of pollution experienced since initial construction of the building or since previous cleaning, although it is likely that crust growth is not a linear process (Whalley, et al., 1992). Black crusts can comprise a variety of substances such as flyash derived from the combustion of fossil fuels, dust, pollen, biota and inorganic precipitates. The most common inorganic component is gypsum formed through reaction between atmospheric sulphur and calcareous components of stone and mortars. Crusts not only detract from the appearance of a building but are often associated with features such as granular disintegration and flaking (Del Monte, 1991; Fassina, 1991). They provide a reservoir of potentially damaging organic and inorganic substances and may also mask subsurface decay processes. Debate persists concerning the value of crust removal during cleaning as crusts inherited from former more polluted conditions may protect weakened substrates which once exposed will experience accelerated decay (Maxwell, 1992; Whalley, et al., 1992).

In addition to chemical alteration associated with crust development, it is important to note that darkening of stone surfaces through soiling and crust growth increases absorption of solar radiation and may create more extreme surface temperature conditions and enhance the effectiveness of specific weathering mechanisms such as salt crystallisation and insolation effects (Davison, 1986; Warke, et al., in press).

Inheritance effects arising from intervention measures

Decay and soiling of stone detracts from the aesthetic appeal and architectural value of buildings which often comprise important components of our cultural heritage. These signs of structural degradation frequently result in well-intentioned but often inappropriate conservation treatments. Aggressive procedures have undoubtedly been applied to buildings without a full understanding of their immediate effects on the stone and their influence on future rates and patterns of decay. Abrasive cleaning, for example, can alter surface pore characteristics, effectively increasing permeability and providing the potential for accelerated decay (Maxwell, 1992). Similarly, inappropriate high pressure washing of stone may drive surface salts into the substrate and create the potential for future accelerated stone decay. In addition, consolidants, biocides and other chemical treatments may be applied to a building without an appreciation of their long-term chemical interactions with constituents of the stone and with prevailing environmental conditions, the full effects of which may not become apparent for many years.

CONCLUSION

Building stone decay, while unsightly and in some cases structurally compromising, is the natural result of exposure to subaerial conditions. In many instances, however, urban environmental conditions accelerate the decay process through the introduction of a wide range of gaseous and particulate pollutants. Current rates and patterns of decay, therefore, reflect the effects of a variety of spatially and temporally variable weathering processes. They are also often related to the cumulative effects of former weathering events, environmental conditions and treatment of stone prior to emplacement.

The gradual accumulation of structural and mineralogical inheritance effects alters a stone's durability making it more susceptible to decay by reducing its ability to resolve imposed stress. Stone with a complex exposure history will be less able to resolve stress arising from, for example, interstitial salt crystallisation than stone of the same lithology freshly exposed at the quarry face. Acceleration of decay processes may not, therefore, be indicative of more aggressive environmental conditions. Instead it could reflect a general decline in stone durability and influence of inherited pollutants stored within the stone fabric.

Despite this obvious complexity, there is still a tendency in studies of stone decay to relate rates and patterns of breakdown to prevailing environmental conditions, probably because current environmental variables can be easily measured whereas the weathering/exposure history of the stone or building is less tangible and, therefore, almost impossible to quantify. Inheritance effects, however, can have a profound influence on stone response to contemporary conditions and must be considered when attempting to predict the likely outcome of conservation procedures and their effect on future patterns and rates of decay.

References

BERG (1989) *The Effects of Acid Deposition on Buildings and Building Materials in the United Kingdom.* Building Effects Review Group Report. HMSO, London.

Bierman, P. and Gillespie, A. (1991) Range fires: a significant factor in exposure-age determination and geomorphic surface evolution. *Geology* **19**: 641–644.

Bradley, W.C. (1963) Large-scale exfoliation in massive sandstones of the Colorado Plateau. *Geological Society of America, Bulletin* **74**: 519–528.

Cooke, R.U. (1979) Laboratory simulation of salt weathering processes in arid environments. *Earth Surface Processes and Landforms* **4**: 347–359.

Davison, A.P. (1986) An investigation into the relationship between salt weathering debris production and temperature. *Earth Surface Processes and Landforms* **11**: 335–341.

Del Monte, M. (1991) Stone monument decay and air pollution. In F. Zezza (ed.) *Weathering and Air Pollution.* Community of Mediterranean Universities, Bari, pp. 101–110.

Dragovich, D. (1993) Fire-accelerated boulder weathering in the Pilbara, western Australia. *Zeitschrift für Geomorphologie N.F.* **37**: 295–307.

Drever, J.I. (1994) Durability of stone and textural perspectives. In W.E. Krumbein, P. Brimblecombe, D.E. Cosgrove and S. Staniforth (eds) *Durability and Change. The Science, Responsibility and Cost of Sustaining Cultural Heritage.* J. Wiley & Sons, Chichester, pp. 27–37.

Fassina, V. (1991) Atmospheric pollutants responsible for stone decay. Wet and dry surface deposition of air pollutants on stone and the formation of black scabs. In F. Zezza (ed.) *Weathering and Air Pollution.* Community of Mediterranean Universities, Bari, pp. 67–86.

Goudie, A.S. (1974) Further experimental investigation of rock weathering by salt and other mechanical processes. *Zeitschrift für Geomorphologie N. F.* **21**: 1–12.

Goudie, A.S. (1977) Sodium sulphate weathering and the disintegration of Mohenjo-Daro, Pakistan. *Earth Surface Processes and Landforms* **2**: 75–86.

Honeyborne, D.B. and Harris, P.B. (1958) The structure of porous building stone and its relation to weathering behaviour. *The Colston Papers* **10**: 343–365.

Lautridou, J.P. and Ozouf, J.C. (1982) Experimental frost shattering: 15 years of research at the Centre de Geomorphologie du C.N.R.S. *Progress in Physical Geography* **6**: 215–232.

Mai, Y.W. and Jacob, L.J.S. (1980) Thermal stress fracture of solar control window panes caused by shading of incident radiation. *Materials and Structures* **13**: 283–288.

Maxwell, I. (1992) Stone cleaning – for better or worse? An overview. In R.G.M. Webster (ed.) *Stone Cleaning and the Nature, Soiling and Decay Mechanisms of Stone.* Donhead Publishing, London, pp. 3–49.

McGreevy, J.P. (1982) Hydrothermal alteration and earth surface rock weathering: a basalt example. *Earth Surface Processes and Landforms* **7**: 189–195.

McGreevy, J.P. and Smith, B.J. (1984) The possible role of clay minerals in salt weathering. *Catena* **11**: 169–175.

Potts, A. S. (1970) Frost action in rocks: some experimental data. *Institute of Britrish Geographers Transactions* **49**: 109–124.

Rose, C. (1985) Acid rain falls on British woodlands. *New Scientist*, 14 November, pp. 52–57.

Simmons, G. and Richter, D. (1976) Microcracks in rocks. In *The Physics and Chemistry of Minerals and Rocks.* J. Wiley & Sons, Chichester, pp. 105–137.

Simmons, G. and Cooper, H.W. (1978) Thermal cycling cracks in three igneous rocks. *International Journal of Rock Mechanics, Mineral Science and Geomechanics Abstracts* **15**: 145–148.

Smith, B.J. and McGreevy, J.P. (1987) The production of silt-size quartz by experimental salt weathering of a sandstone. *Journal of Arid Environments* **12**: 19–214.

Sperling, C.H.B. and Cooke, R.U. (1985) Laboratory simulation of rock weathering by salt crystallisation and hydration processes in hot arid environments. *Earth Surface Processes and Landforms* **10**: 541–555.

Warke, P.A. (1994) *Inheritance effects in the weathering of debris under hot arid conditions.* Unpublished PhD Thesis, The Queen's University of Belfast.

Warke, P.A., Smith, B.J. and Magee, R.W. (in press.) Thermal response characteristics of stone: implications for weathering of soiled surfaces in urban environments. *Earth Surface Processes and Landforms.*

Whalley, W.B., Smith, B.J. and Magee, R.W. (1992) Effects of particulate air pollutants on materials : investigation of surface crust formation. In R.G.M. Webster (ed.) *Stone Cleaning and the Nature, Soiling and Decay Mechanisms of Stone.* Donhead Publishing, London, pp. 227–234.

Contact address
School of Geosciences
The Queen's University of Belfast
Belfast
BT7 1NN
United Kingdom

SECTION TWO

MECHANISMS OF STONE DECAY

(A) Surface Change

'...And the roots' fingers, sopped with rain,
Crumble the stone to mud again.'

N. Nicholson, Coniston Flag,
Selected Poems, 1972

4 Black crusts formed during two different pollution regimes

E. BELL, P. DOWDING and T.P. COOPER

ABSTRACT

Black crusts formed on a limestone building in Trinity College, Dublin under two different pollution regimes are examined. The first crust formed over 160 years, from 1732 to 1892 while the second developed over 260 years from 1732 to 1992. Originally the ground floor of the building com prised an open colonnade but this was enclosed in 1892 with subsequent glazing of archways. Black crusts were not removed from what had become interior walls leaving them intact and protected from outdoor conditions but crusts on exerior walls remained exposed to pollutants and weathering processes. This differentiation in crust development provides a unique opportunity for comparing the influence of two pollution regimes where the former (1732–1892) occurred prior to the advent of oil combustion while the latter (1892–1992) includes the combined effects of oil and coal combustion.

INTRODUCTION

The aim of this study was to examine black crusts formed during two different pollution regimes but with exactly the same location, microenvironment and underlying stone material. The first black crust was formed during the period 1732 to 1892, while the second was formed during the period 1732 to 1992. Both crusts were taken from a building in Trinity College, Dublin, designed by Thomas Burgh and built between 1712 and 1732 of a local limestone with a high shale content. Originally the ground floor con-

Processes of Urban Stone Decay. Edited by B.J. Smith and P.A. Warke. © 1996 Donhead Publishing Ltd.

sisted of an open colonnade but in 1892 this was enclosed to provide further space for housing the growing book collection. After enclosure the archways were glazed, however no attempt was made to remove the black crusts which had built up over the previous 160 years from what was now an interior wall. These black crusts therefore remained intact and largely unaffected by outdoor conditions. On the other side of the window, the black crusts remained exposed to pollutants and weathering processes thus providing a unique opportunity to compare crusts developed under two different pollution regimes.

EXAMINATION OF THE CRUSTS FROM THE COLONNADES

Two samples were taken from the library building from a sheltered north facing wall, one inside the building, the other outside the building, at a distance of 10 cm apart. These were examined using Scanning Electron Microscopy (SEM) and microprobe analysis.

SEM and microprobe analysis

Sample A, taken from inside the library, consisted predominantly of crystals of gypsum with embedded aluminosilicate spherical particles. These particles were composed primarily of Si, Al, Fe, K, Ca, Ti and S (in that order) as illustrated by Figure 4.1. The particles had a smooth spherical appearance with a diameter of approximately 15 µm formed during combustion as a transformation product of clays and other minerals present as impurities in coal (Fassina, 1992). Iron particles ranging in size from 4–6 µm were also common. Smaller iron pyrite particles were found. Their presence may be as a result of release from the underlying argillaceous rock. Sample B, taken from outside the library, was similar to sample A with gypsum crystals predominating. Iron particles were present but not as common as in sample A. Spheres of an aluminosilicate composition similar in abundance and morphology to those in sample A were noted, however sulphur rich carbonaceous particles with a diameter of up to 27 µm were more common. These particles had a C, S, Fe and Ca composition, as illustrated in Figure 4.2. The SEM micrograph (Figure 4.3) shows the smooth surface of the particle pitted with circular pores.

Determination of carbonate and non-carbonate sources of carbon

Carbonate carbon (from the underlying rock) and non-carbonate carbon (primarily from combustion sources) was determined by a method devised by Zappia, Sabbioni and Gobbi (1993). This involves the elimination of carbonates by placing the ground sample for 48 hours in an atmosphere saturated with HCl vapours. The sample was then dried over KOH to remove

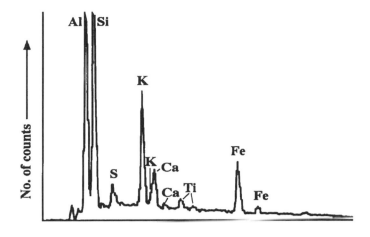

Figure 4.1 Qualitative energy dispersive X-ray (EDX) analysis of coal flyash particle in black crust located inside the Old Library.

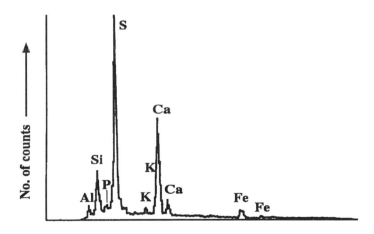

Figure 4.2 Qualitative energy dispersive X-ray analysis (EDX) of oil flyash particle in black crust located outside the Old Library.

humidity and any residual HCl. Non-carbonate carbon was subsequently determined by combustion and IR spectroscopy. Untreated samples were also combusted to determine the total carbon content and from the two figures the carbonate content of the crust was calculated.

The non-carbonate carbon concentration in sample A (inside) was found to be 24 mg g^{-1} dry weight of crust, while the non-carbonate carbon concentration in sample B (outside) was 25 mg g^{-1} dry weight. The light weight of oil derived particles may account for this lack of difference.

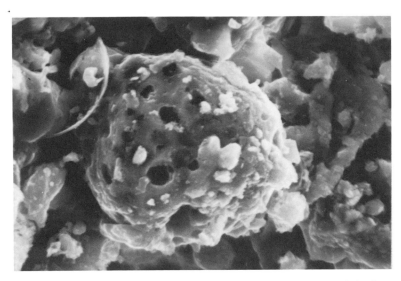

Figure 4.3 Scanning electron micrograph of an oil flyash particle from the black crust located outside the Old Library. (Picture width 40 μm)

Although there was no significant difference in the non-carbonate content there was a difference in the carbonate carbon content with sample A (inside) yielding 11 mg g^{-1} dry weight and sample B (outside) yielding 3 mg g^{-1} dry weight. This suggests that a higher percentage of the total carbon content of the crust formed in the period 1732 to 1892 originated from the stone. The sulphate content of the crusts was determined by ion chromatography after elution in deionised water. The sulphate content of the crust taken from inside the Colonnades was 25.87 mg g^{-1} dry weight while that of the crust taken from outside was 26.38 mg g^{-1} dry weight, a difference of 1.93%.

Comparison of the condition of the underlying stone

The underlying stone was examined ($\times$ 25 magnification) after micro-blasting at low pressure to remove the black crust. The depth of the crust at both sites was similar (2 mm approx.). After removal of the crusts the surface appeared the same in both cases with no evidence of any serious damage. The Calp limestone is a dense stone that is relatively resistant to weathering.

DISCUSSION

Before the enclosure of the Colonnades in 1892 it can be assumed that the contribution of sulphur and smoke from oil burning was minimal. The major source of atmospheric particulates was from the burning of coal, peat and wood. This is reflected in the black crusts taken from inside the Colonnades. The black crusts taken from outside the Colonnades contained as many particles derived from coal burning but in addition, many derived from oil combustion. This is despite the fact that in 1987 oil/diesel burning contributed only 11% to total smoke output in Ireland while coal combustion accounted for 34% of smoke output. The larger number of oil derived particles present is probably as a result of their greater powers of adhesion brought about by their larger surface area.

The atmospheric oxidation mechanism of SO_2 as a precursor to gypsum formation is not thought to be an important mechanism in Dublin. This is evidenced by the relatively high pH of 5.4 recorded in Dublin (Cooper, *et al.*, 1991). The surface oxidation mechanism therefore will predominate. As discussed previously, this mechanism requires the presence of catalysts and moisture at the stone/air interface. Particles from the burning of oil products provide this. The particles found in the black crusts from outside the Colonnades contained metal catalysts and their large surface area and potential hygroscopic nature could be considered ideal for aiding the oxidation of SO_2. The presence of sulphur compounds in the particles can provide a further source of sulphur so that even when atmospheric levels may be low the formation of $CaSO_4 2H_2O$ may continue (Del Monte and Sabbioni, 1984).

By comparing the thickness of the two crusts it can be seen that the thickness of the crust does not increase indefinitely but appears to reach a steady state, with the older gypsum crystals breaking off with time. This is in agreement with the findings of Camuffo, *et al.* (1983). No difference could be discerned at $\times$ 25 magnification in the underlying stone after the removal of the crusts. This would suggest that no additional damage has been caused by the advent of oil combustion, however it is not possible to determine accurately how much material loss has occurred at each site. More thorough examination with SEM may have yielded some difference, however it was not possible to take cores at this site.

From the above it would seem that the ban on the sale of bituminous coal in 1990 and the subsequent drop in smoke output of 74% (Ahlstrom, 1992) would have little effect in reducing the formation of black crusts. It must be noted that in the Dublin area in 1987 67% of SO_2 was derived from fuel oil while only 18% was derived from coal combustion (ENFO, 1990). Even though coal combustion produces three times more smoke than oil product combustion, it is oil derived particles that adhere to the stone/gypsum surface in greater numbers. Therefore while the reduction in smoke output from the burning of bituminous coal may improve air quality for humans and reduce soiling of building façades, a reduction in SO_2 and smoke from oil combustion would be required to produce any impact on the formation of gypsum. It should also be noted that peat which is considered a smokeless fuel for the purposes of the Air Pollution Act, in fact produced 55% of all smoke output in 1987. Smoke from this source is not monitored on a regular basis and therefore is not taken into account when reductions in smoke output are being calculated.

CONCLUSIONS

An assessment of the crust samples using SEM showed that sulphur rich carbonaceous particles were present in the samples taken from outside the Colonnades. Aluminosilicate particles were present in both the inside and outside samples. The results of the visual assessment were not as clearly defined by chemical analysis. The difference in the non-carbonate carbon and the sulphate content of the crusts was small while there was significantly more carbonate carbon in the crusts formed during the 1732 to 1892 period. The presence of the sulphur rich particles in the crusts from the outside samples had not influenced the sulphate content of the crusts to any great extent. However, the presence of these particles may become more important when other sources of sulphur are reduced. Sulphate and non-carbonate carbon levels in both crust types were similar.

References

Ahlstrom, D. (1992) Coal ban has cut Dublin smog by 70%. *Technology Ireland.* September, 1992.

Camuffo, D., Del Monte, M. and Sabbioni, C. (1983) Origin and growth of the sulfated crusts on urban limestone. *Water, Air and Soil Pollution* **19**: 351–359.

Cooper, T.P., Bell. E., Duffy, A. Lyons, F., O'Brien, P., Dowding, P., Lewis, O., Mulvin, L., O'Daly, G., Dillon-Malone, P. and Murphy, C. (1991) *Effects of air pollution on historic buildings and monuments.* Final report to the EC for Research Contract EV4V0 048 IRL.

Del Monte, M. and Sabbioni C. (1984) Gypsum crusts and flyash on carbonatic outcrops. *Archives for Meteorology, Geophysics, and Bioclimatology.* Series B **35**: 105–111.

ENFO (1990) *Air quality data.* Fact sheet 13 6/90.

Fassina, V. (1992) The weathering of the statues of Prato della Valle and the criteria used for consolidation. In R.G.M. Webster (ed.) *Stone Cleaning and the Nature, Soiling and Decay Mechanisms of Stone.* Donhead Publishing, London, pp. 268–282.

Zappia, G., Sabbioni, C. and Gobbi, G. (1993) Non-carbonate carbon content on black and white areas of damaged stone monuments. *Atmospheric Environment* **27A**: 1117–1121.

Contact address
Director of Buildings
West Chapel
Trinity College
Dublin 2
Ireland

5 The black soiling of sandstone buildings in the West Midlands, England: regional variations and decay mechanisms

D.P. HALSEY, S.J. DEWS,
D.J. MITCHELL and F.C. HARRIS

ABSTRACT

The distribution of sandstone weathering forms has been examined for churches built of ferruginous sandstone in the West Midlands, England. The surveyed buildings had not been heavily restored or cleaned, and the majority were built in the nineteenth century of Quartz Arenites. The survey recorded percentage cover of each weathering form in 1 m² quadrats for thirty buildings situated in two 40 km by 10 km transects across the West Midlands. One transect ran from north to south and the other from east to west. Around 1400 quadrats were completed and regional weathering patterns were examined using cluster analysis and contour mapping. The transects show that black soiling covers < 10% of sandstone façades in rural areas to the west of the conurbation, > 40% of stone in the centre of the conurbation and < 20% in rural areas to the east. Façades in southern areas of the conurbation typically have < 20% black soiling, whereas façades in the north have > 40%. An increase in black soiling caused by urbanisation is clearly demonstrated and there is some evidence that the location of industry may have increased black soiling in certain areas of the conurbation. Coal has historically been the dominant industrial and residential fuel of the West Midlands and Scanning Electron Microscopy shows that coal flyash is prevalent on black soiled sandstone in this area.

INTRODUCTION

The application of sensitive measurement techniques, over short periods of time, is essential to improve our understanding of stone weathering mecha-

Processes of Urban Stone Decay. Edited by B.J. Smith and P.A. Warke. © 1996 Donhead Publishing Ltd.

nisms. However, to evaluate and explain the occurrence of various forms of weathering it is necessary to carry out objective assessments of weathering features that have formed over significant time periods. Stone buildings, of a known age, provide a means to carry out these assessments, but much of the research on the weathering of buildings is in the form of case studies, involving single or small numbers of buildings. This investigation reports some of the findings from a survey of weathering forms affecting 30 sandstone buildings and relates these findings to various sandstone decay mechanisms.

METHODOLOGY

To achieve a distribution of comparable buildings across rural and urban environments two transects, 40 km long and 10 km wide, were drawn on a map of the West Midlands. A north–south and an east–west transect, centred on the West Midlands conurbation (NGR SP 010890), crossing both rural and urban areas, were selected. An initial examination of buildings along these transects revealed that most sandstone buildings were churches. Therefore, it was decided that the survey should concentrate on churches, which are generally free standing in graveyards and orientated according to the cardinal points. Examination of churches in or very close to these transects provided 30 suitable buildings, which showed no evidence of cleaning or major restoration. All were constructed from ferruginous sandstone, typically quartz arenites (presumably quarried from local Permo-Triassic Sandstone formations). Twenty-four of the churches were built in the nineteenth century, while the remaining six were older.

To record the type and amount of weathering, a system to classify the different weathering forms was devised. An existing classification with over 40 different types of weathering, was considered and reduced to 18 forms of sandstone weathering by removing those inappropriate to sandstone and generalising the less common forms of deterioration. This study investigates the findings of three of these forms (black soiling, black flaking and black scaling), but will also refer to total blackened stone, which is the sum of these three forms (Table 5.1). For each building the amount of stone affected by each weathering form was recorded as percentage cover to the nearest 5%. This was done by analysing one metre quadrats of sandstone, between the heights of 0.2 and 1.2 metres, and 1.2 and 2.2 metres, at two metre intervals along the wall. These heights were selected so that the lower one represented stone influenced by the capillary rise of ground water, while the upper one was less influenced. The quadrat interval of two metres was found to be sufficient to account for the spatial variability on most walls. The survey concentrated on vertical walls, but the weathering of horizontal or sloped surfaces, if present, were recorded separately and are not considered in this investigation. Four of the buildings were re-surveyed to check the repeatability of the technique, and t-tests showed no statistically significant difference between original results and those from the repeated survey.

54

Weathering forms	Description
Black flaking	Detaching black surface layer (thickness of detaching stone < 3mm).
Black scaling	Detaching black surface layer (thickness of detaching stone > 3mm).
Black soiling	Black coating on the sandstone surface.
Total blackened stone	Sum of black soiling, black flaking and black scaling (not a true weathering form).

Table 5.1 Definitions of sandstone weathering forms used in the study.

RESULTS

Data from approximately 1400 quadrats were collected and spatial distributions were analysed using cluster analysis. For each building the average percentage cover, per metre squared, for each of the three weathering forms was collated into a data set and analysed with hierarchical clustering methods. Three conceptually different methods (unweighted arithmetic averaging technique, single linkage method and Ward's method) were used to identify the structure of the data and the number of clusters. All three methods produced similar results, exemplified by the dendrogram produced by the unweighted arithmetic averaging technique (Figure 5.1). Three distinct clusters in the data can be identified. A K-means cluster analysis was carried out to check the composition of the three clusters and provide descriptive statistics and analysis of variance (ANOVA) for the final clusters (Table 5.2). Members of cluster 1 have on average 47% total blackened stone, cluster 2 members 25% and cluster 3 members 11%. ANOVA shows the difference between the means of the three clusters to be statistically significant for all three weathering forms (Table 5.2), giving evidence that the amount of black flaking, scaling and soiling does vary between clusters of buildings. However, a post-hoc comparison of means, Tukey Honest significant difference test for unequal sample sizes, (Table 5.3) shows which cluster means are particularly different from each other. It is apparent that there is strong evidence for a difference in means for black soiling and total blackened stone for each cluster, but the evidence for black flaking and black scaling is not so strong.

To evaluate spatial distributions, building location and cluster membership were plotted onto the survey base map (Figure 5.2). Buildings in

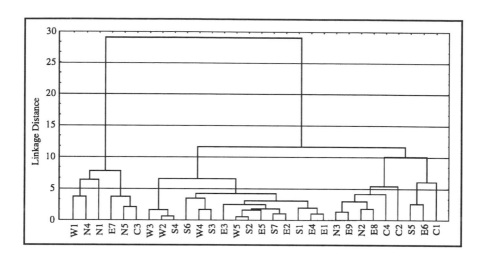

Figure 5.1 Dendrogram produced by unweighted pair-group average technique, using Euclidean distance.

	Cluster 1		Cluster 2		Cluster 3		ANOVA
Weathering forms	Mean cover	Standard deviation	Mean cover	Standard deviation	Mean cover	Standard deviation	p value
Black flaking	4.4%	0.6	7.5%	4.7	3.6%	1.9	< 0.05
Black scaling	4.1%	2.8	1.7%	1.2	1.1%	0.9	< 0.01
Black soiling	38.6%	3.9	16.0%	2.7	6.4%	2.7	< 0.01
Total blackened stone	47.0%	4.9	25.1%	4.5	11.1%	4.7	< 0.01

Table 5.2 Descriptive statistics and ANOVA for each cluster formed by K-means clustering. (p values of < 0.01 give strong evidence of a significant difference between means of the three clusters whereas p values of < 0.05 only give some evidence of a significant difference.)

Weathering forms	Cluster 1 Cluster 2	Cluster 1 Cluster 3	Cluster 2 Cluster 3
Black flaking	----------	---------	< 0.05
Black scaling	< 0.05	< 0.01	---------
Black soiling	< 0.01	< 0.01	< 0.01
Total blackened stone	< 0.01	< 0.01	< 0.01

Table 5.3 Results of post-hoc comparison of means. Tukey Honest significant difference test for unequal sample sizes was used. (p values of < 0.01 give strong evidence of a significant difference between the means of two clusters whereas p values of < 0.05 only give some evidence of a significant difference.)

cluster 1, with the highest percentage of total blackened stone, are situated in central areas of the conurbation with one exception just north of the conurbation. Members of cluster 2, with an intermediate amount of total blackened stone, are generally inside the conurbation, but also extend to the north and are skewed slightly towards the east. Members of cluster 3, with little total blackened stone, are generally outside the conurbation or on the fringes to the east, south and west (Figure 5.2). This pattern suggests that urbanisation may increase the amount of total blackened stone, but to examine this further isometric lines, representing the percentage of total blackened stone for each building, were plotted onto the base map (Figure 5.3). There is a noticeable gradient, with values increasing from less than 10% in rural areas to the west to greater than 40% in the centre of the conurbation and decreasing to less than 20% in rural areas to the east. Changes from south to north are less clear, but it can be seen that in rural areas to the south values are typically below 20%, increasing in the centre to more than 40%, which is maintained to the north of the conurbation.

DISCUSSION

The isometric lines of total blackened stone and the cluster analysis results suggest that buildings in urban areas of the West Midlands experience up to four times more total blackened stone than buildings in rural areas. This general pattern is complicated by local factors exerting an influence within the conurbation. The isometric lines show that the highest cover of total

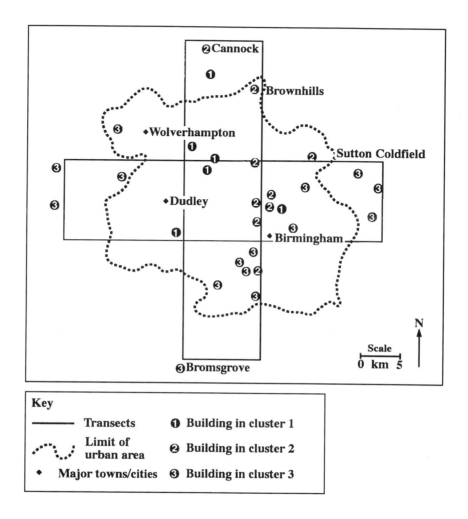

Figure 5.2 Map showing survey area, with transects, building distribution and cluster membership.

blackened stone occurs in an area crossing the middle of the conurbation from approximately north to south. A limb of relatively high cover also extends from the centre of the conurbation east above Birmingham (Figure 5.3). Various factors, such as relief or degree of exposure, could cause this distribution, but the most convincing factor is the location of industry. Major industrial emitters were identified in the 1960s by the national survey of air pollution. The location of these emitters compares closely to the iso-metric lines of total blackened stone (Figure 5.4). The central region has the

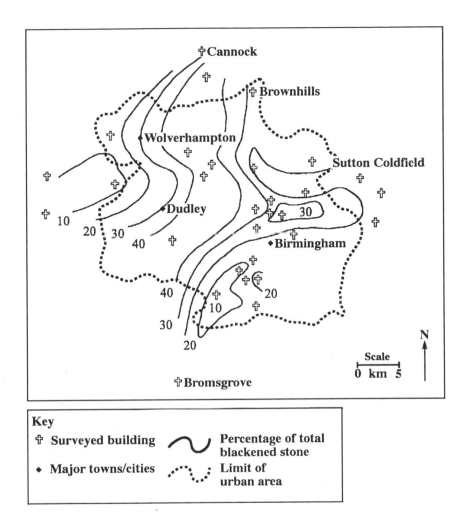

Figure 5.3 Map of survey area showing isometric lines representing percentage of total blackened stone.

densest concentration of emitters and the limb of relatively high total blackened stone north of Birmingham has a relatively high concentration. To fully explain the role of industry, however, it is necessary to consider the location of industry for the last 150 years (coinciding with the age of these buildings), and the type and amount of atmospheric pollutants they released. Data on the latter are especially limited, and industrial locations and activities have changed over time. A survey of the conurbation in the 1940s mapped the location of industry, indicating its historical distribution (Figure 5.5). It is noteworthy that the heavier industries, such as iron production,

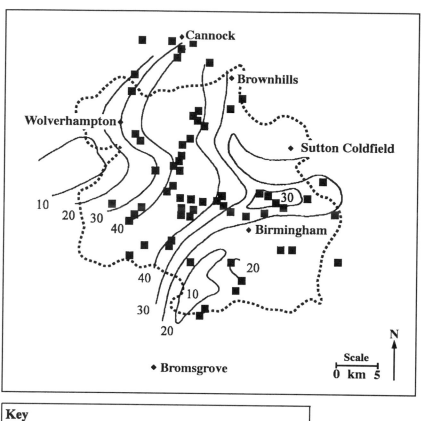

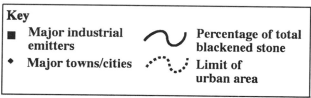

Figure 5.4 Map of survey area showing the distribution of major industrial emitters identified by the national survey of air pollution 1961–1971 (Warren Spring Laboratory, 1973). Isometric lines represent percentage of total blackened stone.

occupied a central location, especially between Birmingham and Wolverhampton, which may account for the highest percentage of total blackened stone occurring in this area.

The increase in total blackened stone, due to urbanisation and industrialisation, alters the appearance of the buildings, but the possible damaging influences of soiling warrants further consideration. Previous research

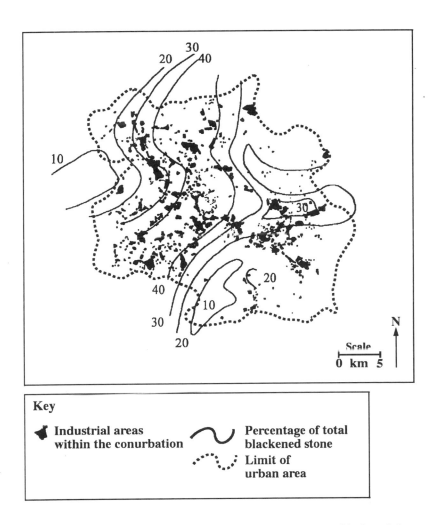

Figure 5.5 Map of survey area showing the distribution of industrial areas within the conurbation in the 1940s (West Midlands Group, 1948). Isometric lines represent percentage of total blackened stone.

reports black crusts to have a varied composition, but generally consist of inorganic particles such as flyash, organic materials such as algae and precipitates such as gypsum. A microcatchment experiment carried out on ferruginous quartz arenites, similar to those used in these buildings, has found that on average 66 mg m^{-2} week^{-1} of solid particulate matter was deposited and held by sandstones exposed in Wolverhampton. These particulates were rich in silicon, aluminium and iron, with considerable deposits of calcium. On these sandstones, with little calcareous material, deposition of particulate matter may be an important source of calcium necessary for gypsum formation. Further to this, the deposition of iron may catalyse gypsum formation. Scanning Electron Microscopy (SEM) examination of a black scale collected from Wednesbury (NGR SO 987934), near the centre of the conurbation, showed the presence of a range of particulate matter, predominantly coal fly ash, identified by its glassy and spherical form. This is not surprising, since historically the local source of fuel has been the indigenous Carboniferous Coal Measures.

In addition to chemical influences, black soiling may increase stone deterioration by physical weathering mechanisms. Black soiling lowers the albedo of stone, increasing absorption of incident solar radiation. Using a scale from zero to one, where zero is the minimum absorption of incident solar radiation and one the maximum, a red sandstone was found to have an absorptivity of 0.7, while coal flyash has a value of 0.95. This increase in the stones absorption of incident solar radiation may increase the importance of heating/cooling cycles, differential thermal expansion and wetting/drying cycles. These cycles produce stresses in the stone, but also increase dissolution/crystallisation cycles and hydration/dehydration cycles of gypsum, hence exacerbating stress. Previous research has commented on the possible damaging effects of black soiling trapping moisture behind the soiled outer layer of the stone. If black soiling totally covers sandstone, water absorption can be reduced from 0.68 1 m^{-2} hour $^{-1}$ for unsoiled sandstone to 0.07 1 m^{-2} hour $^{-1}$. Any drying occurs at the most permeable area, enhancing gypsum concentrations in this area and hence localised stone breakdown. This may be one reason why enhanced deterioration is often seen at the edges of ashlar, as the stone/mortar interface may provide a gap in the layer of black soiling. Additionally, during low temperatures, freezing may occur, forcing water to expand in a confined space behind the black soiling. This generates further stresses which may enhance deterioration and indeed rapid stone breakdown has been reported following a severe frost.

Considering these potentially deleterious effects of black soiling enables a generalised three stage model of the breakdown of black soiled sandstone to be proposed (Figure 5.6). This model provides a convenient summary of the mechanisms operating, however, the actual importance of each process, and whether they occur at all, will depend upon the properties of the stone and the environment it is exposed to. Presumably, these variables will also be decisive in whether black flaking or black scaling is formed. To examine whether these forms of detachment are proportional to the amount of total blackened stone, the share (%) of total blackened stone attributed to each weathering form was calculated for the three clusters of building (Table 5.4). Black scaling is reasonably consistent for all clusters and typically accounts for about 9% of the total blackened stone. Black flaking is less consistent, accounting for approximately 30% of the total blackened stone for clusters 2 and 3, but only 9% for cluster 1. The reasons for this are unclear, but it must be considered that the surveying technique only recorded the weathering forms present at the time of surveying. Therefore, if black flakes had already detached from many of the more

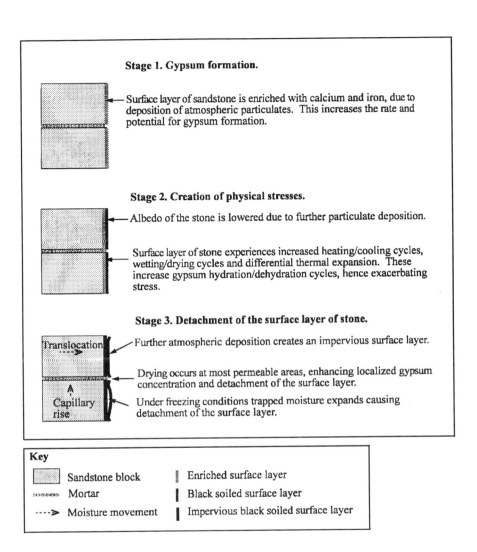

Stage 1. Gypsum formation.

Surface layer of sandstone is enriched with calcium and iron, due to deposition of atmospheric particulates. This increases the rate and potential for gypsum formation.

Stage 2. Creation of physical stresses.

Albedo of the stone is lowered due to further particulate deposition.

Surface layer of stone experiences increased heating/cooling cycles, wetting/drying cycles and differential thermal expansion. These increase gypsum hydration/dehydration cycles, hence exacerbating stress.

Stage 3. Detachment of the surface layer of stone.

Further atmospheric deposition creates an impervious surface layer.

Drying occurs at most permeable areas, enhancing localized gypsum concentration and detachment of the surface layer.

Under freezing conditions trapped moisture expands causing detachment of the surface layer.

Key

Sandstone block		Enriched surface layer
Mortar		Black soiled surface layer
Moisture movement		Impervious black soiled surface layer

Figure 5.6 Generalised three stage model of the breakdown of heavily soiled sandstone.

severely soiled buildings in cluster 1, this form of weathering would be underestimated. Although it is often apparent that flaking or scaling has occurred, recording the actual type of flaking or scaling is not possible. It may be this limitation causing the poorer statistical significance for black flaking and black scaling shown by the post-hoc comparison of means (Table 5.3).

Weathering forms	Cluster 1	Cluster 2	Cluster 3
Black flaking	9.3%	29.8%	32.4%
Black scaling	8.7%	6.7%	9.9%
Black soiling	82.0%	63.5%	57.7%

Table 5.4 Percentage share of total blackened stone attributed to each weathering form.

CONCLUSIONS

Recording the percentage of stone covered by various weathering forms has enabled a quantification of the amount of total blackened stone, with values from less than 10% in rural environments to values greater than 40% in urban areas. These data are supported by observations in Italy where black soiling of sandstone was noted to be more severe in urban than in rural areas. There is also evidence that sandstones in more industrial areas experience the highest amounts of total blackened stone. In the West Midlands the use of coal as the dominant domestic and industrial fuel appears to have been an important source for much of this soiling, and this has a potentially deleterious effect upon the stone.

Acknowledgements

This work was funded by the Engineering and Physical Sciences Research Council, UK. We are grateful to the architects and officials who granted permission for buildings to be used in the survey and helped with historical details. Thanks to Ms S. Padfield for help with surveying and the following staff at the University of Wolverhampton for technical assistance: Mr D. Crane, Dr C. Williams, Mr B. Bucknall, Dr A. Williams, Mrs D. Spencer and Mr K. Muggleston.

References

Bluck, B. and Porter, J. (1991) Sandstone buildings and cleaning problems. *Stone Industries* **26**: 21–27.
Cheng, R., Mohnen, V., Shen, T., Current, M. and Hudson, J. (1976)

Characterisation of particles from power plants. *Journal of the Air Pollution Association* **26**: 787–790.

Elfving, P., Panas, I. and Lindqvist, O. (1994) Model study of the first steps in the deterioration of calcareous stone: III. Manganese and iron mediated sulphation of natural stone. *Applied Surface Science* **78**: 373–384.

Fitzner, B., Heinrichs, K. and Kownatski, R. (1992) Classification and mapping of weathering forms. In J. Rodrigues, *et al.* (eds) *7th International Congress on Deterioration and Conservation of Stone*, Lisbon, Portugal, 15–18 June, pp. 957–968.

Halsey, D., Dews, S., Mitchell, D. and Harris, F. (1995) Real-time measurements of sandstone deterioration: A microcatchment study. *Building and Environment* **30**: 411–417.

Halsey, D., Mitchell, D., Dews, S. and Harris, F. (1995) The effects of atmospheric pollutants upon sandstone: Evidence from real-time measurements and analysis of decay features on historic buildings. In J. Kamari, *et al.* (eds) *Proceedings of the 10th World Clean Air Congress, Volume 3,* Espoo, Finland, 28 May–2 June, FAPPS, Helsinki.

Howard, P. (1991) *An Introduction to Environmental Pattern Analysis.* The Parthenon Publishing Group, New Jersey.

McGreevy, J.P. (1985) Thermal properties as controls on rock surface temperature maxima, and possible implications for rock weathering. *Earth Surface Processes and Landforms* **10**: 125–136.

Sabbioni, C. and Zappia, G. (1992) Decay of sandstone in urban areas correlated with atmospheric aerosol. *Water, Air and Soil Pollution* **63**: 305–316.

Siegel, R. and Howell, J. (1972) *Thermal Radiation and Heat Transfer.* McGraw-Hill, New York.

Smith, B.J., Magee, R.W. and Whalley, W.B. (1994) Breakdown patterns of quartz sandstone in a polluted urban environment: Belfast, N. Ireland. In D. Robinson, and R.B.G. Williams (eds) *Rock Weathering and Landform Evolution.* J. Wiley & Sons, Chichester, pp. 131–150.

Threlkeld, J. (1970) *Thermal Environmental Engineering* (2nd edn). Prentice Hall, New Jersey.

Warren Spring Laboratory (1973) *National survey of air pollution 1961–71.* HMSO, London.

West Midlands Group (1948) *Conurbation: a planning survey of Birmingham and the Black Country.* The Architectural Press, London.

Contact address
School of Construction, Engineering and Technology
University of Wolverhampton
Wulfruna Street
Wolverhampton
WV1 1SB
United Kingdom

6 Aberdeen granite buildings: a study of soiling and decay

D.C.M. URQUHART, M.E. YOUNG,
J. MacDONALD, M.S. JONES
and K.A. NICHOLSON

ABSTRACT

Observations at city centre sites in Aberdeen has established the nature of the decay and soiling of granite façades. Most buildings were constructed between circa 1830–1890 using local granites from a number of quarries and built in ashlar with relatively narrow joints. Older granite properties are constructed from another local granite which is more vulnerable to weathering and decay because of the presence of muscovite mica along grain boundaries. Generally, the manifestations of decay are spalling of the ashlar face, scaling, loss of detail at arrises, granular disaggregation (often associated with mortar joints) and decay associated with the formation of gypsum crusts. Soiling on Aberdeen granites is of two main types. The most common form comprises a thin, compact layer (10 μm – several 100 μm in thickness), tightly bound to the stone surface. The second type of soiling are crusts up to 6 mm in thickness. Soiling was studied using scanning electron microscopy (SEM), energy dispersive X-ray analysis (EDX) and X-ray diffraction (XRD) and depth profiling was used to determine the nature and amount of soluble ions present at particular depths in the granite. Evidence suggests that mortar joints are implicated in the decay of granite.

INTRODUCTION

The work described in this paper forms a small part of a research commission, (Urquhart, *et al.*, 1995) sponsored by Historic Scotland, Scottish Enterprise and Grampian Enterprise, investigating the cleaning of granite buildings and monuments. The need for this research reflected concern that

Processes of Urban Stone Decay. Edited by B.J. Smith and P.A. Warke. © 1996 Donhead Publishing Ltd.

uncontrolled and aggressive cleaning techniques may be damaging façades already at risk from surface decay. It was found during the course of this work that there was a general preconception amongst building professionals that as granite is a hard stone it is therefore infinitely durable and that durability of granite masonry is not a significant issue.

The majority of buildings in Aberdeen, Scotland, built prior to circa 1940 are constructed from granite taken from local quarries, of which over 100 have been identified, although not all were producing granite for building purposes. In the main, granites used on later city centre buildings (from around 1820 AD–1900 AD) were extracted from the Aberdeen Granite outcrops (e.g. Rubislaw Granite); a medium to coarse-grained, foliated, grey, muscovite-biotite-granite and from Kemnay Granite, a light silver-grey, medium grained, muscovite-biotite granite. Occasionally a pink, medium-grained, foliated muscovite-biotite granite from the Corrennie quarry is used, usually in feature panels but occasionally as a complete façade. Older properties, mainly built in the eighteenth and early nineteenth centuries, are built with a light grey-brown, weathered, medium-grained, biotite-muscovite granite with secondary muscovite oriented along grain boundaries, typical of that from the Loanhead quarry. This latter granite is generally in an advanced state of surface decay, with extensive iron staining.

Whilst the research project incorporated both laboratory and field investigations, this paper focuses on typical case studies of buildings that were selected for stone cleaning trials, to assess the efficacy of a range of cleaning regimes.

SOILING AND DECAY OF GRANITE

It is recognised that the soiling of granite on a building façade is a complex phenomenon, that occurs at or near the surface of the stone, where the low porosity and permeability of granite tends to concentrate water run-off, and leads to particular areas of heavier soiling at the margins of run-off zones. Soiling takes two main forms; particulate soiling and biological soiling. In practice both types may be present, either separately or in combination. This paper will concentrate on particulate soiling as biological soiling of façades is not a major problem on the relatively plain Aberdeen façades, where the annual rainfall is relatively low (long-term average, 795 mm per annum).

Observations on the nature of particulate soiling on façades at a number of city centre sites in Aberdeen indicate that the soiling falls into two main categories. The most common form of soiling on buildings that have not been cleaned in the past is a thin, compact layer tightly bound to the stone surface. Generally, this form of soiling is not uniformly distributed over the façade; there tends to be more intense soiling at base courses and projecting architectural features, such as sills. In addition, variations in the physical and chemical nature of the stone and in the micro-climate influence the location and intensity of the soiling layer. The second category of soiling observed are crusts up to 6 mm in thickness, typically found in association with mortar joints and in sheltered areas adjacent to run-off zones. Figure 6.1 shows a typical mix of cleaned and uncleaned façades and, on the uncleaned façade, indicates a fairly uniform level of soiling over most stones and areas of more intense soiling representing incipient crust formation. It is interesting to note the early reappearance of this form of soiling on the cleaned, right-hand façade.

There is no evidence to suggest that there is a direct correlation between soiling on the surface of the granite and decay of the granite. In the case of crust formations, it has yet to be established whether this is the direct cause of observed damage to the underlying granite. In general terms, the manifestations of decay are similar to those observed by other workers throughout the world, and are similar to that found on sandstone. In Aberdeen the most frequently observed forms of decay are:

• Spalling or flaking.
• Scaling similar to contour scaling of sandstone with plate type detachment.
• Loss of detail at arrises.
• Granular disaggregation (granulation), often associated with mortar joints.

Examples of contour scaling are reported in Hungary (Smith, et al., 1993); India (Gauri, 1990); Ireland (Cooper, et al., 1993); Portugal (Sequeria Braga, et al., 1993); and Spain (Casal Porto, 1989, 1993). A typical example of this phenomenon in Aberdeen is shown in Figure 6.2.

Figure 6.3 shows both surface spalling of the ashlar block and loss of detail at the raised feature at a granite arched entrance, built of a Rubislaw type granite. The increased grain loss at the mortar joint is a common feature observed in many other situations.

The decay of granite through contact with the jointing mortar is a recognised phenomenon (Cooper, et al., 1989, Duffy and Perry, 1994), where both lime and cement mortars provide a source of calcium which, on reaction with pollutants deposited through wet and dry deposition, create a range of salts depending on the composition of the acidic solution. The most common salt formation is gypsum, however calcium chloride and calcium nitrate may also form (Jones, 1990). Many examples of this form of decay exist in the Aberdeen granites. It is often the case that, prior to any grain loss from the surface, stones are seen to have a distinct and colour-altered rim around the stone where it is in contact with the mortar joint.

A postulated granite decay model, illustrating the sequential decay process, is presented in Figure 6.4 and is based upon site observations of granite masonry of a variety of ages and conditions. In the model, the original joint profile (1) is still sharp and well defined. Frequently a clearly defined zone around the perimeter of the granite block, adjacent to the mortar joint (the hatched area), is observed. This zone is the 'active' zone where changes in the stone are taking place, possibly as a result of interaction between the stone and the mortar. As the mortar joint weathers, fine cracks develop at the granite–mortar interface that allow a greater penetration of moisture and pollutants resulting from run-off down the face of the granite.

Figure 6.1 Typical city centre elevation, King Street, Aberdeen.

Figure 6.2 Granite scaling.

Figure 6.3 Advanced decay to projecting detail. Note also surface spalling.

The gradual loss of grains from the exposed granite arris (2 and 3), through increased exposure to moisture, pollutants and salts leaves the mortar unsupported and causes a gradual erosion of the joint over many years. Repointing is typically carried out in hard, cement based mortars applied over the face of the eroded granite (4) and the hard mortar helps to promote the time of wetness of the granite in contact with the mortar. Shrinkage cracking of the mortar, at an early stage in the life of the mortar, will again cause run-off to be directed into the shrinkage crack (5).

These observations on the granite–mortar interface indicate that the effects of the mortar on the granite decay process are very complex, with little available evidence to support the precise mechanism. Further work on the effects of mortar on granite decay is needed. Maxwell (1994) reports a similar effect at sandstone–mortar interfaces.

CASE STUDY

A number of buildings were studied within Aberdeen city centre as part of a granite cleaning research project and the findings of one study, the Medico-Chirurgical Hall, 27–29 King Street (Figure 6.5), are indicative of the condition of granite façades in the city centre area, constructed from this granite type.

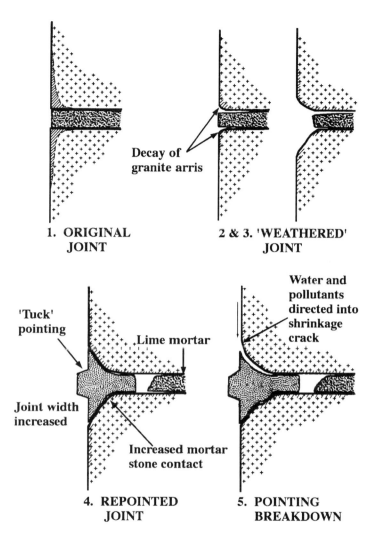

Figure 6.4 Granite–mortar joint interaction.

The Medico-Chirurgical Hall is an important Category 'A' listed building by Archibald Simpson, built between 1818 and 1820 as a library and meeting place. The granite used for this building was a Rubislaw type granite and all of the ashlar stonework for the main street façade was of a similar granite type, with a smooth, finely tooled surface. Overall, the degree of soiling was low but with localised areas where distinct run-off patterns had resulted in slightly heavier soiling levels. Incipient crust formations, often in association with mortar joints, were also evident in places (Figure 6.6).

Figure 6.5 Main elevation of the Medico-Chirurgical Hall.

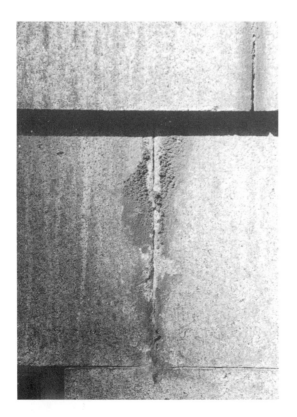

Figure 6.6 Typical crust formation in association with mortar joint. Depth profiling analysis.

Colour analysis of the granite surface employing the L*a*b* colour space system (also known as CIELAB) was carried out using a Minolta Colorimeter. Using this system the lightness of the surface (L*), reflecting the level of soiling, can be quantified. In the case of this façade the average L* value of the soiled granite was 44.2 and the unsoiled value was 51. A granite surface that is perceived to be heavily soiled has a lightness value of 30.

Whilst, in general terms, the granite forming the façade exhibited little observable large scale decay, a number of individual stones were showing signs of surface decay, most of which tended to be in regions adjacent to the joints and mainly took the form of spalling and loss of detail at joint arrises. A sample, 25 mm diameter by 50 mm deep, extracted by dry coring was subjected to analysis by scanning electron microscopy (SEM) and electron dispersive X-ray fluorescence (EDX).

One of the most obvious characteristics of this sample was the presence of sulphur bearing compounds, distributed in discreet patches on the surface of various mineral grains (Figure 6.7). EDX analysis, Figure 6.8, showed the presence of calcium (Ca) and sulphur (S), indicating that this material is a form of calcium sulphate. The presence of a small chlorine

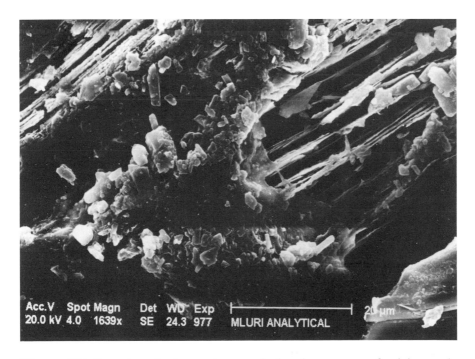

Figure 6.7 Scanning electron micrograph showing an area of calcium sulphate adhering to a mica crystal on the surface of soiled granite. (Picture width 65 µm)

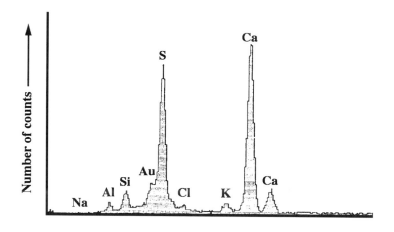

Figure 6.8 Qualitative energy dispersive X-ray analysis (EDX) of crystalline structure shown in Figure 6.7.

peak probably indicates the presence of sodium chloride (NaCl), most likely due to the coastal environment in which the building is located. Generally the surface of the soiled granite contained patches of calcium sulphate randomly distributed over the surfaces of all mineral types.

Core samples from the granite and from the jointing mortar were extracted. The amount of soluble ions present in the granite and in the mortar were determined by ion chromatography at sampling intervals between 0–10 mm, using a depth profiling technique (Figures 6.9 and 6.10). The ions analysed were fluoride, chloride, nitrate, sulphate and sodium, which, apart from fluoride, are those most likely to be responsible for potentially damaging salts (Winkler, 1994).

In the case of the granite, within the surface zone (0–1 mm), a relatively high sulphate level, in comparison with other ions, of about 2000 ppm and a sodium level of about 600 ppm were determined. All other soluble ions were present in amounts varying from a little over 100 ppm (chloride) to around 20 ppm (fluoride).

The mortar sample presented a much higher level of ion concentration within the surface zone (0–5 mm) and the results here are typical of mortar samples from other buildings. In this case the level of sulphate was just under 30,000 ppm, soluble sodium was 800 ppm, chloride was about 1000 ppm and nitrate 600 ppm. The amount of soluble fluoride was very low.

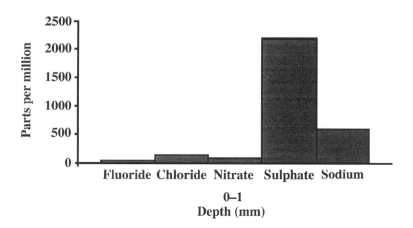

King Street: Granite before cleaning

Figure 6.9 Depth profile of soiled granite before cleaning.

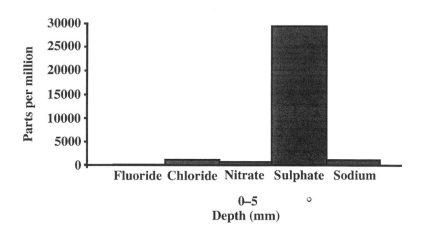

King Street: Mortar before cleaning

Figure 6.10 Depth profile of mortar joint before cleaning.

CONCLUSIONS

From the evidence of this work it may be postulated that a significant factor in the decay of granite is the association between the granite and the mortar joint. The level of atmospheric pollution in a city centre situation, and the deposition of sulphur, in particular, on the façade appears to act in combination with the mortar constituents with the resultant formation of calcium sulphate. Whilst a complete understanding of the decay processes is, as yet, not available; the common occurrence of decayed granite in the joint region lends weight to the hypothesis that it is the action of this salt within microcracks at the granite surface that is a primary means of decay. This conclusion is supported by other workers (Haneef, *et al.*, 1992). The distinct colour alteration of the granite within the zone of influence of the joint, may be a further indicator of incipient decay. It is also clear from the high levels of soluble ions present in the mortar, in comparison to the granite, that the mortar joint is acting as a reservoir for soluble pollutants being absorbed by the joint as a result of surface run-off from the relatively impermeable granite.

Whilst soiling levels on most granites within the city centre area can not be considered to be high, it is sufficient to reduce the level of brightness of the granite surface. The occurrence of 'streaking' at the edges of run-off zones is a common feature of granite soiling, and has been found in the form of a gypsum crust (Urquhart, *et al.*, 1995). When these crusts are well established they are often associated with decay of the granite substrate.

References

Casal Porto, M., Delgado Rodrigues, J., Silva Hermo, B. (1992) Construction materials and decay problems of Salome Church in Santiago de Compostela. In J. Delgado Rogrigues, F. Henriques and F. Telmo Jeremiads (eds) *Proceedings of the 7th International Congress on Deterioration and Conservation of stone*. Lisbon, Portugal. 15–18 June, pp. 3–10.

Cooper, T.P., Duffy, A., O'Brian, P., Bell, E., Lyons, F. (1993) Conservation of historic buildings at Trinity College, Dublin. In M.A. Vicente Hernández, E. Molina Ballesteros and V. Rives Arnau (eds) *Actas del Workshop Alteración de Granitos y Rocas Afines*. Consejo Superior de Investigaciones Científicas, Madrid, pp. 59–65.

Duffy, A.P. and Perry, S.H. (1994) The effects of mortars on granite decay. In Bell, E. and Cooper, T.P. (eds) *Granite Weathering and Conservation*. Trinity College, Dublin, pp. 1–9.

Gauri, K.L. (1990) Decay and preservation of stone in modern environments. *Environmental Geology and Water Science* **15**: 45–54.

Haneef, S.J., Johnson, J.B., Jones, M.S., Thomson, G.E., Wood, G.C. and Azzaz, S.A. (1993) A laboratory simulation of degradation of Leinster granite by dry and wet deposition processes. *Corrosion Science* **34**:

511–524.

Jones, M.S. (1990) *The degradation of building stone.* Unpublished Ph.D. Thesis, UMIST.

Maxwell, I. (1994) The interaction of lime mortar and Scottish sandstones. *SPAB News* **15**: 16–18.

Sequeira Braga, M.S., Simões Alves, C.A., Begonha, A. (1993) Weathering of the Oporto granite and the deterioration of the Hospital de Santo António: historical monument built with granitic materials. In M. A. Vicente Hernández, E. Molina Ballesteros and V. Rives Arnau (eds) *Actas del Workshop Alteración de Granitos y Rocas Afines.* Consejo Superior de Investigaciones Científicas, Madrid, pp. 153–154.

Smith, B.J., Magee, R.W., Whalley, W.B. (1993) Decay of granite in a polluted environment in Budapest. In M. A. Vicente Hernández, E.M. Ballesteros and V.R. Arnau (eds) *Actas del Workshop Alteración de Granitos y Rocas Afines.* Consejo Superior de Investigaciones Científicas, Madrid, pp. 159–162.

Urquhart, D.C.M., Young, M.E,. MacDonald, J., Jones, M., Laing, R., Nicholson, K. (1995) *Research report: Cleaning of granite buildings.* Scottish Enterprise. Historic Scotland and Grampian Enterprise.

Winkler, E.M. (1994) *Stone in Architecture: Properties, Durability*, (3rd edn). Springer-Verlag, Berlin.

Contact address
Faculty of Design
The Robert Gordon University
Garthdee Road
Aberdeen
AB9 2QB
United Kingdom

7 Fluorescence characteristics of algae commonly found on sandstone: application to algae mapping

D.McSTAY, R.D. WAKEFIELD,
E. BRECHET and M.S. JONES

ABSTRACT

This paper reports some initial results from an investigation into the spectral characteristics of algae commonly found on stone and the application of this information to the development of instrumentation for quantifying the distribution of the algae on stone. Four algal species have been examined and all found to exhibit similar broadband fluorescence spectra with emission bands centred around 310 nm, 380 nm and 685 nm. The origin of the first two bands is likely to be pigments in the algae while the 685 nm band is known to be due to chlorophyll-a. For a fixed excitation intensity it has been shown that the fluorescence intensity is proportional to the concentration of the algae. Freshly cut stone has been found to possess a weak fluorescence which limits the sensitivity of the present system, however this should be greatly reduced by incorporation of improved optical filtering. Nevertheless the use of the fluorescence from algae has been shown to provide a potential means of quantitatively mapping the distribution of algae on stone. The technique therefore has potential for enhancing the non-destructive study of colonisation of stone by algae, the effectiveness of various biocidal treatments in preventing algal recolonisation and as an early warning system in the recognition of colonisation of culturally sensitive materials.

INTRODUCTION

Biological communities; algae, lichen, fungi and bacteria, are known to play a role in the decay of various materials on buildings and are therefore of great interest to those involved in the conservation of stone (Lewis, *et al.*

Processes of Urban Stone Decay. Edited by B.J. Smith and P.A. Warke. © 1996 Donhead Publishing Ltd.

1989; Sand and Bock, 1991; May, *et al.,* 1993). Algae in particular are the quickest to recolonise fresh or recently cleaned stone and their appearance is often the motive for the application of biocidal chemicals which aim to prevent or slow down the recolonisation process.

The accurate measurement of the extent, distribution and variation with time of photosynthetic biological communities on stone is an essential requirement in the study of the efficacy of many masonry surface treatments including biocides, water repellents and cleaning agents. The comparative effectiveness of different products in preventing re-soiling, and associated decay, by biological growths can be determined by monitoring their appearance on treated façades. Conventional methods to assess the distribution of algae are largely subjective, rely on close access, visual interpretation, hand mapping, sampling and later analysis and colour measurements, all of which are labour intensive. These factors limit the number of measurements which can practically be performed and the reliability and accuracy of the data. There is therefore a requirement for the development of novel, objective and less labour intensive techniques for mapping such biological communities on buildings which can be used in building surveys and in the assessment of product efficacy.

The use of infra-red cameras has proven useful in the assessment of the effectiveness of ultra-violet light as a biocide on plaster walls colonised by algae and cyanobacteria (Van der Molen, *et al.,* 1980). Although worthwhile, this technique can only be semi quantitative and has not the potential to be species specific. In recent years laser techniques have increasingly found favour in a wide range of measurement applications such as biomedical diagnosis and in particular, are increasingly being employed in environmental applications such as the monitoring of plume dispersion from industrial sites and the measurement of marine algal distributions (McStay, *et al.,* 1995). Optical and laser techniques are also routinely employed to study a wide range of surface parameters, for example, surface roughness, stress or corrosion induced micro-cracking of metal surfaces and surface contamination, but as yet have not been applied to the routine characterisation of stone surfaces.

Laser based techniques have a number of features which lend themselves to conservation applications: they are non-contact and highly directional. This allows the potential for developing measurement systems which can be deployed remotely from the stone to be monitored, avoiding the cost and risk associated with the construction of scaffolding used by conventional systems to access many sites. In addition, by incorporating optical spectral analysis, the chemical composition of a soiling layer or specific algal species can be probed. Photosynthetic pigments present in algae of the class *chlorophyceae*, typically those found on stone, are the chlorophylls (both chlorophyll-a and -b) and smaller amounts of accessory pigments, carotenes and xanthophylls, which can vary in quantity from species to species and between algal groups, environment and nutrient status (Round, 1973). Finally fluorescent pigments have previously been used as indicators of metabolic state, there is therefore scope for developing laser based systems which would have the potential to probe the speciation and metabolic state of algae (i.e. live or dead) on stone. For such an approach to be investigated it would, however, be necessary to acquire a detailed spectral data base of those algae commonly found on stone. At present no such data base exists. The development of a data base containing specific spectral characteristics of different photosynthetic biological communities found on buildings could aid in the identification of specific organisms and the colonisation/re-colonisation rates on masonry.

In this paper we report some initial results from the spectral analysis of several algae commonly found on masonry and the use of a laser based system to map the distribution of algae on sandstone.

FLUORESCENCE SPECTRA OF COMMON ALGAE

The spectral properties of selected algae commonly found on sandstone was determined from pure cultures of single celled *Chlorococcum hypnosporum* and *Pleurococcus spp.* and filaments *Ulothrix giga* and *U. convervicola*, all green algae of the class *chlorophyceae* (Sciento Educational Services). The algae were maintained in Bolds Basal medium and the excitation and emission spectra for each species measured using a standard spectrofluorimeter. The samples were stirred periodically throughout the measurements to ensure a uniform distribution in the cuvette.

The measured excitation and emission spectra in the 260–550 nm region for the four algal species are shown in Figures 7.1a–d. Figure 7.1a shows the measured spectra for *Chlorococcum hypnosporum*. From this figure it can be seen that the algae possesses a broadband fluorescence spectra extending from around 280–530 nm. The spectra comprises two distinct bands, one centred around 315 nm and one centred around 380 nm which extends well into the visible region. The spectra presented has not been corrected and thus the actual magnitudes of the peaks are not absolute. The absence of a peak at 685 nm due to chlorophyll-a on these graphs is due to the relatively small intensity of this peak compared to the others and the relative insensitivity of the instrument at this wavelength. The 685 nm peak for chlorophyll-a for *Chlorococcum hypnosporum* can be seen on Figure 7.2, obtained using a second spectrofluorimeter. As can be seen the peak is much smaller than that of the shorter wavelength bands.

The measured excitation and emission spectra for *Pleurococcus* is shown in Figure 7.1b. The spectra for this species again comprises two distinct broadband emissions which are centred around 330–380 nm. In contrast to *Chloroccum* the shorter wavelength emission is observed to be slightly less intense than the longer wavelength band. As can be seen from Figure 7.1c, which shows the measured spectra for *Ulothrix convervicola*, two broadband fluorescence emissions are observed centred around 307 nm and 380 nm. For this species it is observed that both bands have a similar intensity. Finally, the measured spectra for *Ulothrix giga* is shown in Figure 7.1d, yet again a two fluorescence band structure is observed, with one band

(a) *Chlorococcum hypnosporum*

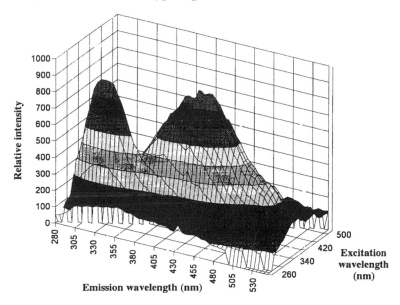

(b) *Pleurococcus spp.*

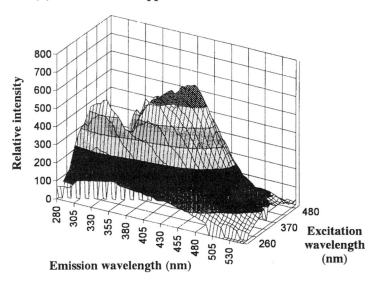

Figures 7.1a and 7.1b The measured excitation and emission spectra of (a) *Chlorococcum hypnosporum* and (b) *Pleurococcus spp.*

(c) *Ulothrix convervicola*

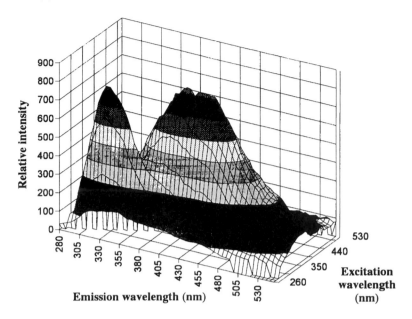

(d) *Ulothrix giga*

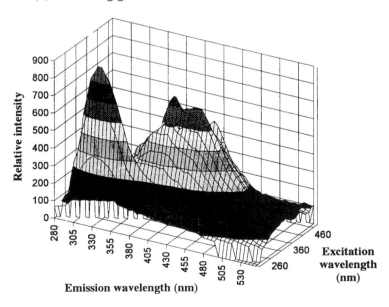

Figures 7.1c and 7.1d The measured excitation and emission spectra of (c) *Ulothrix convervicola* and (d) *Ulothrix giga*.

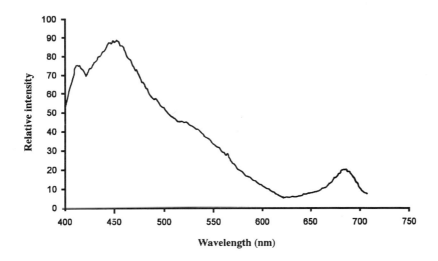

Figure 7.2 The extended spectra for *Chlorococcum hypnosporum* excited at 360 nm.

centred around 310 nm and the other at 380 nm. In this case the shorter wavelength band (310 nm) is significantly more intense.

From the figures it is apparent that the algal species examined possess a similar excitation and fluorescence spectrum. The exact origin of these bands are at present unknown but are likely to be due to the photosynthetic pigments in the algae. The 685 nm emission band is however, known to be due to chlorophyll-a (Boney, 1983). Chlorophyll-a is a pigment universally found in all higher plants, algae and blue-green algae, and consequently is commonly used as a standard for measuring plant populations. The actual concentration of algae in the samples used in this work can thus be determined by extracting the chlorophylls and carotenoids in replica samples in organic solvents using standard techniques (Boney, 1983).

The variation in the measured fluorescence intensity at 400 and 360 nm with concentration of algae (*Chlorococcum hypnosporum*) is shown in Figure 7.3. As can be seen from the figure the fluorescence intensity is related to the amount of algae present.

FLUORESCENCE MAPPING SYSTEM

In order to test the feasibility of employing the intrinsic fluorescence from algae as a means of mapping its distribution on a stone sample, a bench top laser based fluorescence detection system, as shown schematically in Figure 7.4, was constructed. The system comprises a conventional microscope into

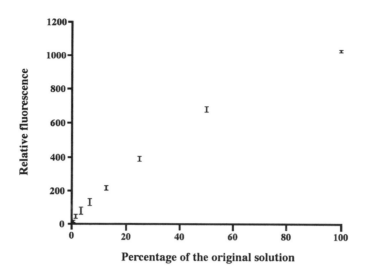

Figure 7.3 The variation in fluorescence intensity of *Chlorococcum hypnosporum* with concentration.

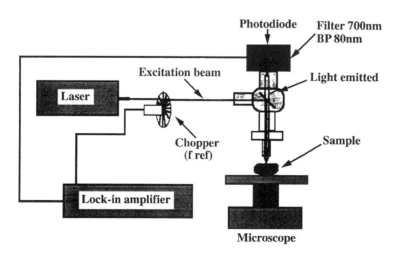

Figure 7.4 Schematic diagram of the laser-based fluorescence microscope system used to map algal distribution on stone.

which 488 nm light from an Argon-ion laser is coupled *via* a beam splitter. The 488 nm light from the laser is amplitude modulated at 0.9 kHz using an optical chopper. The 488 nm excitation light is directed onto the sample under investigation, which is mounted on a translation stage, *via* the microscope objective. The resultant fluorescence is collected by the objective and directed *via* the beam splitter and a wavelength selective system to a photodiode (RS Components BPX21). The broadband nature of the fluorescence of the algae allows the use of a simple interference filter arrangement (bandpass filter 500–550 nm mounted in front of the photodiode) as the wavelength selection system, resulting in a low cost spectroscopic system with both a high rejection and throughput. The output from the photodiode was connected to a lock-in amplifier (EG and G 5101) which took a reference from the chopper. The use of a translation stage allows the sample surface to be mapped.

Sandstone samples of different types were selected which are currently used as building stone and in ongoing conservation research projects, which include effects and efficacy of biocides on stone. Visual examination of the samples showed them to be relatively uniformly distributed with algae, on at least one face.

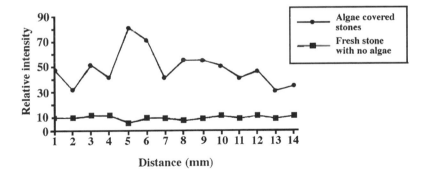

Figure 7.5 Typical results obtained using the laser-based fluorescence microscope system on freshly cut and algae covered sandstone.

Figure 7.5 shows typical results obtained using the laser system for a freshly cut sandstone sample and for a sample of the same sandstone colonised by algae. From the figure it can be seen that the freshly cut stone produces a relatively weak and constant fluorescence signal. This is due to intrinsic fluorescence from components of the stone and associated defect centres. From Figure 7.5 it can be seen that the fluorescence for the sample colonised by algae is much more intense than the freshly cut sample. The fluorescence signal for this sample is observed to vary across the stone with the variation in algae coverage. As shown in Figure 7.3 fluorescence intensity is related to algae concentration thus the results shown in Figure 7.5 demonstrate that it is possible to map out the algae population using the laser microscope. Unlike conventional visual inspection or photographic fluorescence microscope systems the present system is capable of being configured to produce a numerical value related to the algae concentration and distribution. This background fluorescence from the stone will necessarily limit the ultimate sensitivity of the system, however this can be greatly reduced by replacing the current optical filters with narrower band pass and higher rejection filters designed to suppress the fluorescence due to components of the stone. The broadband nature of the fluorescence spectra of the algae means that suppression of this background fluorescence may also be achieved by varying the excitation wavelength employed.

CONCLUSIONS

The four algal species examined all exhibited similar broadband fluorescence spectra with emission bands centred around 310 nm, 380 nm and 685 nm. The origin of the first two bands is likely to be pigments in the algae while the 685 nm band is known to be due to chlorophyll-a. For a fixed excitation intensity it has been shown that the fluorescence intensity is proportional to the concentration of the algae. Freshly cut stone has been found to possess a weak fluorescence which limits the sensitivity of the present system, however this should be greatly reduced by incorporation of improved optical filtering. Nevertheless the use of the fluorescence from algae has been shown to provide a potential means of quantitatively mapping the distribution of algae on stone. The technique therefore has potential for enhancing the non-destructive study of colonisation of stone by algae, the effectiveness of various biocidal treatments in preventing algal recolonisation and as an early warning system in the recognition of colonisation of culturally sensitive materials.

References

Boney, A.D. (1983) *Studies in Biology, No. 52.* Edward Arnold, London.
Lewis, F.J., May, E., Daley, B. and Bravery, A.F. (1989) The role of heterotrophic bacteria in the decay of sandstone from ancient monuments. *Occasional Publication of the Biodeterioration Society* **3**: 45–53.
May, E., Lewis, F.J., Pereira, S., Tayler, S., Seaward, M.R.D. and Allsopp ,D (1993) Microbial deterioration of building stone – a review. *Biodeterioration Abstracts* **7**: 109–123.
McStay, D., Milne, R., Dunn, J. and Wright G.W. (1995) A single probe fibre optic fluorosensor for marine and freshwater measurements of

phytoplankton populations. *International Journal of Remote Sensing* **16**: 957–965.

Round, F.E. (1973) *The Biology of the Algae,* (2nd edn). Edward Arnold, London.

Sand, W. and Bock, E. (1991) Biodeterioration of mineral materials by micro-organisms – Biogenic sulphuric and nitric acid corrosion of concrete and natural stone. *Geomicrobiology Journal* **9**: 129–138.

Van der Molen, J.M., Garty, J., Aardema, B.W. and Krumbein, W.E. (1980) Growth control of algae and Cyanophyta on historical monuments by a mobile UV unit (MUVU). *Studies in Conservation* **25**: 71–77.

Contact address

School of Applied Sciences
The Robert Gordon University
St Andrew Street
Aberdeen
AB1 1HG
United Kingdom

8 Decay of sandstone colonised by an epilithic algal community

R.D. WAKEFIELD, M.S. JONES
and G. FORSYTH

ABSTRACT

Evidence of, and investigations into algal stone decay mechanisms is limited compared to that of lichens, bacteria and fungi but their direct and synergistic action in biodeterioration is of great importance. Work on orange-
coloured spalled stone from extensively decayed areas of the north façade of
Hermitage Castle in the Scottish Borders shows decay to be associated with
the alga *Trentepohlia*, the cells of which accumulate a carotenoid oil. Quartz
crystals in decayed stone appear to be forced apart by aerial filaments of
Trentepohlia growing towards the surface and calcium encrustation
observed around algal cells and fungal hyphae may indicate calcium mobilisation from an inorganic source in the stone or mortar. From these initial
studies, it appears that physical alteration to surface layers of stone may be
caused by the directed growth of algal filaments between stone grains.
Forces applied by wet–dry cycling of mucilage and the mobilisation of calcium and its concentration in the proximity of the community are possibly
additional factors in stone decay.

INTRODUCTION

Stone exposed to the atmosphere exhibits weathering in many forms, some
of which are directly related to the activities of microbial and plant communities growing over large areas of the surface and deeper, in cracks and
pores. Surface growths on a macroscopic scale comprise mainly higher
plants and moss, lichen thalli and mats of algae. Phototrophic organisms are

Processes of Urban Stone Decay. Edited by B.J. Smith and P.A. Warke. © 1996 Donhead Publishing Ltd.

among the primary colonisers of stone, associated with these are microscopic colonies of bacteria, fungi and other micro-organisms which exist in symbiotic and mutualistic relationships. Such communities are commonly embedded in a mucilaginous matrix of complex polysaccharide gels which allows attachment to the substrate, protection from environmental stress and competitive strategies of neighbouring organisms and may also play a highly interactive role in acquisition of nutrients from the immediate environment.

Initial studies have associated the distribution of an algal community, of which the predominating species is *Trentepohlia,* with sandstone decay. *Trentepohlia,* a filamentous alga of the class *Chlorophyceae,* grows as filaments which appear from below the surface of the stone. The filaments below the stone surface are green in colour and became orange through the accumulation of oil globules containing carotene as they reach higher light levels at the stone surface. The distribution of the algae is synonymous with extensive spalling of the surface of the stone. *Trentepohlia* has been identified on the surface of sandstone in the Republic of Ireland and Arran in the west coast of Scotland, granite on the east coast of Scotland, limestone and concrete buildings in the south of England and on concrete in the sub-tropics, where it is currently subjected to extensive eradication programmes due to its unsightly appearance.

A BRIEF REVIEW OF ALGAL STONE DECAY

The role of algae in stone decay has been mostly recognised through its supporting role in the nutrition of 'more aggressive' organisms such as fungi and bacteria, through the production of mucilage and readily assimilable carbon (Hueck van der Plas, 1968; Outega-Calvo, *et al.,* 1993; Warscheid, *et al.,* 1993). However, it is also appreciated that the role of the algae themselves in stone decay mechanisms is more direct, although comparatively little work has been carried out on their full potential as biodeteriorative agents, particularly with regard to the production of acidic compounds which are considered to be the most significant in biological decay (Outega-Calvo, *et al.,* 1993).

Mucilage production by algae, and associated microbial communities, has been acknowledged as a significant contributor to stone decay through a complex array of chemical and mechanical processes. Extracellular substances can absorb considerable amounts of water on wetting and subsequently undergo large changes in volume on wetting and drying. The increased water retention at the stone surface can aid dissolution of minerals by water and hydrated, mucilaginous films can exacerbate damage by both freeze–thaw and wet–dry cycling (Koestler, *et al.,* 1985; Griffin *et al.,* 1991; Danin and Caneva, 1990; Outega-Calvo, *et al.,* 1993). Frequent drying and wetting cycles can stimulate more mucilage production and so increase the potential for more associated damage (Krumbein and Lange, 1978).

The chemical action of mucilage, and products of algal metabolism have been suggested as potential stone decay agents. Sugars and proteins produced from the photosynthetic process and secreted into the mucilage, and the polysaccharides themselves, may act as chelating agents, solubilising minerals such as calcium, iron, manganese, magnesium and potassium, which are nutritionally important (Strzelczyk, 1981; Koestler, et al., 1985; Kaplan, et al., 1987; Bock and Sand, 1993). The production of carbonic acid from carbon dioxide, organic acids, including glycolic acid from photosynthesis, and chelating agents by algae have also been reported (Hueck-van der Plas, 1968; Krampitz and Yarris, 1983; Caneva, et al., 1993).

Although there appears to be a great potential for algae to decay stone, direct observations of stone decay associated with them are not well documented, most reports being of cyanobacteria (blue-green algae) which for example, have been found in self formed pits in marble (Krumbein and Lange, 1978; Danin and Caneva, 1990; Caneva, et al., 1993) although little work has been carried out on the exact mechanisms involved. Associated decay with green algae is even less well documented, with reports concentrating on colour changes and enhancement of water retention at the stone surface. *Trentepohlia* has been associated with pitting of outer layers of calcareous stone (Degelius, 1962).

FIELD STUDIES

Site location

Hermitage Castle is situated in the Scottish Borders and is currently in the care of Historic Scotland. It was built around the end of the thirteenth century as an important Border fortress and is frequently referred to in the records of the War of Independence, exchanging hands between Scotland and England several times until the end of the sixteenth century. The building consists of four intact outer walls and fifteenth century towers, at the base of which was originally a moat. A number of ruinous inner walls and staircases constitute the remains of a thirteenth century manor house, built of coursed red ashlar blocks. The outer walls and towers are constructed mainly of rubble sandstone of unknown origin with large blocks of sandstone for the cornerstones.

Stone description

Sandstone on the outer walls at Hermitage was characterised as a medium grained, quartz-rich sandstone. Interestingly, the survey of a single course around the entire building showed that the colour of the sandstone varied throughout a single block from white, grey to yellow or ochre to red. This variation in colour is due to the presence of iron within the stone in various forms (Fe^{2+} to Fe^{3+}). Distinct iron pan zones 5.0 mm to 15.0 mm thick were also found within the stone. Samples of stone were obtained for character-isation purposes which were relatively fresh and were not colonised by *Trentepohlia*.

Thin sections of the white sandstone analysed by the cross polarising microscope indicated the presence of quartz and alkali feldspar (microcline) with most grains exhibiting pressure solution with little cement present. Scanning electron microscopy of the 'fresh' white sandstone indicated that the grains closely abut one another with little cementing material present. The yellow sandstone thin section was examined and contained in addition to quartz and feldspar some clay minerals which were subsequently identi-fied by X-ray diffraction (XRD) as illite and kaolinite. There was a trace of calcite identified by XRD in the yellow sandstone. Further characterisation of fresh and spalled sandstone colonised by *Trentepohlia* is ongoing.

Biological survey of the stonework

A brief survey of the biological growths present on the external walls of the building was carried out in order to establish patterns of decay and coloni-sation. The survey showed that there were very few areas of green algal growth on any of the façades of the building, the most obvious being a dis-crete area high up on the north façade located in the water run-off zone beneath an owls nest. Large areas of the façades were colonised by well established crustose lichens. Small samples of lichen and spalled stone sup-porting growths of the orange alga were removed for identification and were found to be black growths of *Candelariella aurella* and *Verrularia spp.*, white growths of *Tephromela atra* and *Ochrolechia parella* and yellow growths of *Caloplaca citrina*.

Trentepohlia appeared most frequently on the north façade of the build-ing growing often with *C. citrina*. Stonework situated in the lower 6.0 to 10.0 metres of the north façade was colonised mainly by a species of yellow crustose lichen and orange growths of the algae *Trentepohlia*. The alga appeared over large areas of the north façade of the castle, and over small, discrete areas elsewhere, giving the sandstone a bright orange colouration. Associated with the decay was spalling, where discrete patches of the sur-face stone (between 0.5 to 5.0 cm diameter, 0.1 to 0.2 cm in depth) were falling away. In examples where the lichen occurred on the same stone as *Trentepohlia*, spalling decay occurred only on areas colonised by the latter.

Decayed stone was easily removed and revealed vivid green areas of algal colonised stone beneath. The spall appeared friable when dry, and became soft and gelatinous when wet. The pattern of growth on the most heavily colonised area of the façade followed patterns expected from capil-lary rise of water (Figure 8.1), particularly with a higher rise of water at cor-ners. The wall is in contact with a grassy bank at the base, which slopes towards the wall, most marked at the base of the north west tower. Beneath this tower runs a drainage ditch, originally for drainage of waste water from the castle into the surrounding moat.

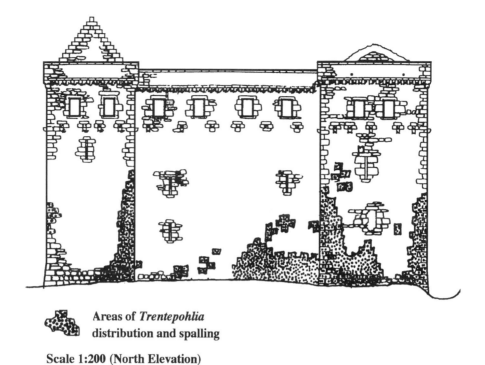

Areas of *Trentepohlia*
distribution and spalling

Scale 1:200 (North Elevation)

Figure 8.1 Diagram showing the pattern of *Trentepohlia* distribution (and spalling decay) on the north façade of Hermitage Castle (shaded areas). (Modified diagram from Historic Scotland.)

Spalling decay associated with *Trentepohlia* occurred much less frequently on other parts of the building and was largely limited to individual stones on east and north facing areas. The growths of *Trentepohlia* were well established on both sandstone and mortar, with filaments growing between sandstone grains at the surface and as small, discrete colonies on the mortar, which remained sound.

Examples of grain loss and some spalling were evident on the west and south façades. This decay was mainly associated with the occurrence of an unidentified lichen with no visible surface thallus or obvious fruiting bodies, which coloured the stone dark grey. Unlike decay occurring on algal colonised stone, spalled zones were not easily removed and did not become soft when moist.

EXPERIMENTAL OBSERVATIONS

Light microscopy examination

Spalled stone appeared brittle and friable when dry and very soft and gelatinous when wet. The high absorbency of the material was indicative of large amounts of mucilage. Samples of wet spall examined under the light microscope showed that individual grains in the spall were enveloped in mucilage, most of which appeared to be associated with the green growth on the spall underside, which consisted of green coloured filaments of *Trentepohlia*, coccoid algal cells and blue-green colonies of *Nostoc*. The large *Trentepohlia* filaments present consisted of both regular and irregularly shaped cells, the orange coloured filaments present on the outside of the spall contained discrete orange oil droplets of varying size, with many of the larger cells having lost green chloroplasts completely. Growth of *Trentepohlia* was prolific, with the outside of the spall being exclusively colonised by this organism. Filaments were closely attached to the quartz grains of the spall.

Scanning electron microscope examination

Intact samples of the external surface of the spall examined using SEM showed *Trentepohlia* filaments growing between individual stone grains (Figure 8.2). Examination of the underside of the spall revealed algal filaments and single algal cells, as observed under the light microscope, and also clumps of bacteria and networks of fungal hyphae which were quite extensive in some areas. The hyphae appeared to be growing in bundles which were enveloped in calcium-rich deposits (Figure 8.3) identified by electron dispersive X-ray analysis. Calcium deposits were also evident throughout the spall, largely concentrated on and around the microbial community. In some areas, the remains of 'sheets' of a calcium rich substance were evident, which could be the remains of the mucilaginous material which had undergone dehydration during the SEM preparation. Quartz grains in close proximity to the biological community did not appear to be significantly pitted or etched and at the present time from these initial studies, there is little evidence for the production of substances aggressive to stone, such as acidic metabolites or chelating agents.

Trentepohlia filaments showed thick, cross woven cellulose walls, the terminal cells of which were of a larger diameter than the green coloured filaments (20.0 μm diameter compared to 10.0 μm). Considering their large size and the thickness of the cell walls, these filaments could be particularly destructive to the stone matrix when growth is directed between grains or into cracks and fissures, which is evident from surface examination of spalled stone. Examination of spalled stone showed many examples where joins between previously closely abutted quartz grains had opened considerably.

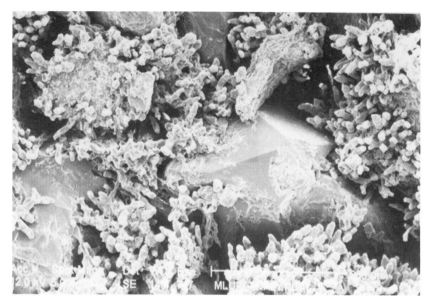

Figure 8.2 Scanning electron micrograph showing the surface of an intact spall with filaments of *Trentepohlia* growing between quartz grains (picture width 650 µm).

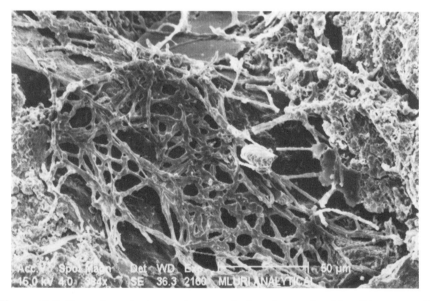

Figure 8.3 Scanning electron micrograph showing underside of intact spall with bundles of fungal hyphae covered in calcium-rich deposits (picture width 230 µm).

CONCLUSIONS AND ONGOING WORK

Trentepohlia is a terrestrial algae and is found largely on soil and rocks in northern and western Britain due to the damper climates typical of these regions (Belcher and Swale, 1978). It has been reported as being found in association with pitting in calcareous rocks (Degelius, 1962) and the cause of much interest in Singapore through aesthetic damage to concrete buildings (Lee and Wee, 1982; Loh and Lee, 1987). The alga has also been found relatively recently on limestone buildings in England (Jones, 1990), granite monuments in the east of Scotland and causing similar lesions to those observed at Hermitage on natural sandstone outcrops in the western Isles of Scotland (authors' observations). The latter observation is of great interest since it is uncommon to find characteristic decay patterns associated with a particular type of growth.

From initial observations, the decay process appears to be largely mechanical, with directed growth of the relatively large filaments of *Trentepohlia* between quartz grains. However, the interactions occurring between growths and the substrate at the spall interface, where the activities of fungi, bacteria and algae are most concentrated are also of great importance and are being investigated as part of this research. The incidence of calcium deposits on and around microbial cells in this vicinity may be indicative of calcium mobilisation or absorption, the source of which may be the lime mortar, since the stone appears to contain very few minerals rich in calcium. Calcium, derived from mortar, could be present dissolved in the pore water and be a readily available source to microorganisms in the vicinity. Alternatively, insoluble sources could be mobilised by biological mechanisms, essentially occurring through the production of substances with acidic or chelating properties. However, from the initial SEM studies, there is little evidence to suggest these mechanisms to be significant in this particular decay process.

Ongoing laboratory work involves culture of individual isolates of bacteria, fungi and algae with samples of hermitage stone and analysis for calcium. Substances with potential for chelation or dissolution of mineral elements are also being identified from individual isolates as well as intact spall samples. Also ongoing are detailed studies of climate at the field site itself, where daily fluctuations in light levels, humidity and temperature are being logged on north and south façades. It is the aim that from such studies, the factors influencing the growth of *Trentepohlia* at the stone surface, and the decay mechanisms of most importance will be elucidated.

Acknowledgements

The authors wish to acknowledge the support and access to Hermitage Castle given by Historic Scotland, Dr W. McHardy and Dr M.J.Wilson of the Macauly Land Use Research Institute in Aberdeen for loan of SEM facilities and valuable advice, to Dr Frances Davis of Luton University, for lichen identification and finally to the EPSRC for funding this research (ref. GR/J91500).

References

Belcher, H. and Swale, E. (1978) *Freshwater Algae – A Beginner's Guide.* Institute of Terrestrial Ecology. HMSO, London.

Bock, E. and Sand, W. (1993) The microbiology of masonry biodeterioration. *Journal of Applied Bacteriology* **74**: 503–514.

Caneva, G., Nugari, M.P., Ricci, S., Salvadori, O. (1993) Pitting of marble Roman monuments and the related microflora. In *Proceedings of the 7th International Congress on Deterioration and Conservation of Stone.* Lisbon, Portugal, 15–18 June, pp. 521–530.

Danin, A. and Caneva, G. (1990) Deterioration of limestone walls in Jerusalem and marble monuments in Rome caused by cyanobacteria and cyanophilous lichens. *International Biodeterioration* **26**: 397–417.

Degelius, G. (1962) Über Verwitterung von Kaik- und Dolomitgestein durch Algen und Flechten. In U.A. Hedval (ed.) *Chemie Im Dienst der Archäologie, Bautechnik und Denkmalpflege.* Göteborg, pp. 156–163.

Griffin, P.S., Indictor, N. and Koestler, R.J. (1991) The biodeterioration of stone: a review of deterioration mechanisms, conservation case histories, and treatment. *International Biodeterioration* **28**: 187–207.

Hueck-van der Plas, E.H. (1968) The micro-biological deterioration of porous building materials. *International Biodeterioration Bulletin* **4**: 11–28.

Jones, M.S. (1990) *The degradation of building stone* Unpublished PhD. Thesis. UMIST.

Kaplan, D., Christiaen, D. and Arad, S.M. (1987) Chelating properties of extracellular polysaccharides from *Chlorella* spp. *Applied and Environmental Microbiology* **53**: 2953–2956.

Koestler, R.J., Charola, A.E., Wypyski, M. and Lee, J.J. (1985) Microbiologically induced deterioration of dolomitic and calcitic stone as viewed by scanning electron microscopy. In *Proceedings of the 5th International Congress on 'Deterioration and Conservation of Stone',* Lausanne **2**: 617–626.

Krampitz, L.O. and Yarris, C.E. (1983) Glycolate formation and excretion by *Chlorella pyrenoidosa* and *Netrium digitus. Plant Physiology* **72**: 1084–1087.

Krumbein, W.E and Lange, C. (1978) Decay of plaster, paintings and wall material of the interior of buildings via microbial activity. In W.E. Krumbein (ed.) *Environmental Biogeochemistry and Geomicrobiology.* Ann Arbor Science, Michigan USA, pp. 687–697.

Lee, K.B. and Wee, Y.C. (1982) Algae growing on walls around Singapore. *Malayan Nature Journal* **35**: 125–132.

Loh, W.S., and Lee, K.T. (1987) Factors contributing to the fouling of walls on Singapore buildings by algal growth. In *Fourth International Conference on 'Durability of Building Materials and Components'*. Singapore, pp. 1040–1048.

Ortega-Calvo, J.J., Hernandez-Marine, M., Sanz-Jimenez, C. (1993) Experimental strategies for investigating algal deterioration of stone. In *Proceedings of the 7th International Congress on 'Deterioration and Conservation of Stone'*. Lisbon, Portugal, 15–18 June, pp. 541–549.

Strzelczyk, A.B. (1981) Stone. In A.H. Rose (ed.) *Economic Microbiology* **6**. Academic Press, London, pp. 61–80.

Warscheid, T.H., Barros, D., Becker, T.W., Braams, J., Eliasaro, S., Grote, G., Janssen, D., Jung, L., Mascarenhas, S.P.B., Mazzoni, M.L., Petersen, K., Simonoes, E.S., Moreira, Y.K., and Krumbein, W.E. (1993). Biodeterioration studies on soapstone, quartzite and sandstones of historical monuments in Brazil and Germany. Preliminary results and evaluation for restoration practices. In *Proceedings of the 7th International Congress on 'Deterioration and Conservation of Stone'*. Lisbon, Portugal, 15–18 June, pp. 491–500.

Contact address
School of Applied Sciences
The Robert Gordon University
St Andrew Street
Aberdeen
AB1 1HG
United Kingdom

9 Spatial variability of weathering of Portland stone slabs

A. SHELFORD, R.J. INKPEN
and D. PAYNE

ABSTRACT

A series of experiments using Portland stone slabs are described which investigate the nature and extent of spatial variability in stone weathering. Analysis of surface change using stereoscopic photographs, before and after weathering sequences, provide a basis for identifying zones of alteration. Preliminary investigation of three separate areas of the slabs suggest that surface alteration, and hence weathering loss, is highly variable over an individual slab.

INTRODUCTION

Studies of stone weathering using experimental slabs have concentrated upon measuring alteration through the chemical composition of run-off (Livingston, 1983; Reddy, 1988). Temporal variations in weathering can be derived from such studies, but assessment of relative changes across the slab are not possible. Micro-erosion meter studies such as those by High and Hannah (1970), Viles and Trudgill (1984) and Trudgill, *et al.*, (1989) have permitted some assessment of spatial variation in surface change, but are severely limited due to a relatively small number of repeated point measurements. Because of this only variations in surface topography at the same scale or a larger scale than the spacing between points can be identified. Data from such studies have been used to determine 'average' loss of material, normally on the assumption that surface loss is uniform in space and time. Stone is not, however, physically or chemically homogeneous. Reddy (1988) states, for example, that in a carbonate-bound sandstone, the

Processes of Urban Stone Decay. Edited by B.J. Smith and P.A. Warke. © 1996 Donhead Publishing Ltd.

actively weathered proportion is confined to the carbonate component, with the quartz grains merely falling out of the weakened matrix. This view is reinforced by micro-erosion meter studies at St Paul's Cathedral, London (Trudgill, *et al.*, 1989) which suggested that surface loss at the same point was discrete and followed a staircase-like descent in which each step is roughly as large as individual ooids. This implies a discrete and possibly spatially differentiated pattern to surface loss related to textural and chemical variations in the stone. This study uses photogrammetric analysis of the surface of two slabs under simulated weathering processes to assess spatial variability in surface change.

METHODOLOGY

Experimental set-up

Two slabs (15 × 15 cm) of Portland stone (Whit Bed) from the Upper Jurassic of Southern England (sourced from Independent Quarry, Isle of Portland) were cut from the same block yielding two slabs of similar grain size and structure. Each slab was exposed with the bedding horizontal and weathering agents were delivered from two rainfall simulators (Table 9.1).

Drops of approximately 1 mm diameter were delivered at a fixed rate of 4.5 ml per minute from each of 12 needles, providing 54 ml per minute. Runoff from each slab was collected via a gutter at the base of each slab. Each weathering cycle consisted of twenty-five minutes of simulated rainfall and sixty minutes drying time. This sequence was repeated twenty-five times. During the rainfall phase runoff samples were collected every five minutes. Overall surface loss could be determined by measuring the Ca^{2+} concentration in the runoff from each slab relative to the rainfall composition. After initial rainfall sequences of distilled water and sulphuric acid (pH 4.5) for slabs A and B respectively, both were exposed to simulated rainfall of 0.5 M sodium chloride solution. It is assumed that any increase in surface loss of slab B relative to slab A during treatment with the salt solution would be attributable to changes in surface structure during the previous weathering by sulphuric acid. The weathering cycles, therefore, cover both individual treatments and the possible impact of sequences of weathering treatments.

Photogrammetric analysis

Photogrammetric analysis was carried out using a KERN DSR–14 Analytical Stereo Plotter. Before the start of the two sets of weathering experiments stereoscopic photographs of each slab were taken using a vertically mounted Polaroid MP3 camera, with a low angle incident light source to give maximum clarity of surface relief. The photographs not only permit the construction of the relief models, but also provide a permanent record of

EXPERIMENTAL PROCEDURE AND TREATMENTS	
(i) First Stereo Photographs taken	
BLOCK B **(EXPERIMENTAL)**	**BLOCK A** **(CONTROL)**
1. Acid rain simulation H_2SO_4/HNO_3 mixture pH 4 3 cycles: 25 mins wetting 60 mins drying	1. Rain simulation Distilled water pH 7 3 cycles: 25 mins wetting 60 mins drying
2. Salt weathering simulation 0.5 M NaCl solution 1 cycle: 25 mins wetting 60 mins drying	2. Salt weathering simulation 0.5 M NaCl solution 1 cycle: 25 mins wetting 60 mins drying
3. Acid rain simulation H_2SO_4/HNO_3 mixture to pH 4 3 cycles: 25 mins wetting 60 mins drying	3. Rain simulation Distilled water pH 7 3 cycles: 25 mins wetting 60 mins drying
(ii) Final Stereo Photographs taken	

Table 9.1 Experimental procedure showing type and duration of treatments, and indicating points at which photographs were taken.

the nature of the surface before and after each weathering experiment.

To be of use in photogrammetry, stereo photos must fulfil three main requirements. Firstly, because the technique works on the basis of assigning Cartesian coordinates to points, stringent surface controls are required as fixed points which will not experience change, either vertically or laterally.

For this reason the slabs were both placed in a purpose-built frame when they were photographed. This consists of a plate with a series of pins of known height fixed on to it which would appear within the photographic image, but were not in contact with the slab surface, and do not influence experimental results.

These fixed points fulfil the requirements of the KERN DSR–14 software which is used for analysis. They are necessary to provide constant x, y and z references in the model, by which absolute orientation is achieved so that planar and vertical positioning of points becomes possible, by which technique the surface can be mapped for topographic change. Relocation on the horizontal plane using this method is accurate to plus or minus 10 µm. Vertical measurement is less accurate however, and it was not possible to introduce an absolute baseline against which to assess change. Instead heights are calculated as relative values above or below the mean surface height.

The second requirement is that there are fiducial marks on the photographs. These are needed for re-establishment of relative orientation, i.e. lateral positioning of the model each time it is loaded. Finally, the KERN software also requires inputting of the parameters of the camera to allow compensation for parallax distortions within the image, that is, the bending of light causing points to converge or diverge from the principle point of the image. Two key parameters are the lens focal length, fixed in this case, and the position of the principle point of the lens.

Once the model is established, the KERN is used to collect the set of height points for the surface of the slabs from the stereo photos. The software allows any point to be relocated within the images by assigning x and y coordinates to each data point collected, allowing remeasurement of the same points within a sequence of photographs of the same surface, as clearly x and y are non-changing positions in space, with only the z measurement undergoing change. The main advantage of this technique of data collection is that measurement is possible without disruption to the surface and that data collection can be repeated in case of error as the surface is preserved as a static image. In this manner it should be possible to not only identify the nature of change across a surface, but also to quantify such changes and contextualise their relationship with specific features.

Digital Terrain Models (DTMs) are produced using SURFER from the position and height data collected *via* the KERN.

RESULTS

Surface change

A brief examination of the main surface features and their alteration upon weathering indicates the main macro-scale changes on the slabs. This paper focuses on the relative change in three distinct weathering zones on the slabs namely the top, middle and base of the slab surface. The top of the slab represents an area where water only flowed occasionally from raindrop impact. The area may sometimes be wetted but only by seepage into the stone, not by run-off. The middle of the slab is an area washed by run-off from above and potentially subject to dissolution, if flow was not saturated. At the base of the slab, as run-off reached the edge of the slab a slight ponding occurred. The base would also be a zone of potentially saturated subsurface flow and might experience reprecipitation of material. Detailed examination of these areas used over 450 point measurements in areas as small as 8 cm^2 (57 points/cm^2).

Macro-surface change

Before treatment the main surface features identified were saw marks and protruding grains. The saw marks trend from side-to-side across both slabs. After the weathering treatments saw marks are still visible, although their preservation is different on different areas of the slabs. Ooids standing proud of the surface are a less dominant feature after weathering and imply a possible smoothing of the surface. There were distinct surface salt accumulations at the tops of the slabs after completion of the simulations. Absence of any efflorescence at the base of the slabs suggests that leaching of salts is more effective in this zone of greater surface run-off and seepage.

Micro-surface change

The 'before' and 'after' states of the surface of the slabs constructed by the DTMs, illustrate the variability of surface change. There are three possible ways in which surface form alters. Firstly, smoothing of the surface could result in a flattened plane or at least subdued relief. High peaks could be reduced to a greater extent than depression by dissolution to produce such a change. Similarly, either rock flour, reprecipitated calcite or debris could be deposited in surface depressions reducing relative relief. Secondly, the surface could retain its form, with no change in surface morphology during weathering. Form retention could result from material moving across the surface without causing erosion. Alternatively, erosion may proceed uniformly over the surface as a whole. Thirdly, surface relief may increase in magnitude. Differential erosion of the surface could result in surface roughening if erosion is concentrated in depressions or ruts.

Each area of the control and experimental slabs appears to respond differently to the same weathering history. Visual interpretation of Figures 9.1a–c and 9.2a–c provide the basis for assessing changes in surface form for each area. On the slab treated with sulphuric acid there appears to be a smoothing of the surface towards the base (Figure 9.2a) possibly from reprecipitation of calcite or deposition of debris. The presence of a thin line of debris in this zone supports this latter view. The 'control slab', however, appears to roughen upon weathering (Figure 9.1a).

Top of control slab, before

Surface shows relatively smooth profile.
Saw-lines form distinct valleys giving
strong linear form to the surface.

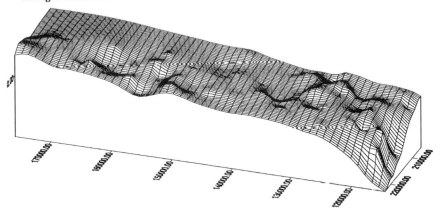

Top of control slab, after

Surface pitted and lined. Central
trough has developed, possibly as a
result of lateral water flow across
the surface. Pit **P** may be due to the
loss of a single large grain.

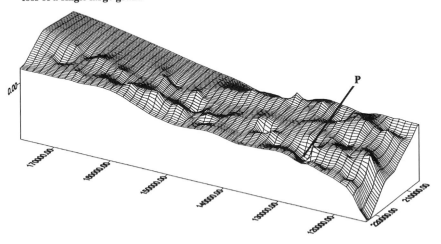

Figure 9.1a DTMs showing top of control slab before and after experimentation.

Centre of control slab, before

**Surface relatively smooth. Saw-lines
distinct and punctuated by small pits (P).**

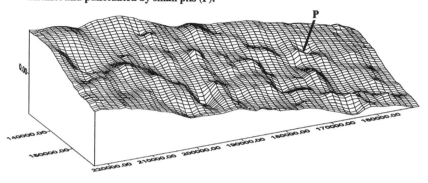

Centre of control slab, after

**Surface shows roughening. Trough visible in 'before'
model has extended and deepened (T). Central portion
shows roughening from pitting and deposition,
particularly the right side which shows some infilling.**

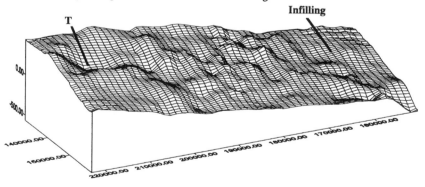

Figure 9.1b DTMs showing centre of control slab before and after experimentation.

Base of control slab, before

**Relatively smooth initial surface.
Saw-line trends visible.**

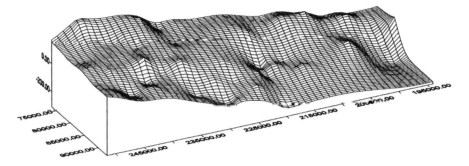

Base of control slab, after

**Surface shows increasing relief after deposition.
Saw-line trend remains visible but with some
modification. Pit and dome features have remained
the same, but have increased in magnitude.**

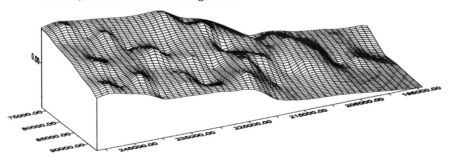

Figure 9.1c DTMs showing base of control slab before and after experimentation.

Top of experimental slab, before

DTM looking towards upper end of slab. Relief is produced mainly by the cutting process with lines left by the saw blade. Surface is relatively flat and smooth.

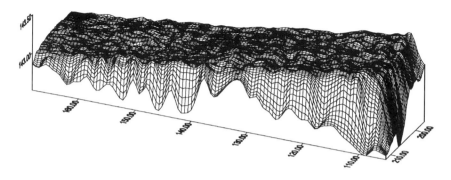

Top of experimental slab, after

View along upper edge of slab. 'Valleys' are more pronounced due to selective removal of material along saw-lines. 'Ridge' along upper edge results from deposition in zone of low flow (see text). Infilling of slab edge produced by the same process. Surface shows overall roughening through a combination of erosion and deposition.

Figure 9.2a DTMs showing top of experimental slab before and after treatment.

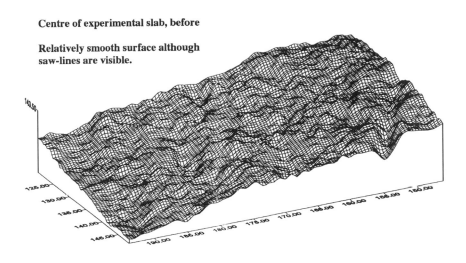

Centre of experimental slab, before

Relatively smooth surface although saw-lines are visible.

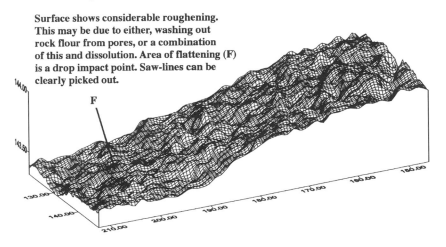

Centre of experimental slab, after

Surface shows considerable roughening. This may be due to either, washing out rock flour from pores, or a combination of this and dissolution. Area of flattening (F) is a drop impact point. Saw-lines can be clearly picked out.

F

Figure 9.2b DTMs showing centre of experimental slab before and after treatment.

Base of experimental slab, before

**Undulose domed surface, possibly
resulting from debris accumulation.
Relatively smooth surface apart
from saw marks.**

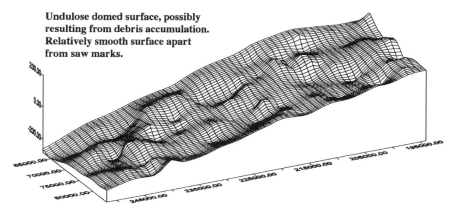

Base of experimental slab, after

**Surface has undergone some flattening and infilling.
Dome previously noted has been extended to form
a 'ridge-like' feature, possibly the result of deposition
of material along a saw-line.**

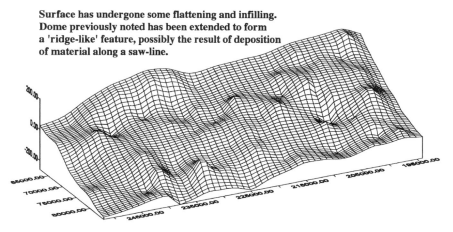

Figure 9.2c DTMs showing base of experimental slab before and after treatment.

Removal of rock flour or lack of debris deposition and reprecipitation may help explain this roughening. An increase in visible pits may point, however, to increased surface and subsurface dissolution. Alternatively, this may represent increased exposure of the slab surface as weathering removes surface rock flour left from the cutting and preparation procedures. The centre of both slabs (Figures 9.1b and 9.2b) show little change in form after weathering, although the surface of the experimental slab seems to be slightly rougher. Similarity in form may imply the centre area is a region through which material is moved rather than one of erosion or deposition. Some evidence of dissolution is visible, however, in the emergence of ooids and pits suggesting that these areas are maintaining their form despite some surface loss.

The top of each slab shows roughening of the surface, but to differing degrees (Figure 9.1c and 9.2c). On both slabs salt deposition in a region of the slab relatively unwashed by run-off appears to account for most of the peaks in height observed. On the control slab there are also areas of heavy pitting away from the zone of salt deposition.

CONCLUSION

Photographs of slabs of Portland stone before and after weathering provide the basis for identification and potentially quantification of surface change at a variety of scales. Stereoscopic images, with appropriate internal and external controls, can be used to construct three dimensional models of weathered surfaces. In the experiment outlined above, visual inspection of three distinct weathering zones in these models of the slabs imply that the changes in surface topography vary over slabs subjected to the same weathering processes. In addition, there is some evidence that the magnitude of surface alteration may depend on the weathering treatment to which the slabs have been subjected. Most importantly, however, the results demonstrate the potential of photogrammetric techniques in monitoring surface decay of stone.

References

High, C.J. and Hanna, K.K. (1970) A method for the direct measurement of erosion on rock surfaces. *British Geomorphological Research Group, Technical Bulletin* **5**. Geoabstracts, Norwich.

Livingston, R.A. (1983) Evaluation of building deterioration by water runoff. Building performance: function, preservation and rehabilitation. *ASTM Special Technical Publication* **901**: 191–198.

Reddy, M.M. (1988) Acid rain damage to carbonate stone: a quantitative assessment based on aqueous geochemistry of rainfall runoff from stone. *Earth Surface Processes and Landforms* **13**: 335–354.

Trudgill, S.T., Viles, H.A., Cooke, R.U. and Inkpen, R.J. (1989)

Remeasurement of weathering rates, St Paul's Cathedral, London. *Earth Surface Processes and Landforms* **14**: 175–196.

Viles, H.A. and Trudgill, S.T. (1984) Long-term remeasurement of micro-erosion meter rates, Aldabara Atoll, Indian Ocean. *Earth Surface Processes and Landforms* **9**: 89–94.

Contact address
Department of Geography
University of Portsmouth
Buckingham Building
Lion Terrace
Portsmouth
PO1 3HE
United Kingdom

SECTION TWO

MECHANISMS OF STONE DECAY

(B) Physical Breakdown

10 Background controls on stone decay in polluted environments: preliminary observations from Rio de Janeiro

H.L. NEILL and B.J. SMITH

ABSTRACT

Weathered Precambrian augen gneiss from salt-rich coastal sites near to Rio de Janeiro are compared with the same stone from buildings in the polluted centre of the city. The urban samples exhibit granular disintegration and contour scaling that appears to be associated with exploitation by crystalline gypsum of a widespread microfracture network. This network is essential in creating a secondary microporosity that allows ingress by pollution-derived salts. The absence of this network from the coastal samples and a corresponding reduction in active, salt-induced disruption, suggests that microfracturing is related to the placing of stone in the built environment. It could result from the loading of stone near to ground level, where decay is concentrated, but may equally be inherited from quarrying and preparation procedures. The necessity for prior microfracturing highlights the essentially exploitative nature of salt weathering and the possibilities for synergistic interactions between weathering mechanisms within complex, polluted urban environments.

INTRODUCTION AND BACKGROUND

While the incidence of pollution-induced decay on monuments and buildings has been well documented in recent years, structures composed of granitoid rocks have received scant attention. These rocks are, however, often utilised in buildings for their good mechanical properties and low porosities and they have the reputation of being amongst the most durable of the major rock types (Lazzarini, 1993; Smith, *et al.,* 1993). Despite this, such materi-

Processes of Urban Stone Decay. Edited by B.J. Smith and P.A. Warke. © 1996 Donhead Publishing Ltd.

als do decay within the urban regime, at rates that are controlled by combinations of MATERIAL PROPERTIES (mineralogy, texture, porosity), CLIMATIC CONDITIONS (temperature, humidity) and LOCAL VARIABLES (microclimate of structure, aspect, exposure). Of these controls, porosity is of particular significance. The decay of many building stones is facilitated by an inherent primary porosity that permits dissolution/alteration by percolating acidified waters and/or the ingress and subsequent disruptive crystallisation of salts. However, in granitoid and similar lithologies with low or no effective permeability, decay is either restricted to exposed surfaces or is dependent upon the existence of a secondary porosity. The latter could be created, for example, by dilatation (pressure release), chemical alteration and volume increase of minerals such as biotite or, more conjecturally, differential thermal expansion of constituent minerals. Once created, inter- and intra-crystalline fractures can then be enlarged and extended by solution and salt-related weathering mechanisms. Therefore, when considering physical decay in low permeability stone it is important to distinguish between mechanisms of fracture initiation and those responsible for subsequent fracture exploitation.

In this paper the distinction is investigated through examination of surface breakdown of augen gneiss from buildings in the polluted centre of Rio de Janeiro. This breakdown is compared with weathering patterns in natural outcrops of the same stone in a salt-rich coastal environment. In this way it is hoped to distinguish between natural contributions to decay and those elements attributable to exposure in a polluted urban atmosphere. Any exposed rock experiences continuous deterioration through combined chemical, mechanical and biological processes. This weathering encompasses complex interactions between rock surfaces and atmosphere, hydrosphere and biosphere systems and affects both 'natural' rock outcrops as well as stones utilised within the 'built' environment. Stone in the built environment is, however, subject to a range of additional, anthropogenic factors which influence weathering – principally through modification of atmospheric composition which varies widely with location. Indeed, in recent years, we have come to appreciate that the urban atmosphere of the twentieth century creates special environmental conditions at exposed stone surfaces due to the rapid increase in the levels of atmospheric pollution within many urban locations. This alters and accelerates weathering rates to many times those of rural environments (Jaynes and Cooke, 1987; Moses (this book)). Thus, decay of stone in urban environments should combine natural weathering, pollution-related decay and possibly the two sets of processes acting either in sequence, or possibly in combination.

LOCATION OF STUDY

Rio de Janeiro (Figure 10.1) is an urban centre which has been identified by Moreira-Nordmann, *et al*., (1988) as experiencing in recent years high levels of atmospheric pollution. It has a distinctly maritime location and a

114

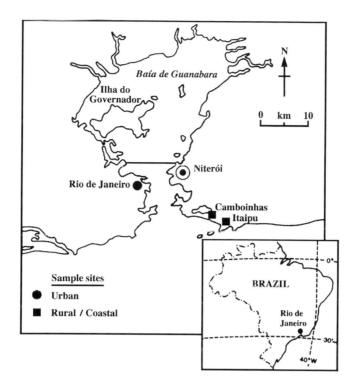

Figure 10.1 Location map and study sites.

humid sub-tropical climate, with monthly temperatures uniformly around 25°C and average annual rainfall of 1500–2000 mm concentrated between October and April. What makes Rio de Janeiro so susceptible to atmospheric pollution is the complex interplay between the natural topography of high, dome-shaped mountains, narrow, flat-floored valleys and the man-made environment superimposed upon it. Situated in the lee of the domes, high-rise, high density buildings concentrate and channel pollution along 'urban corridors' to produce frequent photo-chemical smogs and distinctive weathering forms on buildings (Smith and Magee, 1990).

METHODOLOGY

To distinguish between natural and anthropogenic weathering effects, samples of a Pre-Cambrian augen gneiss were collected from buildings within the polluted centre of Rio de Janeiro, at heights of between 0.5 m and 2.0 m above road level. Sites were chosen which were clearly undergoing active breakdown adjacent to busy streets. The augen gneiss is characteristically coarse-grained and displays a high metamorphic grade. The matrix is essentially composed of quartz-plagioclase, with variable amounts of medium to coarse potassium feldspars that are ovoid to sub-rectangular in shape and with other mega-crystals can comprise between 50–90% of the rock volume. The main mafic mineral is biotite, which can comprise up to 10% of the rock volume although garnets (generally < 2%) are ubiquitous. A comparative set of samples was also taken from natural outcrops of the same stone, in the salt-rich splash and spray zones of coastal sites at Camboinhas and Itaipu (Figure 10.1). Samples were collected from the exposed surface of rock in both locations and in the urban site where contour scaling was present on buildings (Figure 10.2). Whole scales were collected so that the outer and interior surfaces could be examined using a Jeol 6400 scanning electron microscope (SEM). Mineralogy of powdered subsamples was also determined by X-ray diffraction (XRD) using a Siemens D5000 Diffractometer and by qualitative energy dispersive X-ray analysis (EDX) during SEM examination. The results obtained are discussed in the following sections.

Figure 10.2 Detail of contour scaling near base of building in central Rio de Janeiro.

RESULTS

Characteristic weathering features on exposed surfaces within the urban environment include black crust development, contour scaling and granular disintegration. Of these, the most obvious and unsightly feature is the presence of superficial gypsum-based black crusts (Figure 10.3). These are observed at varying stages of development, ranging from isolated rosettes of interlocking gypsum crystals, to an almost continuous cover of plate-like crystals on highly polluted samples (Figure 10.3a). Incorporated within these crusts are carbonaceous flyash particles derived from the combustion of fuel oil, with some of the gypsum appearing to grow out of the flyash (Figure 10.3b). It is the accumulation of these pollutants that provides the calcium and sulphur on a non-calcareous substrate which can be mobilised in solution to form the gypsum that comprises the crusts (Smith and Magee, 1990). It is also possible to observe how these crusts interact directly with the underlying mineral components. Gypsum crystals are, for example, seen to accumulate in the inter- and intra-crystalline fractures of quartz and feldspar crystals and to bridge gaps between open cleavage planes in micas (Figure 10.3c and 10.3d). It is, in fact, micas which are often the most obvi-

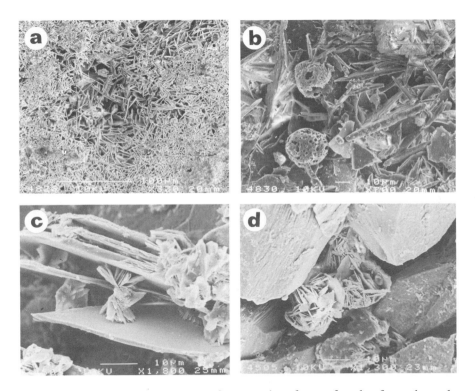

Figure 10.3 SEM micrographs of exposed surfaces of scales from the polluted centre of Rio de Janeiro. (a) Interlocking lattice of gypsum crystals on surface of sample (picture width 290 µm). (b) Detail of gypsum crust showing the open plate-like structure with enclosed flyash particles (picture width 140 µm). (c) Gypsum crystal bridging gaps between open cleavage planes of mica (picture width 60 µm). (d) Crystallisation of gypsum within inter- and intra-granular spaces (picture width 80 µm).

ous avenues of entry for agents of decay since, once their structure has been deformed, they could either form potential fluid pathways into the rock substrate, or undergo volumetric change to induce mechanical decay. Mineralogical analysis (Table 10.1) does not indicate the clay mineral concentration that one would expect to be associated with such alteration and expansion of micas, but it does confirm the presence of gypsum in the urban samples.

Compared to exposed surfaces, SEM investigation of the interiors of scales illustrates a distinctive micro-environment, characterised by a lack of large-scale gypsum accumulations, despite the presence of extensive microfracturing. The paucity of gypsum would seem to imply that salt weathering alone does not produce contour scaling. Similarly, it seems unlikely that chemical alteration could be the causal link since only traces of kaolinite were identified in the chemical analyses of contour scales (Table 10.1) and little evidence of alteration of primary minerals was observed under SEM. What seems to be a more logical explanation is that granular disintegration and contour scaling are associated with a combination of formative processes (Figure 10.4). Inherent structural weaknesses and microfractures could, for example, be initiated prior to any ingress of salts or atmospheric pollutants, as illustrated by the highly developed network of salt-free inter- and intra-granular microcracks observed in contour scales (Figure 10.4a). In addition to widespread microcracking, however, disaggregation was also seen to occur by the 'unlocking' or 'decoupling' of individual crystals along their boundaries (Figure 10.4d). Once such discontinuities are initiated, salts such as gypsum can then be precipitated within them from percolating solutions. Flyash particles (oil and coal) may also be either blown or washed in behind scales once they have formed, where they are again associated with gypsum crystallisation (Figure 10.4b). This two-stage sequence of events could similarly permit some chemical processes to operate, such as solution etching observed on quartz crystals and along cleavage lines in potassium feldspars (Figure 10.4c). Pollution-derived gypsum is, therefore, seen to be exploiting a network of fractures and cracks to extend granular disintegration and to lift scales away from the underlying stone. Its effectiveness in causing breakdown is, however, dependent upon the pre-existence of a fracture network.

In contrast, similar fracture networks were not observed at the coastal sites, where contour scaling was limited and SEM characteristically identified surface abrasion rather than granular disintegration. The only salts observed are occasional surface deposits of halite (Table 10.1), the effects of which are neither continuous, nor deeply penetrating into the rock structure (Figure 10.5a). While there is some evidence of limited disruption of mica plates which could provide pathways to the ingress of salts, there is no widespread fracturing or dislocation of crystals around micas. Rather, any microcracks or discontinuities are exploited more by algal growths than by salt penetration. Biological weathering would, therefore, seem to assume greater significance within the coastal environment (Figure 10.5b–10.5d).

	PRIMARY MINERALS						CLAYS		SALTS	
	Quartz	Orthoclase	Anorthoclase	Albite	Muscovite	Phlogopite	Kaolinite	Vermiculite	Gypsum	Halite
PONTA de ITAIPU										
Intertidal zone	++			++	+++					
Splash zone	+++	++		++	+++		++			++
Spray zone	+++	++		++	+++		+	+		
Supra–spray zone	++	++		++	+++					
CAMBOINHAS										
Intertidal zone	+++	++		++	+++		+			++
Splash zone	++		++	++	+++			+		
Spray zone	++		++	++	+++		++			++
Supra–spray zone	+++		++	++	++					
RIO de JANEIRO										
Site 1: Scaling flakes	+++		+++	+++		+++	+			
Site 2: Scaling flakes	+++		++	++		+++				
Site 2: Granulated material	+++		+++	+++		++			++	
Site 2: Black crust	+++		+++	+++		+++			+++	

+++ Major peaks   ++ Minor peaks   + Trace

Table 10.1 Summary of chemical analyses.

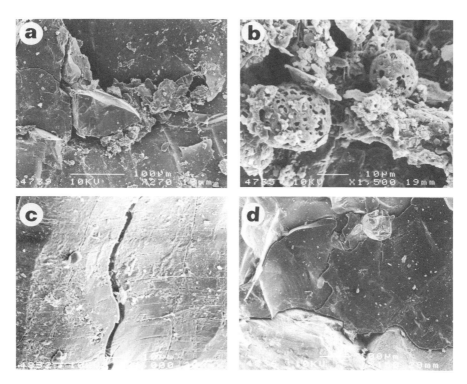

Figure 10.4 SEM micrographs of interior surfaces of the scales from the polluted centre of Rio de Janeiro. (a) Microcracking and decoupling of minerals on interior face of scales (picture width 400 μm). (b) Deposition of fly-ash (either washed or blown) on interior face of scale (picture width 70 μm). (c) Solutional etching along cleavage planes of feldspar mineral grain (picture width 90 μm). (d) Disaggregation caused by decoupling of quartz and feldspar minerals and fracturing along crystal boundaries (picture width 700 μm).

DISCUSSION AND CONCLUSIONS

This brief study suggests that the urban environment of Rio de Janeiro imposes distinct controls on the nature of breakdown in granitoid rocks. Exposed surfaces are characterised by unsightly black crusts which clearly indicate the influence of atmospheric pollution on stone decay processes. However, while pollutants and particularly pollution-derived salts such as gypsum represent potential agents of decay, they are initially confined to the stone surface. For them to act to cause breakdown, they require a point of weakness in the rock mass to gain entry and initiate mechanical and chemical change. This may be achieved *via* a profusion of microcracks and grain boundary dislocations, which infer a much higher porosity than would nor-

120

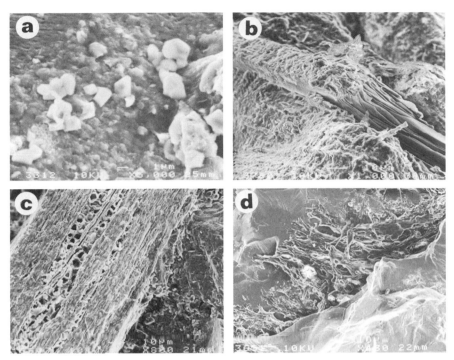

Figure 10.5 SEM micrographs of exposed surfaces at coastal locations. (a) Isolated clusters of halite crystals adhering to the rock surface (picture width 20 µm). (b) Abrasion of surface and evidence of algal cover (picture width 100 µm). (c) Algal growths exploiting and colonising gaps between mica plates (picture width 120 µm). (d) Inter-crystalline fractures exploited by algal growths (picture width 190 µm).

mally be perceived for such rocks.

Rodrigues (1993) outlined the importance of porosity in consideration of building stone decay, since the pore space of such materials is not a static component, but changes in response to the weathering environment (Table 10.2). In terms of a dynamic porosity, this study has indicated that a principal difference between the coastal and urban locations is the occurrence of processes responsible for widespread microcracking and grain boundary dislocations which instigate the distinctive stone decay observed on polluted buildings. Why these processes operate in the urban environment remains unclear, but it would seem that special factors operate to facilitate fracture initiation. These could be related to pressure-release consequent upon quarrying of stone, or result from the way in which the stone is dressed. The possibility of pressure-release initiating microfracturing is particularly applicable to rocks such as augen gneiss, which not only accumulate stresses during their original, deep-seated emplacement but are subject to additional

GENESIS	PERMEABILITY	LOCATION
Primary porosity	*Open porosity*	*Interparticle porosity*
Created by petrogenesis	Total system of all pores being interconnected with access to the stone surface accessible for all gaseous and liquid agents	Pore space between the particles of a stone, main type of porosity
Secondary porosity	*Intermediate*	*Intraparticle porosity*
Modification of porosity after crystallization	Through flow pore channels and non through flow pore channels	Pore space within particles
Weathering porosity	*Closed porosity*	*Intracrystalline porosity*
Created by weathering processes	Inaccessible pores	Pore space within crystal lattice

Table 10.2 Classification of rock porosity (after Fitzner, 1993).

stressing by subsequent metamorphism. The effects of this are evident in the Rio de Janeiro area where *in situ* deep weathering of the gneiss, especially where it is rich in potassium feldspars, can produce regolith profiles in excess of 30 m depth that are dominated by disaggregated sand-sized quartz and feldspar crystals, with only limited clay mineral formation (Power and Smith, 1994). This pressure release may not, however, be present in all natural outcrops or its effects may be reduced where exposure is achieved gradually by natural processes of erosion. Prior stressing of stone may also be accomplished by other, natural weathering mechanisms. Warke and Smith (1994) have shown, for example, how prior subjection of samples of fresh granite to freeze–thaw cycles made them more prone to salt-induced decay compared to samples that were not pre-stressed.

In addition to dilatation and weathering stresses it is also possible that loading of the stone within a building contributes to the development of initial fracturing and scaling. If so, this might be a factor in the concentration of decay near to the bases of the buildings sampled. Previously this concentration near ground level has been interpreted as a response to increased pollution levels associated with traffic. It might be, however, that it is the combination of loading and pollution/salt availability that creates conditions amenable to accelerated stone decay. This acceleration appears to be triggered by the formation or at least availability of a network of microfractures. Once initiated, these are effectively exploited by pollution-derived salts to produce the extensive decay currently observed. The necessity for prior fracture initiation could explain the frequently observed lack of susceptibility of samples of fresh granitoid rocks to salt weathering under laboratory conditions and their good performance in many durability tests. The high durability indicated by these tests is often at variance with observations of extensive decay on, for example, granite buildings (e.g. Cooper, *et al.*, 1993). Similarly, it must also question the simplistic attribution of urban stone decay solely to the action of atmospheric pollution or pollution products.

Clearly, many questions remain to be answered. Not least is what mechanisms operate to concentrate fractures at a constant depth below the surface to produce contour scales? Could this boundary, as proposed by Dragovich (1969), coincide with a frequent wetting depth or could it relate perhaps to patterns and depths of thermal cycling? One way in which these questions may be addressed is through laboratory simulation experiments, including the salt weathering of pre-altered or stressed granites and other stones as opposed to the freshly quarried samples traditionally used in such experiments. Additionally, as an alternative to the use of small, unconstrained blocks, it may be worthwhile to employ larger blocks with dimensions commensurate with those of the contour scales found on stonework. If these blocks could be placed under a compressive stress it might then also be possible to more closely replicate conditions experienced on buildings.

Acknowledgements

The writers are grateful for fieldwork assistance provided by José Antonio Baptista Neto and for financial support from The British Council, Universidade Federal Fluminense, Niteroi and The Queen's University of Belfast. We are also indebted to the staff of the Electron Microscope Unit at Queen's for their analytical assistance and to Gill Alexander for preparation of diagrams.

References

Cooper, T.P., Duffy, A., O'Brien, P., Bell, E. and Lyons, F.   (1993) Conservation of historic buildings at Trinity College, Dublin. In M.A. Vicente Hernández, E. Molina Ballesteros and V. Rives Arnau (eds) *Actas del Workshop Alteración de Granitos y Rocas Afines.* Consejo Superior de Investigaciones Científicas, Madrid, pp. 59–65.

Dragovich, D. (1969) The origin of cavernous surfaces (tafoni) in granitic rocks of southern Australia. *Zeitschrift für Geomorphologie* **13**: 163–181.

Fitzner, B. (1993) Porosity properties and weathering behaviour of natural stones – methodology and examples. In F. Zezza (ed.) *Stone Material in Monuments: Diagnosis and Conservation.* Community of Mediterranean Universities, Bari, pp. 43–54.

Jaynes, S.M. and Cooke, R.U. (1987) Stone weathering in southeast England. *Atmospheric Environment* **21**: 1601–22.

Lazzarini, L. (1993) The deterioration and treatment of granitic columns. In F. Zezza (ed.) *Stone Material in Monuments: Diagnosis and Conservation.* Community of Mediterranean Universities, Bari, pp. 160–168.

Moreira-Nordmann, L.M., Forti, M.C., DiLascio, V.L., Monteiro do Espirito Santo, C. and Danelon, O.M. (1988) Acidification in south-east Brazil. In H. Rhode and R. Herrera (eds) *Acidification in Tropical Countries.* J. Wiley & Sons, Chichester, pp. 257–296.

Power, E.T. and Smith, B.J. (1994) A comparative study of deep weathering and weathering products: case studies from Ireland, Corsica and Southeast Brazil. In D.A. Robinson and R.B.G. Williams (eds) *Rock Weathering and Landform Evolution.* J. Wiley & Sons, Chichester, pp. 21–40.

Rodrigues, J.D. (1993) Measurement and significance of physical properties on granitic rocks. In F. Zezza (ed.) *Stone Material in Monuments: Diagnosis and Conservation.* Community of Mediterranean Universities, Bari, pp. 71–81.

Smith, B.J. and Magee, R.W. (1990) Granite weathering in an urban environment: an example from Rio de Janeiro. *Singapore Journal of Tropical Geography* **2**: 143–153.

Smith, B.J., Magee, R.W. and Whalley, B.W. (1993) Decay of granite in a polluted environment: Budapest. In M.A. Vicente Hernández, E. Molina Ballesteros and V. Rives Arnau (eds) *Actas del Workshop Alteración de Granitos y Rocas Afines.* Consejo Superior de Investigaciones Científicas, Madrid, pp. 163–166.

Warke, P.A. and Smith, B.J. (1994) Inheritance effects on the efficacy of salt weathering mechanisms in thermally cycled granite blocks under laboratory and field conditions. In E. Bell and T.P. Cooper (eds) *Granite Weathering and Conservation.* Trinity College, Dublin, pp. 19–27.

Zappia, G., Sabbioni, C. and Gobbi, G. (1991) Damage to stone surfaces in the urban environment. *Materials Engineering* **2**: 255–262.

Contact address
School of Geosciences
The Queen's University of Belfast
Belfast
BT7 1NN
United Kingdom

11 Characterisation and decay of monumental sandstone in La Rioja, Northern Spain

S. PAVÍA SANTAMARÍA, T.P. COOPER
and S. CARO CALATAYUD

ABSTRACT

Calcareous sandstone from the continental Tertiary of the Ebro Basin has been used as a building material since the Stone Age. Weathered stone from twelfth to eighteenth century buildings and unweathered stone from quarries were examined by X-ray diffraction (XRD), scanning electron microscopy (SEM) and energy dispersive X ray analysis (EDX) and the results compared to establish chemical and petrological composition and changes. Physical tests, including mercury porisimetry, established physico-mechanical properties such as pore size, morphology and distribution. Results show that the stone is highly porous and consists of quartz, calcite, feldspar and mica with fossils, rock fragments and accessory minerals bound by a micritic cement comprised mainly of recrystallised sparite. Because of high porosity and well interconnected pore system its water absorption capacity and capillary suction are high. The stone has a medium to low compression resistance and a low abrasion resistance. Decay is mainly associated with capillary groundwater rise which produces dissolution of the calcite binder and detachment of material. Gypsum crusts also develop through sulphation of the stone and dissolution of calcite cement followed by recrystallisation. These crusts are fractured and replacement of the original texture by gypsum and sparite causes the stone to become softer and more fragile.

INTRODUCTION

Calcareous sandstone from the continental Tertiary of the Upper Ebro Basin has been used as a building material since the Stone Age. Structures built

Processes of Urban Stone Decay. Edited by B.J. Smith and P.A. Warke. © 1996 Donhead Publishing Ltd.

using this stone include megalithic tombs, churches, monasteries and civil buildings.

Pollution levels are low all over La Rioja province apart from Logroño, the capital city of La Rioja, where the main source of pollution is traffic. The climate is continental with Atlantic influences. Summer is hot and freezing conditions are usual in winter. Despite the low levels of regional pollution, there is significant decay of certain buildings. This study examines the physical characteristics of the Tertiary sandstones that may influence their durability and the nature and origins of decay mechanisms. These observations are used to recommend future use of the sandstones.

METHODOLOGY

A survey of buildings sited in urban and rural atmospheres was carried out, and a survey of quarries from which the material was extracted. This was followed by sampling of weathered and unweathered material and mapping of macroscopic decay forms. The mineralogy, petrography, chemical composition and physico-mechanical properties of the stone was then studied together with the stratigraphy of the quarries.

Analytical techniques used were: scanning electron microscopy (SEM) with energy dispersive X-ray analysis (EDX); X-ray diffraction (XRD), petrographic microscopy and mercury porosimetry. These supplemented a range of field observations and physico-mechanical tests. These were carried out using Spanish standards UNE, international standards RILEM and previous studies and covered:

- Real density (RILEM, 1980)
- Bulk density (RILEM, 1980)
- Open porosity (RILEM, 1980)
- Water absorption (UNE, 1984)
- Capillary suction (UNE, 1980)
- Total porosity (Ordaz *et al.*, 1984)
- Saturation coefficient (RILEM, 1980)
- Natural wetness content (Ordaz *et al.*, 1984)
- Compression strength (UNE, 1983)
- Abrasion test (UNE, 1985)

THE STONE

There are more than 84 small quarries in the area. Currently most of them are abandoned but a few are still working. The outcrops are often situated at the top of low hills. They all belong to the continental Tertiary and are of Miocene/Oligocene age. The deposits include a succession of sandstones, mudstones, marls and some silts with parallel bedding. Sandstone strata may include channel structures, laminations, cross bedding and ripples.

Petrographic microscope investigations reveal that the stone is comprised of calcite, quartz, feldspar and mica grains bound by micritic calcite partially recrystallised to sparite. Accessory minerals include tourmaline, zircon and iron oxides. Fossils and ooliths are also present. Quantitative mineral composition was calculated by X-ray diffraction. Means from 30 samples collected from 27 quarries in three areas are shown in Table 11.1.

Pore size distribution obtained by mercury porosimetry showed that in unweathered stone most pores have a radius between 0.1–1 μm. The physico-mechanical properties of the sandstone are shown in Table 11.2.

From these results it can be deduced that the rock has a high porosity and a well interconnected pore system. Water absorption and capillary suction are very important. The rock has a medium to low compression resistance and a low abrasion resistance.

Quarry	% calcite	% quartz	% feldspar	% dolomite	% mica + clay minerals
Lo–Ab	51	36	< 5	< 5	6
Ca–Cu	43	42	< 5	< 5	8
Sa–Fo	42	45	< 5	< 5	6

Lo = Logroño
Ab = Ábalos
Ca = Casalarreina
Cu = Cuzcurrita
Sa = Sajazarra
Fo = Fonzaleche

Table 11.1 Mean mineralogical composition of stone from quarries in three areas, 5% is the X-ray diffraction detection limit.

STONE DECAY

Inspection of buildings revealed that most decay is caused by capillary rise of groundwater which can rise as high as 6 metres in some façades. Building plinths affected by capillary water show strong flaking and arenization up to 10 cm in depth. Gypsum crusts were detected in sheltered areas of buildings situated in the urban area of Logroño, capital city of La Rioja (see Figure 11.1). Where these gypsum crusts develop, the sandstone is

Property	Mean value
Bulk density (g/cm^3)	2.20
Real density (g/cm^3)	2.60
Open porosity (%)	17.93
Total porosity (%)	19.62
Capillary suction (Kg/m^2.s$^{0.5}$)	0.05
Natural wetness content (%)	2.02
Water absorption (%)	6.91
Compression strength (Kg/cm^2)	249.75
Abrasion resistance (g.mm)	25.46

Table 11.2 Physico-mechanical properties of the calcareous sandstone.

bleached and exhibits fracturing and granular disintegration. The sandstone is also strongly decayed near areas that were repointed with cement mortars in the 1970s. The worst conditions occur at an apse inside a twelfth to fourteenth century church. This sandstone is partially covered by efflorescences showing flaking and granular disintegration.

A total of 33 weathered samples from three buildings were analysed by X-ray diffraction. Their mean mineral compositions are given in Table 11.3. X-ray diffraction analyses of decayed sandstone were compared with those obtained from unweathered sandstone. The analyses show that, in general, the strongest decay is associated with higher clay mineral, sulphate and hematite contents.

Mercury porosimetry shows that, in the weathered stone, the quantity of pores bigger than 1 μm increased. Given that in the unweathered stone most pores are smaller than 1 μm, it is possible that decay does not produce new voids but increases the size of the pre-existing ones.

Petrographic analyses reveals that the two main decay processes are:

1. Dissolution and recrystallisation of calcite, whereby micritic and microsparitic calcite dissolves and recrystallises as sparite.

2. Sulphation of the stone involving the replacement of calcite cement by gypsum.

Figure 11.1 Gypsum crust developed in a sheltered area of San Bartolomé Church façade in Logroño City.

Building	% Calcite	% Quartz	% Feldspar	% Dolomite	% mica+clay minerals	% sulphate	% haematite
1	52	33	< 5	< 5	7	< 5	t
2	48	37	< 5	< 5	6	t	t
3	40	40	< 5	< 5	9	< 5	t

t = trace

Table 11.3 Percentage mineral content in decayed sandstone from three buildings, 5% is the X-ray diffraction detection limit.

Gypsum crusts result from sulphation and in these crusts both secondary gypsum and sparite replace the original texture of the rock causing it to disintegrate. The crusts were fractured (Figure 11.2) and microspheres in the crusts are derived from atmospheric pollution and contain heavy metals identified using SEM.

Apart from gypsum, other salts, including anhydrite, thenardite and niter, were detected by SEM (Figure 11.3) and analysed by EDX. These were particularly evident in the severely decayed areas that were repointed with cement mortars in the 1970s.

129

Figure 11.2 SEM micrograph of gypsum crust under the petrographic microscope showing cracking (see arrows). (Picture width 2.5mm)

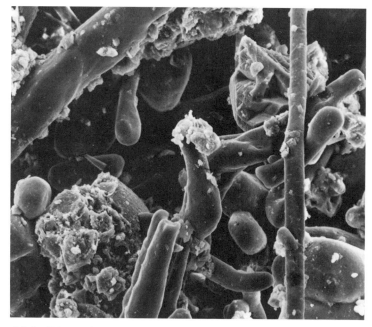

Figure 11.3 SEM micrograph of niter (KNO_3) in a severely decayed sandstone repointed with cement mortar. (Picture width 215 μm)

RECOMMENDATIONS

When using the sandstone for construction the following considerations should be taken into account. Its low abrasion resistance causes the rock to be unsuitable for use as floor tiles, steps or other sites subjected to strong abrasion. Because of its high capillary suction the sandstone should not be used in plinths of buildings. In historic buildings where bases are severely decayed by capillary water, stone replacement is recommended. The replacement should be with whole ashlar; cladding is not adequate. As a new stone for replacement an impermeable aesthetically suitable limestone is recommended.

Acknowledgements

This study was supported by La Rioja Government and Logroño City Council. It was carried out as a part of first author's PhD.

References

Caro Calatayud, S., Pavía Santamaría S., F. Gómez Condon and J. Antolín Alvarez (1992) The preservation of the stone in the Cathedral of 'St M La Redonda', Logroño (La Rioja), Spain. In, *Proceedings of 7th International Congress on Deterioration and Conservation of Stone.* Lisbon, Portugal, 15–18 June, pp. 1327–1334.

Caro Calatayud, S., Pavía Santamaría, S., Valero Garces, B., Pérez Lorente, F. and López Aguayo, F. (1992) Catodoluminiscencia de la arenisca roja usada en la construcción de la Catedral de Santa María de Calahorra, La Rioja Baja, España. *Boletín de la Sociedad Española de Mineralogía* **15**: 54–58.

Castiella Muruzabal, J., Del Valle Lersundi, J., Ramirez del Pozo, J. (1976) *Mapa Geol. de España. E. 1/50.000.* Hoja n° 204 (Logroño). Instituto Geol. y Minero de España.

Ordaz, J, Esbert, R.M., Montoto, M., De Caso, M., Alonso, F.J. (1984) *Estado de alteración y alterabilidad de la piedra de Villamayor: Interpretación petrográfica.* Serie monografías, **3**. Ed. Caja de Ahorros y M.P. de Salamanca, pp. 315–421.

Pavía Santamaría S., Caro Calatayud S., Pérez Lorente, F. (1991) Mortero de la Iglesia de San Bartolomé de Logroño, La Rioja, España. *Actas de la reunión sobre la alteración de granitos y rocas afines empleados como materiales de construcción.* Ed. CSIC, pp. 149–151.

Pavía Santamaría, S., Caro Calatayud, S., Pérez Lorente, F. and López Aguayo, F. (1992) Protection of the stone of 'San Bartolomé' Church in Logroño (La Rioja) Spain. In, *Proceedings of 7th International Congress on Deterioration and Conservation of Stone.* Lisbon. Portugal, 15–18 June, pp. 1335–1340.

Pavía Santamaría, S., Caro Calatayud, S., Valero Garces, B., Pérez Lorente, F. and López Aguayo, F. (1992) Caracterización de la arenisca calcárea de la Iglesia de San Esteban de Abalos por catodoluminiscencia, La Rioja, España. *Boletín de la Sociedad Española de Mineralogía* **15**: 49–53.

Pavía Santamaría S., Caro Calatayud S., Pérez Lorente, F., Duffy A. (1994) More about gypsum crusts on historic buildings (Gypsum crusts on calcareous sandstone from La Rioja, Northern Spain). In V. Fassina and F. Zezza (eds) *International Symposium on the Conservation of Monuments in the Mediterranean Basin*, Venice, pp. 585–588.

Pavía Santamaría, S. (1995) *Material de construcción antiguo de Logroño y La Rioja Alta: petrografía, propiedades físicas geología y alteración.* Ed. Gobierno de La Rioja (IER).

RILEM (1980) Essais recommandés pour mesurer l'alteration des pierres et évaluer l'efficacité des méthodes de traitement. *Materiaux et Constructions, Bulletin RILEM* **13**: 216–220.

UNE (1985) Catálogo de normas. Grupo 7: Ensayos de Materiales. Ed. *Instituto Español de Normalización* (AENOR).

UNE 7068 (1986) Ensayo de compresión. Ed. *Instituto Español de Normalización* (AENOR).

UNE 7069 (1986) Ensayo de desgaste por rozamiento en adoquines de piedra. Ed. *Instituto Español de Normalización* (AENOR).

Contact address
Director of Buildings' Office
West Chapel
Trinity College
Dublin 2
Ireland

12 An analysis of the weathering of Wealden sandstone churches

D.A. ROBINSON and R.B.G. WILLIAMS

ABSTRACT

Hastings Beds sandstones have been used to construct churches in the central Weald from Saxon times onwards. A sample survey of 41 church towers suggests that either the weathering rate of individual stones decreases over time or that weathering was less rapid in the medieval period than today. East facing stonework is more heavily weathered than stonework facing north, south or west. The main weathering phenomena are granular disintegration, cracking, alveolar weathering, and surface crusting and scaling. The stonework on the most weathered nineteenth and twentieth century churches is in worse condition than that on many of the medieval churches.

INTRODUCTION

For many centuries, bands of sandstone that occur within the Hastings Beds of the central Weald of southeast England have been extensively quarried for use as local building material. The relatively high costs of quarrying and transporting the sandstone have tended to restrict its use to major buildings such as churches and large country houses, although in a few places it has also been used to construct small cottages and even boundary walls. Well known buildings constructed of this local stone include Battle Abbey, founded in the eleventh century (the magnificent gatehouse was built in 1338); Bayham Abbey built in the thirteenth century, Penshurst Place and Bodiam Castle both dating from the fourteenth century, Wakehurst Place and Gravetye Manor from the sixteenth century; 'Batemans', Kipling's house at

Processes of Urban Stone Decay. Edited by B.J. Smith and P.A. Warke. © 1996 Donhead Publishing Ltd.

Burwash from the seventeenth century, Kidbrooke Park from the eighteenth century, Ashdown Park dating from 1864 and the now partially ruined house at Nymans which was completed in 1930 (Nairn and Pevsner, 1965; Newman, 1969). The stone has been little used outside the central Weald, possibly because it is softer than most other sandstones, although Stanmer House (1722–7) situated on the South Downs northeast of Brighton, is a notable example. It has never found much favour in London, where very few buildings employ the stone (Elsden and Howe, 1923).

The Hastings Beds are of Lower Cretaceous age and underlie almost the entire area of the central and High Weald. They comprise a complex series of sandstones, siltstones, clays and shales with subordinate ironstones and thin limestones. Some of the sandstones are thin and flaggy with regular partings, others are thicker and more massive. The two most massive sandstones, the Top Ashdown and Ardingly Sandstones, are relatively resistant to weathering and erosion, and frequently outcrop as impressive valley-side cliffs and crags (Robinson and Williams, 1976). They are fine-grained, highly quartzose, and notoriously difficult, if not impossible, to tell apart both in the field and as hand specimens. Milner's suggestion (in White, 1928) that they can be differentiated on the basis of their heavy mineral assemblages remains unconfirmed.

In their original, unweathered state, the Top Ashdown and Ardingly Sandstones are highly porous and contain peculiarly little cementing material between the quartz grains, which makes them unusually friable (Figure 12.1). Their success in forming cliffs and crags is due partly to the massive

Figure 12.1 SEM micrograph of unweathered Ardingly Sandstone. (Picture width 630 µm)

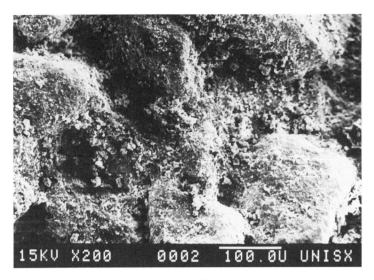

Figure 12.2 SEM micrograph of the silica-crusted outer surface of a natural outcrop of Ardingly Sandstone. (Picture width 580 µm)

nature of the jointing, but also in large measure to their ability to develop a surface crust or weathering rind that strengthens the rock and reduces its permeability (Figure 12.2). The crust results from the precipitation of extra silica cement between the grains when pore-water containing dissolved silica evaporates from the rock surfaces (Robinson and Williams, 1987).

In recent years there have been a number of studies of the weathering of the sandstone cliffs of the central Weald (Bird, 1964; Piper, 1971; Robinson and Williams, 1976, 1981, 1984 and 1987; Pentecost, 1991) and laboratory experiments have been conducted to investigate the behaviour of the stone under simulated weathering conditions (Williams and Robinson, 1981; Robinson and Williams, 1982). However, little consideration has been given to assessing how the stone performs when it is used in buildings. Indeed, compared with the number of studies that have been made of the weathering of limestone building stones, there is a general paucity of studies concerned with the weathering of masonry sandstones. The present paper is a contribution towards redressing this balance by examining the weathering of Hastings Bed sandstone used in the construction of Wealden churches. It is a descriptive analysis carried out as a precursor to more detailed monitoring and investigation of the actual processes at work. Unlike some previous studies of sandstone weathering (e.g. Smith, *et al.*, 1984), which focus on urban and industrial environments, the paper is concerned with the durability of a quartzose sandstone building stone in a relatively unpolluted, non-industrial, rural environment. As such it provides information on weathering features and weathering rates against which weathering of sandstone in polluted urban environments may be compared.

WEALDEN SANDSTONE CHURCHES

The use of local sandstone for the construction of churches in the central Weald began as early as Saxon times and has continued into the present century. The churches thus provide a useful opportunity for studying the ways in which the weathering of building stones develops over a period of up to a thousand years. In addition, they enable one to examine whether the rate and intensity of weathering varies with aspect or orientation. On natural outcrops, the rock surfaces have been exposed to weathering for unknown periods of time, and their orientation is determined by the directions of the joints and the valley sides. Churches provide dateable rock surfaces that, with few exceptions, face the cardinal points of the compass.

The issue of whether stone deterioration on buildings varies with aspect has rarely been discussed in any detail and remains under-researched. Where thermal changes are responsible for the deterioration one would expect to find significant differences in amounts of weathering between the north and south sides of buildings, but little, if any, differences between the east and west sides. Thus, if it is diurnal temperature changes across or above 0°C that are primarily responsible, one might expect the sun-heated south sides of the buildings to be more rapidly and completely weathered than the shaded north sides. If persistent or minimum low temperatures are more important then the cooler north-facing sides of buildings will be more weathered.

In southeast England it is possible that the weathering of buildings is due primarily to exposure to wind and rain rather than thermal stresses. Since the south and west sides of buildings suffer most wind blast and driving rain, and presumably also experience the greatest number of wetting and drying cycles, the stonework on these sides could be supposed to be the most at risk from weathering. However, there is a contrary argument.

In polluted urban areas, sooty sulphate deposits tend to accumulate on stonework on the sheltered sides of buildings, causing the formation of a surface skin, which tends to blister and exfoliate. The skin does not develop on the rain-washed sides of buildings, where the stonework appears to remain in better condition. At one time, it was believed that rain-wash helps to protect stonework against decay (Schaffer, 1932), but the modern view is that the damage is merely less obvious than in sheltered locations because the weathered material is regularly washed away exposing a fresh surface to attack (BERG, 1989).

The impact of salt weathering in a relatively non-polluted area such as south-east England is difficult to predict. In hot deserts salt weathering is most evident on the shaded sides of outcrops and in recesses where moisture lingers longest. This could suggest that the northern sides of the Wealden sandstone churches would be most affected since being cooler they tend to remain damp for longer. However, it is the prevailing south-west wind that brings most salt to the stonework, which could suggest that the south and west sides ought to show the greatest damage.

136

LIMITATIONS OF THE STUDY

In practice, study of the weathering of Wealden churches is less straightforward than might at first appear. A number of problems complicate the exercise:

(1) The churches do not show an even spread of ages. The majority were built in medieval times (twelth to fifteenth century), while a sizeable minority are Victorian or Edwardian. Unfortunately, there is a period of about 300 years, from c. 1500–1800, when relatively few churches were constructed in the Weald (Syms, 1994; Whiteman and Whiteman, 1994), and this limits the extent to which one can draw detailed conclusions about the development of weathering over time.

(2) All the older Wealden churches have been at least partly enlarged or rebuilt, sometimes on several occasions. The Victorians were notoriously unsparing and unprincipled when embarking on their extensive restorations or 'improvements'. As a result, it is frequently impossible to compare like with like. One side of a church may have medieval stonework, while the opposite side is a Victorian addition. The base of a tower may be original, the upper part a reconstruction following a fire, or a later addition simply to add height to the structure.

(3) The source of the sandstone is often unrecorded. In the medieval period the stone was usually quarried close to the building to minimise transport costs. Small quarries were often opened up just to supply stone for the construction or restoration of a single church. In more modern times, as the Wealden roads were improved, stone was fetched from larger quarries over greater distances, but sometimes from more than one source. Although stone from different quarries may appear superficially similar, its durability may vary considerably. Even within a single quarry the beds of stone may differ greatly in their degree of cementation, organic content and susceptibility to weathering (Williams and Robinson, 1981).

(4) Assessment of how weathering varies with aspect must take account of the fact that there is unequal representation of wall area facing the cardinal compass directions. The north and south sides of churches are longer than the east and west facing ends, and other things being equal will have greater numbers of flawed or defective blocks that weather rapidly.

(5) In addition to possibly varying with aspect the rate of weathering undoubtedly varies with other factors, one of the most important of which is height. The most weathered blocks tend to be found towards the base of walls, within the capillary fringe, and towards the top of church towers, especially where there is a parapet. Window surrounds also appear to be particularly susceptible to weathering.

METHODOLOGY

Arguably the most difficult problem is to devise an effective scale for measuring amounts of weathering. It would be unrealistic to expect church authorities to approve the removal of a large number of rock samples for microscopic analysis by, for example, the counting of microcracks, as is required by some engineering classifications of rocks (e.g. Irfan and Dearman, 1978). Because of the crumbly nature of some of the stonework the Schmidt Hammer is of limited usefulness. Mottershead's (1994) 10-point scale of weathering grades for sandstone has the advantage that it relies purely on visual assessment, but unfortunately it applies only to alveolar weathering and cannot therefore be readily employed for the Wealden churches.

The method adopted in the present study is a stone by stone assessment of the percentage area of surface that visibly displays surface weathering phenomena. Surfaces or parts of surfaces that have been stabilised by the development of a hardened crust darken in colour and often become lichen or algae covered. Where there is appreciable surface weathering the rock retains its original grey or buff colour, and as weathering progresses the surface becomes more and more hollowed out. Obvious advantages of the method adopted here are that it is quick to use, non-destructive and based solely on field observation. The main drawback is that small amounts of weathered material removed uniformly from rock surfaces are not easily detected; the method works best if the surface is unevenly weathered. Although considered a satisfactory method for assessing weathering damage to the soft sandstone forming the focus of this study, the method may be much less suitable for harder stones on which stable surfaces do not discolour on exposure.

The present study is concerned solely with the weathering of church towers. These are generally square in plan, which circumscribes the problem that each of the churches is elongated, with more stonework facing north and south than east and west. Generally speaking, the towers are also less affected by additions and rebuilding than the naves and other parts of the churches, and their age is often better documented.

The procedure followed was to assess the damage to 50 stones on each side of each tower around or just below any belfry windows. This avoids the problem that stones towards the base of the towers are weathered more rapidly than elsewhere, but the inaccessibility of the stones has meant that they have had to be examined through binoculars. All corner stones and window surrounds have been ignored, and care has been taken to avoid parapet areas many of which appear to have been rebuilt or to have been adversely affected by runoff and damp from the tower roof or spire. Of the 58 sandstone churches visited 17 could not be included in the survey either because they were not oriented east–west, because the eastern sides of the towers did not rise sufficiently high above the nave roofs to provide enough stonework to assess, because one side of the tower was hidden from view by the rest of the church, or because the stonework had been extensively repaired or rendered and was difficult to date. The location of the 41 churches that were surveyed is shown in Figure 12.3. Fewer churches have been sampled in the eastern part of the study area than in the west.

RESULTS

Weathering phenomena

The sandstone exhibits a number of distinct forms of weathering.

Granular disintegration

This is the most frequent and widespread form of weathering on churches of all ages. Surface grains of quartz become loose and are then washed, blown or simply fall away under gravity. In sheltered locations the loosened grains may continue to adhere to the surface of the blocks for some time; lightly rubbing the surface of blocks with the fingers often releases a shower of grains. On more exposed faces grains are removed as quickly as they become loose, leaving a more stable, but distinctly fresh looking surface. Granular disintegration may affect the entire surface of a block or it may be restricted to the edges, to bands within a stone, bedding planes or patches of the surface.

Weathering cracks

Vertical or near-vertical cracks often cut into or through stone blocks on the churches. They appear to be due to the accumulation of weathering stresses rather than loading or foundation settlement, and probably develop from weaknesses inherent in the stone when it is quarried.

The cracking is most common on medieval churches, but is also found even on churches built in the present century. Some cracks look very fresh and have sharp edges, but in other cases the outer edges of cracks have been widened by granular disintegration. Polygonal cracking (Williams and Robinson, 1989) has developed on the buttresses of the sixteenth century church at Bolney, and on the flat tops of Georgian box tombs at Balcombe.

Alveolar weathering

Several distinct forms of alveolar weathering can be observed. The surfaces of some stones are 'eaten away' by masses of circular hollows separated by narrow ribs of sound rock. The openings of the hollows vary from about 10–30 mm in diameter and they may penetrate the sandstone for up to 20–25 mm, but are most commonly 10–15 mm in depth. This honeycomb weathering, which may affect the entire surface of a block or just part of the sur-

139

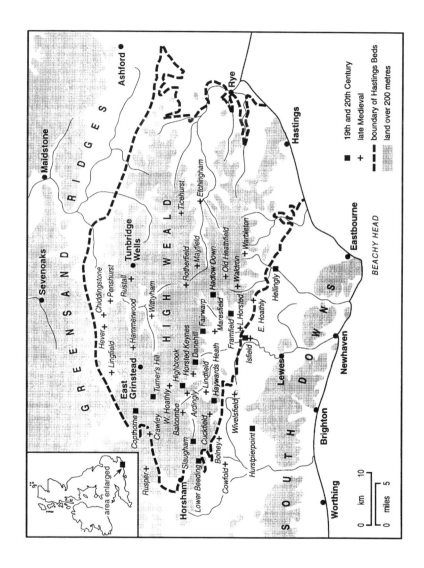

Figure 12.3 Location of the sandstone churches in the central Weald included in the sample.

face, tends to be confined to a limited number of stones on any individual church. Incipient honeycombing has developed on some churches built in the early twentieth century, and deeply hollowed out stones may be seen on Highbrook church (built 1884–5) as well as on most of the medieval churches in the sample. On many medieval churches honeycomb weathering is undoubtedly fossil as the hollows are now stabilised beneath a surface crust (Figure 12.4).

A second form of alveolar weathering observed on the churches consists of lines of hollows developed along particular bands running across the faces of stones (Figure 12.5). These hollows are often larger than those typical of honeycomb weathering being up to 50 mm in diameter, although rarely more than 25–30 mm deep. The fact that the hollows are organised in lines suggests that they are picking out weak layers or bands within the stones.

Isolated alveoles, sometimes exceeding 50 mm in diameter, are also found on some blocks, especially on the older churches. Most are developed on blocks that are extensively crusted and appear totally inactive at the present time.

On a few churches a fourth cause of alveolar weathering is the action of mining bees who sometimes excavate massed pits into small areas of stone. The pits are only 5–10 mm in diameter but often extend 20–30 mm or more into the rock; they are thus much narrower and deeper than the rounded hollows characteristic of honeycomb weathering. At Bidborough church (in Kent) the bees could be seen actively excavating the pits in a number of stones; abandoned pits could be seen in other stones on the same church.

Figure 12.4 Fossilised and degraded honeycombing, medieval church at Mayfield.

Figure 12.5 Alveolar weathering developed along bedding planes, medieval church at Burwash.

Surface crusting

As on natural outcrops, the sandstone case hardens with age. On stable, non-eroding surfaces, the buff coloured fresh sandstone darkens to a greyish colour. Blackening of the surface is much less common than on many of the harder sandstones used in more polluted urban environments. Apart from the colour change, the case hardened layer is difficult to detect except where, with age, it begins to break away from the underlying rock (Figure 12.6).

Figure 12.6 Sandstone block with a hardened crust now spalling to expose a weakened subsurface layer, medieval church tower, Old Heathfield.

Surface scaling

The Hastings Beds sandstones are much less prone to multi-layer scaling or onion-skin flaking than many of the Lower Greensand sandstones, which are also used as building stones elsewhere in the Weald, but deteriorate rapidly. The Victorian churches included in the survey show only limited surface scaling. However, as the stones continue to case harden, the outer surface often becomes detached, revealing a weakened, poorly cemented subsurface layer (Robinson and Williams, 1987). Such single-layer scaling is quite common on medieval churches. Once the crust has been breached some stones undergo multi-layer scaling which hollows out the central part of their surface.

Weathering flutes

Stones on the parapets of some churches (and at Bodiam Castle) exhibit what appear to be incipient flutes (Williams and Robinson, 1994).

Development of weathering over time

The three churches in the survey with towers built early in the twentieth century returned a mean weathering score of 18% (Table 12.1). This is the average amount of weather-damaged surface recorded on the sample stones on all four sides of the three towers (600 stones). For the twelve towers built in the nineteenth century, the average is 23%. Several of these towers were little affected by weathering, but others were quite extensively damaged. The standard deviation of the church means was quite high (11%), largely it would seem because of variations in the quality of the stone provided by different quarries, but perhaps also because of differences in surface preparation. Smooth-sawn ashlar seems less vulnerable to weathering than blocks with decorative, rough hewn or chisel-roughened surfaces. The

Age	Arithmetic mean	Standard deviation	Most weathered	Least weathered	No. in sample
Twentieth century	18%	6%	24%	11%	3
Nineteenth century	23%	11%	46%	10%	12
Medieval	37%	15%	69%	16%	27

Table 12.1 Weathering scores for a sample of Wealden churches.

hollows in these decorative surfaces seem to be preferential sites for the accumulation of salts and the development of alveolar weathering.

The 27 medieval churches returned a mean weathering score of 37% with a standard deviation of 15% (one church in the survey, Isfield, was counted twice as it had a tower with medieval stonework below and Victorian stonework above). The difference between the mean scores of the 'modern' and medieval churches is statistically significant at the 0.001 level. The fact that the medieval churches are more weathered on average than their modern counterparts is entirely predictable. What is surprising, however, is that the least well preserved Victorian churches are much more decayed than the best preserved medieval churches, despite the gap of 300 years or more. Also interesting is the possibility that the weathering rate decreases with time (Figure 12.7). This may be because the stone develops an increasingly thick protective crust which inhibits weathering as time progresses. Another interpretation of the data, however, is that weathering rates this century may have been accelerated as a result of pollution and acid

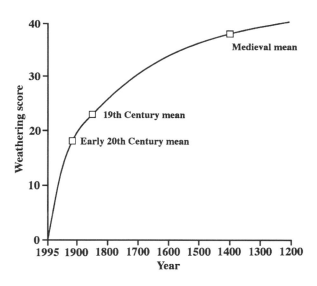

Figure 12.7 Graph showing mean weathering scores for churches of different ages.

deposition, and were lower in the past, despite the intervention of the Little Ice Age. It is also possible that piecemeal replacement of badly weakened blocks has not always been identified in the survey and their inclusion in the sample has reduced the apparent rate of weathering.

On the nineteenth and early twentieth century churches, the first visible sign of weathering is usually the selective etching out of weak bands and bedding planes by granular disintegration. More widespread granular disintegration affecting the entire surface of blocks appears to be rare, although when poorly developed in its incipient stages it is hard to detect and may have been under-recorded in arriving at the weathering scores shown in Table 12.1. Indurated surface crusts tend to be only weakly developed and surface scaling and flaking are generally rare. Honeycombing is usually absent or only very locally developed, but linear alveoles along narrow bands or bedding planes are not uncommon. Vertical cracking occurs on some of the churches.

The medieval churches have generally better developed crusts than the younger churches, but exhibit more surface scaling. Nearly all the churches have some stones that are deeply hollowed out as a result of long-continued granular disintegration or the breakdown of an existing crust (Figure 12.8). Honeycombing is much more widespread and intense than on the modern churches, but is often crusted over, which indicates that it is now fossil. Many of the churches have individual stones that have clearly been replaced or patches of stonework that have been extensively restored. These were ignored in deriving weathering scores.

Figure 12.8 Differential weathering of sandstone blocks on the medieval tower of Mayfield church. Note the central block which is severely weathered and hollowed out.

Weathering of surfaces of differing orientation

The results of the present survey (Table 12.2) are somewhat difficult to interpret. The fifteen church towers built in the nineteenth and twentieth centuries are on average most weathered on their eastern face and least weathered on their southern face. The eastern faces recorded 31% of the overall damage recorded on the four faces of the towers and the southern faces 16%. The probability of such a result arising through chance sampling is small, and it must be presumed that some real process is at work. Perhaps the sun-heated, rain-soaked south-facing sides develop a surface crust more quickly than the other sides and this reduces amounts of weathering.

The medieval churches show a somewhat different pattern of weathering. The north, south and west sides of the towers are on average about equally weathered, each exhibiting a 22% to 25% share of the weathering recorded, with the southern faces again having very slightly the lowest proportion. However, the most noticeable feature is the relatively high proportion (31%) of the weathering that occurs on the eastern sides. This proportion is identical to that recorded on the eastern faces of the younger churches, and in both groups it is the eastern faces that are the most weathered.

DISCUSSION AND CONCLUSIONS

The Hastings Beds sandstone is clearly not an ideal building stone. It is variable in character and the performance of some of the stone, in terms of resistance to weathering, is poor. The area of stonework displaying weathering damage increases with age, but over the time span covered by this study age is not as important a factor as might have been expected. Examples of almost the full range of weathering phenomena described in this paper can

Place and age of church tower	N	S	E	W
Nineteenth and twentieth century				
Copthorne, 1876	40	14	21	25
Danehill, 1892	35	12	26	27
Framfield, 1891-2	33	16	24	27
Hadlow Down, c. 1913	27	7	31	35
Hammerwood, 1879	17	16	35	31
Haywards Heath, 1863	27	20	44	9
Hellingly, early 19C	40	19	27	14
Highbrook, 1884-5	23	10	25	43
Hurstpierpoint, 1843-5	13	37	34	16
Fairwarp, 1935	9	27	25	39
Isfield, c. 1876	39	5	47	9
Lower Beeding, 1840	24	29	28	19
Rustall, 1849-50	29	1	38	32
Slaugham, 1858	33	22	29	16
Turner's Hill, 1923	29	6	28	37
Total	418 (m = 28)	241 (m = 16)	462 (m = 31)	379 (m = 25)
Medieval				
Ardingly, 14-15C	17	35	22	26
Balcombe, 15C	35	18	34	13
Bolney, 1536-8	15	32	28	25
Chiddingstone, 15C	25	10	36	28
Cowfold, 15C	27	32	26	16
Crawley, 15C	36	9	29	26
Cuckfield, 14C	29	24	31	16
East Hoathly, 1645	13	24	38	25
Etchingham, c. 1369	27	8	38	27
Horsted Keynes, 11-12C	33	18	30	20
Hever, 14C	41	8	37	14
Isfield, C. 1493	22	26	25	28
Lindfield, 13C	6	32	29	32
Lingfield, 15C	22	33	31	14
Little Horsted, 15C	16	25	31	28
Maresfield, 15C	18	7	50	25
Mayfield, 13C	23	31	19	27
Penshurst, 17C	31	21	33	16
Old Heathfield, 13C	42	14	29	15
Rotherfield, 15C, 37	15	23	25	
Rusper, c. 1500	30	19	29	21
Ticehurst, 13/14C	18	36	23	24
Waldron, 13/14C	16	37	31	16
Warbleton, 15C	26	22	29	23
West Hoathly, 15C	19	20	33	28
Withyam, 1672	19	23	38	21
Wivelsfield 14-15C	29	13	33	26
Total	672 (m = 25)	592 (m = 22)	835 (m = 31)	605 (m = 22)

Table 12.2 Percentage weathering scores by aspect.

be found on churches of all ages. The stonework of some churches less than 150 years in age is more badly weathered than the stonework of the least weathered medieval churches, some of which are over 500 years old.

On average, weathering is least developed on the south and west sides which are the faces which receive the worst of the wind and rain, and also most insolation. This is a particularly marked feature of some of the younger churches. It suggests that the more persistently damp and cooler stonework on the east and north faces is subject initially to the severest weathering conditions. This receives some support from our observations of the weathering of the natural exposures of the sandstone. In shady woodlands, the surfaces of natural outcrops are frequently eroding and unstable whilst rocks exposed to full sunlight are often crusted and more stable. It may be that the greater number of wetting and drying cycles to which the south and west faces of the sandstone churches are subjected results in the quicker and more complete development of a hardened and protective crust. On the more persistently damp northern and eastern sides crusting would seem to develop more slowly, harden less, and as a result be less complete and protective. With the passage of centuries, however the crusts on the south and west sides begin to spall. This may explain why the south faces of the towers, which have such a low proportion of the weathering on the young churches, should 'catch up' with north and west faces in the sample of older churches. Further investigation is required to test these ideas.

Weathering of stonework is evidently a somewhat erratic process. It would seem to slow down with age, although, as already pointed out, appearances may be deceptive since on the older churches the worst affected blocks may have been replaced so long ago and so skilfully that we have unwittingly included them in our weathering assessment (recent restoration is usually only too apparent). The apparent slow-down may result from the episodic nature of crust formation and destruction. Once developed, the surface crust is protective and in many instances alveolar or granular weathering ceases entirely, as it does also on the natural outcrops of the sandstone (Robinson and Williams, 1976, 1981). However, formation of the crust results in subsurface weakening of the stone (Robinson and Williams, 1987) and, when with time the crusts begin to spall, this can lead to very rapid and catastrophic collapse of the underlying stone requiring replacement, or in some cases complete rebuilding of the towers.

The between-church and between-block variability of weathering is very large. Precisely why this should be awaits further investigation, but on the evidence of laboratory experiments into frost and salt weathering of the stone (Robinson and Williams, 1982; Williams and Robinson, 1981) is almost certainly determined in large part by the varying lithology of different beds of the sandstone, in particular differences in clay content, included organic matter and porosity. For the most part the weathering is not concentrated along the edges of blocks which might be indicative of contamination by mortars. Nevertheless, the use of hard, cement-based mortars from Victorian times onwards does seem to have affected water movement and the weathering of some of the younger churches, and some of those which have been repaired.

In addition to variation within the stone, the local environment surrounding churches and individual stone blocks may have had an important influence on the rate of weathering. Trees often appear to have provided shelter, but in other localities may have accentuated weathering, possibly by acidifying leaf-drip. Victorian and Edwardian photographs reveal that some churches, including the lower parts of their towers, were thickly covered by ivy, which has since been removed. The precise effects of the ivy are uncertain: it may have damaged the mortar but helped shield the stone from weathering attack. Local shading and sheltering of stones by buttresses and other protrusions also influence the rate and form of the weathering of stones in some localities.

The results of this study suggest that in the relatively non-polluted atmosphere of the central Weald where contamination from road salts is also minimal, granular disintegration of sandstone masonry can become well developed in less than 70 years, and on some stones probably commences from the date of building. Alveolar weathering can be visible in 70 years and well developed in a hundred years, but its occurrence and rate of formation is very variable. Surface scaling rarely occurs in less than 200 years and only becomes a noticeable problem on churches more than 500 years old.

References

BERG (1989) *The effects of acid deposition on buildings and building materials in the United Kingdom*, Building Effects Review Group Report, HMSO, London.

Bird, E.C.F. (1964) *Tor-like sandrock features in the central Weald.* (Abstract), 20th International Geography Congress, London, p. 1156.

Elsden, J.V. and Howe, J.A. (1923) *The stones of London.* Colliery Guardian Co., London.

Irfan, T.W. and Dearman, W.R. (1978) Engineering petrography of a weathered granite. *Quarterly Journal of Engineering Geology* **11**: 233–244.

Mottershead, D.N. (1994) Spatial variations in intensity of alveolar weathering of a dated sandstone structure in a coastal environment, Weston-super-Mare, UK. In D.A. Robinson and R.B.G. Williams (eds) *Rock Weathering and Landform Evolution.* J. Wiley & Sons, Chichester, pp. 151–174.

Nairn, I. and Pevsner, N. (1965) *The Buildings of England: Sussex.* Penguin Books, Harmondsworth, Middlesex.

Newman, J. (1969) *The Buildings of England: West Kent and the Weald.* Penguin Books, Harmondsworth, Middlesex.

Pentecost, A. (1991) The weathering rates of some sandstone cliffs, central Weald, England. *Earth Surface Processes and Landforms* **16**: 83–91.

Piper, D.J.W. (1971) Pleistocene superficial deposits, Balcombe area, central Weald. *Geological Magazine* **108**: 517–523.

Robinson, D.A. and Williams, R.B.G. (1976) Aspects of the geomorpholgy of the sandstone cliffs of the central Weald. *Proceedings of the Geological Association* **87**: 93–100.

Robinson, D.A. and Williams, R.B.G. (1981) Sandstone cliffs on the High Weald landscape. *Geographical Magazine* **53**: 587–592.

Robinson, D.A. and Williams, R.B.G. (1982) Salt weathering of rock specimens of varying shape. *Area* **14**: 293–299.

Robinson, D.A. and Williams, R.B.G. (1984) *Classic Landforms of the Weald. Landform Guides, No. 4.* Geographical Association, Sheffield.

Robinson, D.A. and Williams, R.B.G. (1987) Surface crusting of sandstones in southern England and northern France. In V. Gardiner (ed.) *International Geomorphology 1986, Part 2.* J. Wiley & Sons, Chichester, pp. 623–635.

Schaffer, R.J. (1932) *The Weathering of Natural Building Stones.* Department of Scientific and Industrial Research. Building Research Special Report No. 18, HMSO, London.

Smith, B.J., Magee, R.W. and Whalley, W.B. (1994) Breakdown patterns of quartz sandstone in a polluted urban environment, Belfast, Northern Ireland. In D.A. Robinson and R.B.G. Williams (eds) *Rock Weathering and Landform evolution.* J. Wiley & Sons, Chichester, pp. 131–150.

Syms, J.A. (1994) *East Sussex Country Churches.* S.B. Publications, Seaford.

Whiteman, K. and Whiteman, J. (1994) *Ancient Churches of Sussex.* Roedale Books, Brighton.

Williams, R.B.G. and Robinson, D.A. (1981) Weathering of sandstone by the combined action of frost and salt. *Earth Surface Processes and Landforms* **6**: 1–9.

Williams, R.B.G. and Robinson, D.A. (1989) Origin and distribution of polygonal cracking of rock surface. *Geografiska Annaler* **71A**: 145–159.

Williams, R.B.G. and Robinson, D.A. (1994) Weathering flutes on siliceous rocks in Britain and Europe. In D.A. Robinson and R.B.G. Williams (eds) *Rock Weathering and Landform Evolution.* J. Wiley & Sons, Chichester, pp. 413–432.

White, H.J.O. (1928) *The geology of the country near Hastings and Dungeness.* Memoirs of the Geological Survey of England. HMSO, London.

Contact address
School of African and Asian Studies
University of Sussex
Falmer
Brighton
BN1 9QN
United Kingdom

13 Pore properties of limestones as controls on salt weathering susceptibility: a case study

J.P. McGREEVY

ABSTRACT

The susceptibility of six limestones to damage by salt (sodium chloride) crystallisation under laboratory conditions is examined. Variations in relative susceptibilities are discussed in the context of pore and pore-related properties (moisture absorption capacity, effective and total porosity, pore size distribution, saturation coefficient, permeability, capillarity), as are interrelationships between the properties themselves. Clay mineralogy is also considered as a control on weathering behaviour. Although possible susceptibility – property relationships are suggested, it is clear that further work is required before more definite assertions can be made.

INTRODUCTION

'The susceptibility of porous materials to salt crystallisation damage appears to be related to the pore size distribution and pore volume of the material' (Ginell, 1994). This sweeping statement, understandable in the context of a wide-ranging review paper, is probably correct to a large extent. However, it masks the facts that the precise nature of relationships between susceptibility and pore and pore-related properties remains unclear and that the relative significance of these properties in determining susceptibility has yet to be satisfactorily established. Furthermore, the suggestions that clay mineralogy is an important factor and that salt-related chemical (i.e. dissolution) effects should be taken into account, both require scrutiny.

Laboratory-based durability tests provide one useful means of probing these uncertainties by offering insights into how various stone types react to

Processes of Urban Stone Decay. Edited by B.J. Smith and P.A. Warke. © 1996 Donhead Publishing Ltd.

salt crystallisation and the factors which might condition their reaction. The present paper reports on the results of one such test carried out in respect of six limestones the contrasting properties of which afforded the potential for discussing a range of weathering responses.

THE INVESTIGATION

Stone types and properties

The stone types selected for study are as follows: Antrim Chalk (Glenarm, County Antrim, Northern Ireland), Portland limestone (Isle of Portland, Dorset, England), Banc Royal, Fleury and Lorphelin limestones (three varieties of Caen limestone, Calvados, France) and Echoisy limestone (Charente, France). Attention was focused primarily on a number of void-dependent properties and their interrelationships: moisture absorption capacity or water content (w), porosity (both effective and total, n_e and n_t, respectively), saturation coefficient (S), pore size distribution, permeability and capillarity. All are relevant to the absorption, transmission and retention of moisture. Property determinations were based on methods proposed by ISRM (1979), RILEM (1980) and the Centre de Géomorphologie du CNRS (Lautridou and Ozouf, 1980) and are described in full by McGreevy (1982). In addition, X-ray diffraction (XRD) was used to define the clay mineralogy of each stone type and scanning electron microscopy (SEM) used to obtain complementary information on microstructures.

The data in Table 13.1 and depicted in Figures 13.1 and 13.2 highlight

Stone type	w	n_e	n_t	S	k
Antrim chalk	2.60	6.47	8.27	89.41	0.002
Portland limestone	5.17	10.47	17.92	66.50	364.0
Fleury limestone	9.54	19.80	22.28	89.53	0.65
Lorphelin limestone	12.93	24.38	29.32	83.26	3.17
Banc Royal limestone	11.40	22.58	27.07	83.52	2.23
Echoisy limestone	8.59	18.52	20.94	88.56	0.083

w moisture absorption capacity (%)   S saturation coefficient (%)
n_e effective porosity (%)   k permeability (millidarcys)
n_t total interconnected porosity (%)

Table 13.1 Void-dependent property determinations (values for each stone type are means of ten determinations).

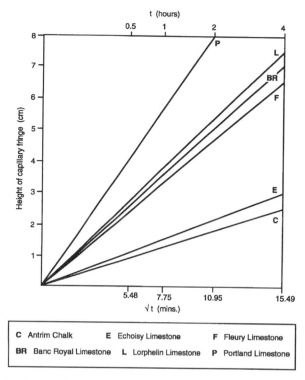

Figure 13.1 Rates of capillary rise of water in six limestones.

the differences between the six limestones. Not surprisingly, the Caen limestones, although quite distinct from each other, comprise a discrete grouping. Their high water content and effective and total porosity values, in particular, contrast with low values obtained for Antrim chalk with the Echoisy and Portland limestones falling between the two extremes. Saturation coefficients generally lie within a narrow range (83–90%), the Portland limestone value of 66.5% proving to be exceptional and hinting at a difference in the nature (as opposed to amount) of pore space. Permeability and capillarity measurements echo each other and are suggestive of variations in pore size and structure. The highly permeable Portland limestone is seen to absorb and transmit moisture much more rapidly than the other stone types. The high porosity Caen limestones are ranked consistently in terms of both properties, whilst the Echoisy limestone and Antrim chalk both display a relatively slow moisture uptake. Capillarity and permeability rankings are also reflected in terms of pore size distributions as evaluated by mercury porosimetry (Figure 13.2).

SEM observations show that the differences in pore throat radii distributions depicted in Figure 13.2 reflect the differences in actual pore sizes. Antrim chalk is shown to be extremely compact with blocky micritic crys-

152

tals interlocking to produce pore spaces usually < 1 μm in diameter and smooth narrow grain boundaries < 0.1 μm wide (Figure13.3a). A compact microstructure is also evident in the Echoisy limestone although not to the same degree (Figure 13.3b). Actual pore sizes appear to lie mostly within the 0.5–3.0 μm diameter range, but also include some relatively large and

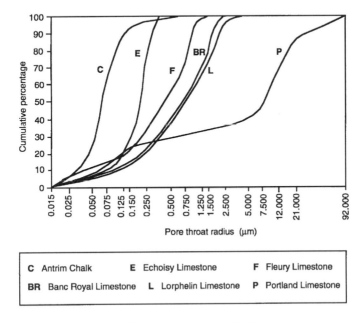

Figure 13.2 Pore size distribution curves of six limestones.

randomly distributed pores, approaching 10 μm in diameter.

The Fleury limestone (Figure 13.3c) shows no grain interlocking, abundant pore spaces and a 0.5–5.0 μm diameter size range which is slightly greater than that estimated for Echoisy limestone. The trend of increasing porosity and pore size continues with the Banc Royal and Lorphelin limestones (Figures 13.3d and 13.3e), the latter showing a well developed system of pores many of which exhibit potential for enlargement through coalescence. Finally, Portland limestone contains extremely large intergranular pores, spaces between ooliths (Figure 13.3f). Where ooliths are in contact these spaces are reduced in size by the presence of well-developed calcite crystals which along with the fine-grained micritic veneer on oolith surfaces, contributes to the significant quantity of micropores evident from the pore size distribution curve (Figure 13.2).

XRD showed three commonly occurring clay minerals: primarily smectite (probably montmorillonite) and illite/mica, but also kaolinite. Relative amounts were estimated using the areas under diffraction peaks on

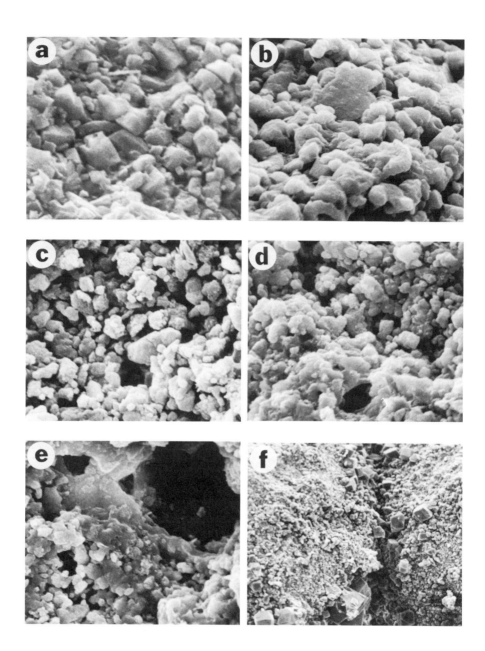

Figures 13.3a–f Scanning electron micrographs of (a) Antrim chalk (picture width 15 μm), (b) Echoisy limestone (picture width 15 μm), (c) Fleury limestone (picture width 15 μm), (d) Banc Royal limestone (picture width 15 μm), (e) Lorphelin limestone (picture width 18 μm) and (f) Portland limestone (picture width 140 μm).

glycolated traces (Table 13.2). Smectite is the predominant clay mineral in the Antrim chalk and Caen limestones (indeed, it is the only one in the Lorphelin limestone). In the Antrim chalk and Banc Royal and Fleury limestones illite/mica is found in smaller amounts whilst in the Echoisy limestone it is the main type, with mixed layer illite/mica-smectite also present along with traces of kaolinite. Portland limestone contains both smectite and illite/mica in equal proportions and a small quantity of kaolinite. Insoluble residue in limestones (of which clay minerals comprise a major component) tends to occur in small quantities and in a random manner (Flugel, 1968). Such is the case in all but the Antrim chalk, in which clay minerals are concentrated along stylolite seams (Scholle, 1974).

Relative proportions of clay minerals				
Rock types	Smectite	Illite/mica	Mixed layer illite/mica-smectite	Kaolinite
Chalk	95%	5%	-----	-----
Banc Royal limestone	90%	10%	-----	-----
Fleury limestone	90%	10%	-----	-----
Lorphelin limestone	100%	(traces)	-----	-----
Echoisy limestone	------	80%	15%	5%
Portland limestone	45%	45%	-----	10%

Table 13.2 Relative proportions of clay minerals found in each stone type.

Property interrelationships

In that they are characteristics of pore systems it is to be expected that the properties described will themselves be interrelated and that there may be some 'redundancy' involved in using them to explain weathering behaviour. It is useful, therefore, to briefly consider these interrelationships.

Moisture absorption capacity correlates well with effective porosity (Figure 13.4) suggesting that one or the other might be regarded as super-fluous. Total porosity could be considered irrelevant in the context of salt crystallisation damage since its evaluation requires vacuum saturation of samples as opposed to 'saturation' under atmospheric pressure (hence the less direct relationship between water content and total porosity in Figure 13.4). However, total porosity does provide some indication of the amount of pore space available to absorb moisture and/or accommodate salt crystal growth, the latter being more appropriately considered in the context of the

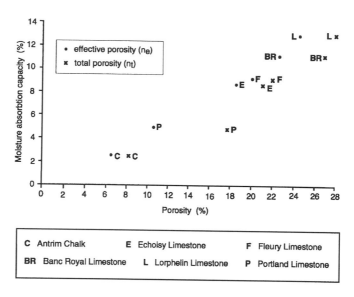

Figure 13.4 Relationships between moisture absorption capacity and effective and total porosity.

saturation coefficient. Low degrees of saturation have been associated with stone types characterised by both high (Aubry and Lautridou, 1974) and low (Honeyborne and Harris, 1958; Niesel, 1981) percentages of micropores. Plots of saturation coefficient against median pore throat radius and microporosity (arbitrarily defined here as $\%n_t < 1$ μm) suggest that the latter view holds for the limestones under study here (Figures 13.5 and 13.6). Finally, it was noted earlier that the same ranking order was evident from permeability measurements and pore size distribution and capillarity curves: the relationship between the first two (Figure 13.7) would seem to reinforce this contention.

Test conditions and procedures

Samples (3 cm cubes) of the limestones were subjected to 100 daily salt crystallisation cycles as follows. Following immersion for one hour in a 10% (by weight) solution of sodium chloride, they were weighed, placed in beakers and put into a Gallenkamp oven where temperature was raised from ambient (21°C) to 54°C over a period of two and a half hours. Temperature remained at this level for 9 hours after which heating was stopped and the samples allowed to cool to ambient temperature.

Release of debris from samples only occurred during the immersion phase of each cycle. During heating, evaporation of solution induces crystal growth and associated damage. However, it would appear that salt crys-

156

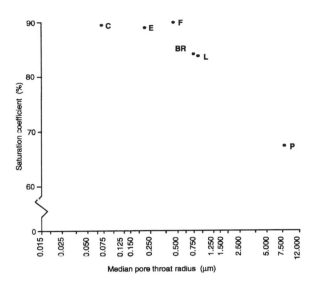

Figure 13.5 Relationship between saturation coefficient and median pore throat radius (see below for key).

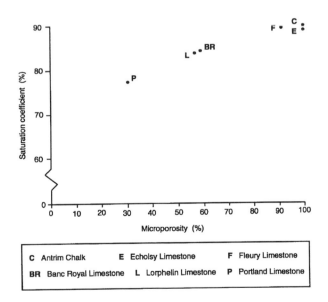

| C | Antrim Chalk | E | Echolsy Limestone | F | Fleury Limestone |
| BR | Banc Royal Limestone | L | Lorphelin Limestone | P | Portland Limestone |

Figure 13.6 Relationship between saturation coefficient and microporosity (percentage $n_t < 1$ μm).

tals also perform a binding or cementing function, preventing detachment of grains during heating and cooling (Rossi-Manaresi and Tucci, 1991). On immersion, salt dissolves with a simultaneous loss of cohesion and release of grains loosened during the crystallisation process.

Following each soaking period, debris generated was filtered. After 100 cycles, the accumulated debris was soaked in distilled water, centrifuged to remove dissolved salt, dried and weighed. Total amounts of breakdown were then expressed as percentages of the initial dry weights of the samples.

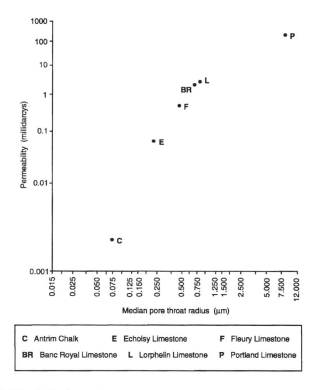

Figure 13.7 Relationship between permeability and median pore throat radius.

RESULTS AND INTERPRETATION

Patterns of breakdown

Percentage weight loss and relative rates of breakdown show varying susceptibilities to salt crystallisation damage (Figure 13.8). Because they were drawn using wet weights recorded following the immersion phase of each cycle (and thus take account of salt and moisture in pore spaces), the disintegration curves do not provide an accurate representation of susceptibilities. Weight loss values represent the true ranking.

Two forms of breakdown were evident – granular disintegration and scaling. The former was predominant and characterised the damage sustained by the Portland and Caen limestones. With Echoisy limestone much of the debris consisted of thin (c. 0.1 cm thick) scales. The Antrim chalk displayed both forms of breakdown with debris released preferentially from the vicinity of stylolite seams while the bulk of the stone remained relatively unaffected.

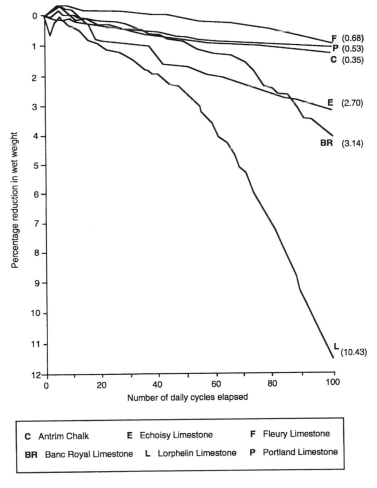

Figure 13.8 Relative rates of breakdown during experiment (values in brackets are percentage weight losses).

Rock properties and susceptibilities to salt crystal damage

Attention is focused here on those relationships between properties and susceptibility which one might expect to be found on the basis of previous work (e.g. Schaffer, 1932; Honeyborne and Harris, 1958; Harvey, et al., 1978; Cooke, 1979; Honeyborne, 1982; Leary, 1983). Thus, possible associations between breakdown amounts and moisture absorption capacity, effective porosity, saturation coefficient, microporosity, permeability and capillarity are examined. Some caution is exercised here because the data used for the above mentioned properties are those contained in Table 13.1 and Figures 13.1 and 13.2. These properties were not measured for the samples used in the experiment. However, problems might have arisen even if they had been evaluated at the beginning of the experiment because initial values are known to change quite considerably during experiments due to modification of pore systems by salt crystal growth (Accardo, et al., 1978; Cooke, 1979).

Dealing first with water content and effective porosity (Figure 13.4), it would appear that no direct relationship holds (Figures 13.9a and 13.9b). Within the group of Caen limestones, a trend is evident whereby breakdown amounts increase with increasing water content and effective porosity. Despite this, however, there are some anomalies. For example, the Echoisy limestone lost more material than the Fleury limestone despite its lower water content and effective porosity. Also, the Antrim chalk and Fleury and Portland limestones all generated similar amounts of debris even though they show wide differences in water content and effective porosity. As it is suggested in Figures 13.9a and 13.9b, it is possible that a form of exponential relationship exists between damage and water content and effective porosity. However, much more work is needed to verify or refute this possibility. Relationships between breakdown amounts and saturation coefficient, microporosity and permeability also seem less than straightforward particularly in regard to permeability (Figures 13.10a–13.10c), whilst the ranking order noted for capillarity is not consistent with relative susceptibilities. An inverse relationship is discernible in respect of both saturation coefficient and microporosity although in both cases the Portland limestone stands apart from the others.

DISCUSSION

Obviously, many more stone types and samples would require examination before generalisations could be justified. In this discussion, therefore, only tentative suggestions are made concerning pore property – salt crystallisation damage relationships.

Water content and effective porosity considered alone may not be particularly relevant. There may be critical values for these parameters above and below which other properties will be of little significance. In such cases, either parameter could provide adequate explanation of weathering behaviour. For example, the water content and effective porosity values of Antrim

160

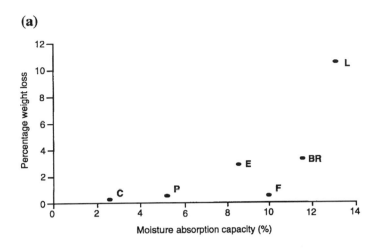

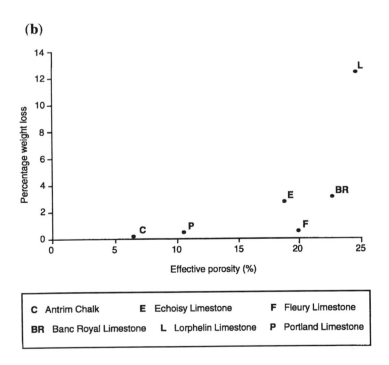

C Antrim Chalk   E Echoisy Limestone   F Fleury Limestone
BR Banc Royal Limestone   L Lorphelin Limestone   P Portland Limestone

Figure 13.9 Relationship between weight loss and (a) moisture absorption capacity and (b) effective porosity.

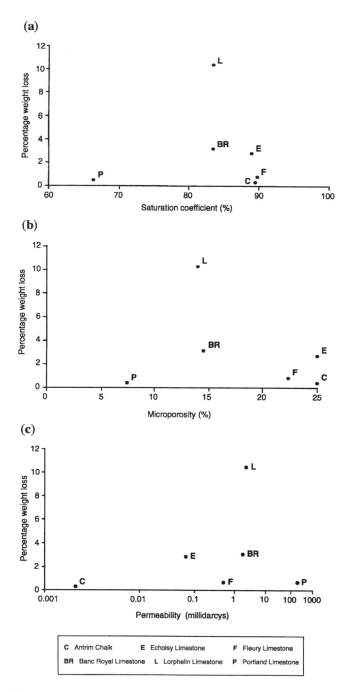

Figure 13.10 Relationships between weight loss and (a) saturation coefficient, (b) microporosity and (c) permeability.

chalk are so low that only small amounts of salt solution could be absorbed to crystallise with limited disintegrative effect (it should be remembered also that often, a corollary to low porosity will be high strength). On the other hand, in a highly porous (and, invariably, low strength) stone capable of absorbing large quantities of moisture, such as the Lorphelin limestone, the opposite situation will prevail. In such instances, it could be argued that evaluation of other properties is unlikely to improve interpretation of responses to weathering. For stone types lying between these extremes, the situation is different and the possibility arises that other properties assume some importance.

As noted by Cooke (1979), it would be expected that a high saturation coefficient value would be detrimental since the extent to which salt crystals might grow into empty pores to relieve stresses would be limited. That this is not the case for the limestones studied here may be explained by viewing saturation coefficient as a rather crude measure of pore structure. Thus, the inverse relationship between microporosity and salt crystallisation damage is paralleled by a similar association between saturation coefficient and damage simply because these two properties are themselves directly related (Figure 13.6). It is suggested, therefore, that the saturation coefficient as initially conceived by Hirschwald (1912) may, in its strictest sense, be of no consequence as a control on the extent of salt crystallisation damage.

As regards the role of microporosity, rigid comparison of results described above with those reported elsewhere, is not possible due to varying definitions of this property (cf. Honeyborne and Harris, 1958; Cooke, 1979; Leary, 1983). For the limestones studied here, SEM observations confirmed the ranking of pore sizes as obtained by mercury porosimetry. Hence rather than considering pore sizes in absolute terms, it is more useful to look at relative differences. In so doing, it is apparent that generally the coarse-pored limestones experience more damage. This generalisation receives some support from the findings of Schulze and Lange (1969) and Price (1978). The latter put forward the interesting suggestion that the significance of pore size lies in its effect on the extent and rate of evaporation of salt solution and that, because they dry slowly, fine-pored stone types will experience less severe conditions. In the context of the more porous stone types used for the present study this would seem not to hold (Figure 13.11). For the French limestones, drying rates are inversely related to pore size, although the rapid rate evident for Portland limestone may be consistent with its characteristic large pores. Similarly, salt crystallisation damage does not relate to drying rates in an obvious way. It could be argued that rapid drying would allow salt solution to migrate to, and crystallise at, the stone surface to cause little or no damage (e.g. Portland limestone) and that, conversely, slow evaporation would promote crystallisation of salt inside the stone with a greater disruptive effect (e.g. Lorphelin limestone). However, the mismatch in rankings of Echoisy, Banc Royal and Fleury limestones in regard to drying rates and salt crystallisation damage would seem to compromise this view.

The Antrim chalk was not used to examine the possible significance of

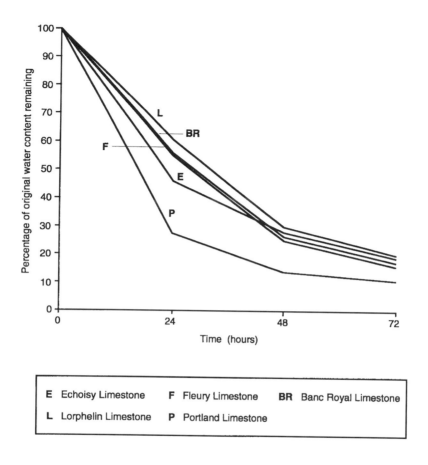

Figure 13.11 Drying rates displayed by five of the limestones.

drying rates. The reason for this lies in the belief that its salt weathering behaviour can be accounted for by reference to other factors. The bulk of the stone was little affected by the salt weathering regime (probably due to its low water content and effective porosity), and most debris was released from stylolite seams. Two observations concerning stylolites are relevant here: as pressure solution phenomena they are associated with (i) a reduction in porosity in their vicinity (Ford, 1971) and (ii) the accumulation of insoluble residue along them (Park and Schot, 1968). For the Antrim chalk, reduction of an already low porosity (effective porosity = 6.47%) would seem to be offset by the presence of smectite within the stylolites. This adds a swelling component to the disruptive effects of salt crystallisation (cf. Fookes and Poole, 1981; McGreevy and Smith, 1984; Douglas, *et al.*, 1987).

CONCLUSIONS

The results reported here do not permit the drawing of any firm conclusions regarding stone property – salt crystallisation damage relationships. Although trends were sometimes discernible, anomalies limited the extent to which generalisations could be made. The small number of limestones studied is an obvious constraint to attempts to relate pore properties not only to damage but also to each other. In making the customary call for further work, therefore, it is clear that a broader range of limestones and, indeed other lithologies, requires investigation and that more attention should be focused on interrelationships between properties. Furthermore, in that salt crystallisation is essentially a drying phenomenon it is suggested that the preoccupation with properties which influence uptake and retention of salt solution should be balanced by a closer examination of those which control its loss. Setting aside the conceptual and practical difficulties of correlating laboratory tests with field performance, it would seem that the use of tests to predict performance is problematic if the results of the tests cannot themselves be satisfactorily explained.

References

Accardo, G., Tabasso, M.L., Massa, S. and Rossi-Doria, P. (1978) Measurements of porosity and of mechanical resistance in order to evaluate the state of deterioration of some stones. In *RILEM/UNESCO Symposium on Deterioration and Protection of Stone Monuments*, Paris, Report 2.1.

Aubry, M.P. and Lautridou, J.P. (1974) Relations entre propriétés physiques, gélivité et caractères micro-structuraux dans divers types de roches: craies, calcaires, crayeux, calcaire sublithographique et silex. *Bulletin du Centre de Géomorphologie du CNRS* **19**: 7-16.

Cooke, R.U. (1979) Laboratory simulation of salt weathering processes in arid environments. *Earth Surface Processes* **4**: 347-359.

Douglas, G.R., McGreevy, J.P. and Whalley, W.B. (1987) The use of strain gauges for experimental frost weathering studies. In V. Gardiner (ed.) *International Geomorphology*. J. Wiley & Sons, Chichester, pp. 605–612.

Flugel, H.W. (1968) Some notes on the insoluble residues in limestones. In G. Muller and G.M. Friedman (eds) *Recent Developments in Carbonate Sedimentology in Central Europe*. Springer-Verlag, Berlin, pp. 46–54.

Fookes, P.G. and Poole, A.B. (1981) Some preliminary considerations on the selection and durability of rock and concrete materials for breakwaters and coastal protection works. *Quarterly Journal of Engineering Geology* **14**: 97–128.

Ford, D.C. (1971) Research methods in Karst geomorphology. In, E. Yatsu, *et al.* (eds) *Proceedings of the First Guelph Symposium on Geo-*

morphology. Science Research Associates, Ontario, pp. 23–47.

Gillott, J.E. (1980) Effect of microstructure and composition of limestone, marble, basalt and quartzite aggregate on concrete durability in the presence of solutions of calcium chloride and magnesium sulphate. *American Society for Testing and Materials. Special Technical Publication* **691**: 605–616.

Ginell, W.W. (1994) The nature of changes caused by physical forces. In W.E. Krumbein, P. Brimblecombe, D.E. Cosgrove and S. Staniforth (eds) *Durability and Change: The Science, Responsibility and Cost of Sustaining Cultural Heritage.* J. Wiley & Sons, Chichester, pp. 81–94.

Harvey, R.D., Baxter, J.W., Fraser, G.S. and Smith, C.B. (1978) Absorption and other properties of carbonate rock affecting soundness of aggregate. *Geological Society of America, Engineering Geology Case Histories* **11**: 7–16.

Hirschwald, J. (1912) *Handbuch der bautechnischen Gesteinsprüfung.* Borntraeger, Berlin.

Honeyborne, D.B. (1982) *The Building Limestones of France.* Building Research Establishment Report. HMSO, London.

Honeyborne, D.B. and Harris, P.B. (1958) The structure of porous building stone and its relation to weathering behaviour. *The Colston Papers* **10**: 343–365.

International Society for Rock Mechanics (Commission on Standardisation of Laboratory and Field Tests) (1979) Suggested methods for determining water content, porosity, density, absorption and related properties and swelling and slake-durability index properties. *International Journal of Rock Mechanics and Mining Science and Geomechanics Abstracts* **16**: 141–156.

Lautridou, J.P. and Ozouf, J.C. (1980) *Définition de normes d'analyses physiques des roches pour les géographes. II. Présentation de nouvelles normes d'analyses physiques des roches pour les géographes.* Centre de Géomorphologie du CNRS Internal Report.

Leary, E. (1983) *The Building Limestones of the British Isles.* Building Research Establishment Report. HMSO, London.

McGreevy, J.P. (1982) *Some field and laboratory investigations of rock weathering with particular reference to frost shattering and salt weathering.* Unpublished PhD. Thesis, The Queen's University of Belfast.

McGreevy, J.P. and Smith, B.J. (1984) The possible role of clay minerals in salt weathering. *Catena* **11**: 169–175.

Niesel, K. (1981) Critères pour le comportement à l'alteration de pierres en oeuvre, compte tenu d'une sélection de valeurs caractéristiques. *Petrography Group of the ICOMOS Stone Committee Newsletter* **2**: 6–14.

Park, W.C. and Schot, E.H. (1968) Stylotization in carbonate rocks. In, G. Muller and G.M. Friedman (eds) *Recent Developments in Carbonate Sedimentology in Central Europe.* Springer-Verlag, Berlin, pp. 66–74.

Price, C.A. (1978) The use of the sodium sulphate crystallisation test for determining the weathring resistance of untreated stone. In

RILEM/UNESCO Symposium on Deterioration and Protection of Stone Monuments. Paris, Report 3.6.

RILEM Commission 25-PEM (1980) Protection and erosion of monuments. Recommended tests to measure the deterioration of stone and to assess the effectiveness of treatment methods. *Matériaux et Constructions* **75**: 175–253.

Rossi-Manaresi, R. and Tucci, A. (1991) Pore structure and disruptive or cementing effect of salt crystallisation in various types of stone. *Studies in Conservation,* **36**: 53–58.

Schaffer, R.J. (1932) *The Weathering of Natural Building Stones.* Building Research Establishment, HMSO, London.

Scholle, P.A. (1974) Diagenesis of Upper Cretaceous chalks from England, Northern Ireland and the North Sea. In K.J. Hsu and H.C. Jenkyns (eds) *Pelagic Sediments: on Land and under the Sea.* International Association for Sedimentology Special Publication 1, pp. 177–210.

Schulze, W. and Lange, H. (1969) Survey of test method for the determination of the frost resistance of aggregates. *Proceedings of an International RILEM Symposium on the Durability of Concrete, Prague,* 1B-63-B-78.

Contact address
Department of Conservation
Ulster Museum
Botanic Gardens
Belfast
BT9 5AB
United Kingdom

167

SECTION THREE

ANALYSIS AND APPLICATION

(A) Analytical Methods

*'Experience without theory is blind
but theory without experience is
mere intellectual play.'*

Immanuel Kant

14 Analytical techniques for the examination of building stone

J.J. McALISTER

ABSTRACT

Methods for the mineralogical and elemental analysis of building stone and similar materials are extensively reviewed. The significance of sample preparation is stressed and the risks and possibilities for contamination identified. The review demonstrates the ever increasing choice of analytical procedures available to those concerned with stone decay It also highlights the need for technical support and the value of a multidisciplinary approach that would, for example, incorporate analytical chemists into any research or conservation 'team'.

INTRODUCTION

Stone is widely perceived as a durable building material. However, over time the cumulative effects of exposure to chemical, physical and biological weathering processes can significantly alter structural and chemical properties, reduce cohesive strength and hence durability. Stone breakdown is therefore necessarily complex, especially in urban environments where, in addition to weathering processes which affect natural stone outcrops, stone is exposed to the effects of a range of gaseous and particulate pollutants derived primarily from the combustion of fossil fuels. Emissions of pollutants such as sulphur dioxide, chlorides and nitric oxide contribute to the acidification of environmental conditions and can enhance decomposition of stone. For example, decomposition of carbonate material by inorganic acids can create sulphate and nitrate salts which crystallise within the stone

Processes of Urban Stone Decay. Edited by B.J. Smith and P.A. Warke. © 1996 Donhead Publishing Ltd.

fabric, weaken intergranular bonds, decrease cohesive strength and ultimately hasten stone decay. The effects of inorganic acids are enhanced in many instances by biological activity where algae and lichens also increase local acidity and contribute to stone breakdown through the combined effects of chemical weathering and physical disruption of stone fabric.

Finally, different lithologies respond to similar environmental conditions in quite different ways and exhibit complex ranges of surface weathering features and residual weathering products. The ability to accurately assess the extent and character of stone deterioration through a range of standardised analytical procedures is therefore extremely important. Many analytical techniques are available to researchers in this area but reliance is often placed on a limited number of these due to a combination of a lack of resources and an unawareness of the relevant techniques. However, because of the great variety of potential chemical and physical changes associated with stone weathering and breakdown in urban environments a range of investigative procedures is often required before the nature of decay mechanisms and their mode of operation can be fully understood. This paper reviews some of the most widely available and commonly used analytical techniques and provides a brief summary of several more recent and less widely known procedures with future potential for researchers in this area.

ANALYTICAL TECHNIQUES

Well established methods for mineralogical analysis include X-ray diffraction (XRD), a range of thermoanalytical procedures, infrared spectroscopy (IR) and scanning electron microscopy (SEM) while changes in chemical characteristics of stone may be investigated using techniques such as X-ray fluorescence (XRF), atomic emission and absorption spectroscopy (AES, AAS) and ion chromatography (IC). Elemental concentrations can be extremely variable within a single sample. This variability cannot be identified by bulk chemical analysis alone, but use of electron probe microanalysis can offer a means of overcoming this problem.

Although mineralogical and chemical analytical techniques are discussed separately it is important to remember that regardless of individual merit, analysis is greatly improved through the concerted use of a range of complementary techniques.

MINERALOGICAL ANALYSIS

X-ray diffraction (XRD)

The principles of this technique and clay mineral identification have been discussed in great detail in other excellent texts (Cullity, 1956; Nuffield, 1966; Klug and Alexander, 1974; Brindley and Brown, 1980; Wilson, 1987) and will only be mentioned briefly in this paper. In short, when an incident beam of electrons impinge on an array of clay mineral crystals that comprise a repetitive order of atoms, scattered waves result. When out of phase, these waves interfere with and destroy each other, but when in phase they combine to form new wavefronts. This constructive interference is known as diffraction and its direction depends on the size and shape of the unit cell of a crystal and its intensity on the nature of the crystal structure. Diffractometers consist of an X-ray generator, a goniometer for sample rotation and measurement of diffraction angles and an X-ray counter tube to detect, amplify and measure diffracted radiation. Computer output diffractograms provide a permanent record of intensity versus diffraction angle.

A few instrumental parameters require consideration, for example, choice of radiation will depend on sample composition. Clays low in iron require copper $K\propto$ radiation which is higher in intensity than cobalt $K\propto$ which is used when iron-rich clays are analysed. However, factors such as cost, complexity and loss of intensity must be considered and sufficient monochromatisation may be achieved *via* a simple metal foil filter system (Brindley and Brown, 1980; Wilson, 1987).

Thermoanalytical techniques

These techniques complement XRD analysis. Whereas the latter give a direct representation of mineral structure and intensity thermoanalytical procedures incorporate physical, chemical and structural factors. As with XRD, a number of excellent texts provide explanations of these techniques (MacKenzie and Mitchell, 1972; Daniels, 1973; Todor, 1976; MacKenzie, 1970, 1980, 1984a, 1984b).

The principle underlying thermoanalytical methods is that temperature is one of the parameters which defines the state of equilibrium and kinetics of material systems. Techniques frequently used in building stone analysis include those that measure temperature difference between the sample and a reference material and sample mass. These include differential thermal analysis (DTA), thermogravimetry (TG), differential thermogravimetry (DTG) and differential scanning calorimetry (DSC). Although equipment design varies, instrumentation generally comprises a measuring system, temperature control and heating unit plus a recording apparatus. An electric furnace provides the heat source with a temperature range from ambient temperatures to 1200°C.

In DTA the temperature difference between the sample and reference material is measured using a differential thermocouple composed from base metals, whereas DSC measures temperature difference using either heat-flux or power-compensation techniques.

Instrumentation for TG and DTG is centred around sensitive electrobalances which continuously measure changes in sample mass as it is heated from ambient temperature to 1000°C in a furnace (MacKenzie, 1970; Redfern, 1970; Daniels, 1973; Paterson and Swaffield, 1987). Mass variation under the influence of thermal energy is recorded in a thermogram that shows an increase, decrease or no change as an incline, a decline or a plateau respectively. DTG curves are obtained simultaneously and this technique provides a more accurate method of qualitative and quantitative analysis since a change in mass is represented by peak area. DTA, DTG and TG determinations can be carried out simultaneously on an instrument known as a derivatograph.

Reproducibility is only possible if certain parameters are strictly adhered to. These include sample heating rate, particle size, packing and size of sample and dilution with reference material (Todor, 1976; McKenzie and Mitchell, 1972; Paterson and Swaffield, 1987; McAlister, *et al.*, 1988).

Infrared spectroscopy (IR)

Infrared spectroscopy is a simple technique commonly used to assess qualitative correlations between samples. A number of detailed accounts of infrared spectroscopy are available (Hadni, 1967; Turrell, 1972; Farmer, 1974; Russell, 1987). This technique which was introduced to clay mineral analysis as far back as 1950, is unique since both crystalline and amorphous structures absorb IR radiation.

Double beam dispersive instruments are generally used. The IR source is a heated solid, detector systems respond to heat rather than photons in contrast to ultraviolet and visible techniques and they scan a spectrum range of between 4000–200 cm. Both natural and synthetic minerals have been studied and this has made IR spectroscopy a very informative technique. The main advantages include small sample size, speed, applicability to crystalline and amorphous compounds and provision of structural information and identification. Degree of crystallinity is also reflected in the sharpness of absorption bands, whereas isomorphous substitution in silicates is observed as broad bands containing reduced detail. IR spectroscopy is particularly useful for clay mineral identification where particle size is < 2 μm.

Scanning electron microscope (SEM)

This technique studies surface or near surface characteristics of specimens. A beam of electrons from a thermionic emission type tungsten filament is accelerated to between 20–40 keV, demagnified and reduced in diameter to between 2–10 nm on point of impact with the sample. This fine beam is scanned across the sample and a detector counts the number of low energy secondary electrons or the radiation given off from each point on the surface. The brightness of a cathode ray tube (CRT) is also monitored by the detector and both the CRT spot and electron beam are scanned as a raster. Image magnification is simple and no lenses are involved. This is achieved by making a raster display of the sample smaller than that displayed on the CRT. See: Borst and Keller, 1969; Gillot, 1969; Bohor and Huges, 1971; Newbury, *et al.*, 1987; McHardy and Birnie, 1987 and Goodhew and

Humphreys, 1988 for more detail.

Electron emission from samples are divided into two energy regions, secondary and back-scattered. Secondary electrons have low energy and only those generated within a few nanometers of the surface escape and participate in the signal. Their yield depends on sample topography. Back-scattered electrons have energies close to the incident electron beam and escape from greater depths and their yield depends greatly on the atomic number of the element. SEM allows high magnitude visual examination of stone surface and substrate, but it is an analytical procedure which is best used in conjunction with other techniques.

Sample preparation for mineralogical analysis

Similar physical and chemical preparation of samples may be used prior to most instrumental analyses. With the possible exception of sample preparation for SEM exmination, building stone analysis inevitably begins with grinding in order to reduce solid samples to a powder form. It is important to know the particle size characteristics of the ground material if results are to be reproducible. Mineralogical analysis often necessitates analysis of different particle size fractions in addition to analysis of the bulk sample.

Size fractionation is a very important preparatory step in mineralogical analysis, for example in thermoanalytical techniques differences in particle size can influence heat transfer characteristics (MacKenzie and Mitchell, 1972). Separation of silt and clay fractions greatly enhances clay mineral identification for all instrumental analyses but it is important to remember that clay minerals in particular can be easily damaged by mechanical and chemical pretreatments and therefore where possible these should be kept to a minimum. Samples may be mixed with a volatile inert organic liquid e.g. isopropyl alcohol prior to grinding to minimise overheating and damage to mineral lattices.

Size fractionation requires samples to be dispersed and care must be taken when choosing a dispersing agent. Spurious peaks may occur when hydroxides of alkali metals are used and a solution of ammonium hydroxide has been found to be suitable as excess ammonia is driven off on drying (MacKenzie and Mitchell, 1972; McAlister, et al., 1988).

Pretreatments may be required to remove organic matter prior to analysis, most commonly by using a hydrogen peroxide solution. However, care must be taken since complex oxalato-aluminates or ferrates may form which are soluble and only removed by thoroughly washing the sample in deionized water (Farmer and Mitchell, 1963). In thermoanalytical techniques, passage of an inert gas such as argon over the sample may be used to suppress peaks that are due to organic components.

Ion exchange and the exchange reaction is of great fundamental importance in the study of clay minerals. A soil or ground stone sample leached with a salt solution can absorb the cation of the percolating solution and in turn liberate an equivalent amount of other cations present in the sample.

The main cations involved in exchange are, hydrogen, calcium, magnesium, sodium, potassium and ammonium. These cations are termed 'exchangeable' because they can replace or be replaced by each other.

Relative humidity governs surface controlled reactions such as loss of adsorbed water. Clays should be homionic and the exchangeable cation used to saturate their exchange complex also has an important bearing on hydroscopic moisture content and hence on their identification. Magnesium ions allow relatively uniform interlayer adsorption of water by swelling layer silicates, while potassium ions restrict adsorption by occupying sites on the basal oxygen sheets (MacEwan, 1946; Walker, 1957; Walker, 1961). Therefore, cation saturation can be used to distinguish expanding from non-expanding 2:1 clay minerals. Supplementary information for identification of swelling clays can be obtained by 'solvation', whereby organic complexes are formed by reacting clays with liquids such as ethylene glycol or glycerol (Norvich and Martin, 1983). After the various pretreatments, different sample mounts are prepared for each instrumental technique.

Clay minerals are frequently platy and acquire a high degree of preferred orientation. This is related to their layer-lattice characteristics and atomic sequence normal to the surface of the clay plate. In XRD analysis orientated mounts are prepared in a number of ways such as the precipitation of clay suspensions onto glass slides (Nagelschmidt, 1941; Brown, 1953), suction onto unglazed ceramic tiles (Gibbs, 1965; Rich, 1975; Rhoton, et al., 1993) and suction onto membrane filters. When clay mineral concentrations are low it is important to use a more sensitive preparation technique such as that reported by McAlister and Smith (1995a, 1995b) where clay suspensions are precipitated on to 25 mm, 0.1 mm membrane filters. Another benefit of this technique is that samples may be subsequently examined by SEM. Pre-concentration amongst fine grained minerals is reduced using this technique, which can present a problem when slide mounts are used (Gibbs, 1965). Other advantages include, speed and simplicity of preparation and the use of low cost equipment.

True randomly orientated mounts for powder samples are difficult to prepare and a number of techniques for filling sample holders have been suggested (Brindley and Brown, 1980). For example, samples have been embedded in plastic material (Brindley and Kurtossy, 1961), polyester foam (Thompson, et al., 1972), mixed with powdered cork (Wilson, 1987) and mixed with acetone before smearing onto a glass slide (Paterson, et al., 1986).

Sample mounting for thermal analyses involves placing a size fractionated powder sample into a crucible. Small sample size and dilution with reference material reduces the problems associated with thermal diffusivity and baseline drift found in DTA (MacKenzie and Mitchell, 1972; McAlister, et al., 1988). Differences in sample packing can also lead to the problems mentioned above but it has been noted that these can be avoided by packing samples into a crucible using a plunger (MacKenzie and Mitchell, 1972). TG and DTG methods require minimum mechanical contact with the sample since it is being weighed, but of great importance in all thermoanalytical techniques is good contact between sample and holder (Paterson and Swaffield, 1987). Heating rate also has an important influence on peak temperature and peak size increases with increased heating rates.

The most widely used method for mounting building stone samples prior to IR analysis is to mix them with an alkali halide such as potassium bromide and press them into a disc (White, 1964). With this technique sample weights of between 0.3–3.0 mg may be analysed. Details of other preparation procedures are given elsewhere (Russell, 1974) but for very small samples of clay a microdisc may be used where as little as 0.1 mg can be pressed into a rectangular pellet with dimensions equal to those of the IR beam at its focus (Russell, 1974).

A wide range of preparatory techniques are available for SEM analysis. These include rinsing with or without ultrasonic vibration, grinding, polishing, etching (ionic, chemical or electrolytic) and various mechanical or frozen fracture methods.

During preparation for SEM analysis the cleanliness of sample surface is very important and this may be achieved by a solvent rinse aided by ultrasonic vibration (where specimen composition permits). Polishing and grinding are usually carried out to expose sample areas and these have been highly developed to produce desired results, depending on sample size and composition. Artificial or natural abrasive powders bonded to block, stone, paper or cloth are used. Alternative techniques that use chemical, electrochemical and etching methods (ion beam, acidic or electrolytic) have been introduced. These methods reveal structural characteristics such as grain boundaries, different minerals and crystal structure (Brady, 1971; Goodhew, 1972). Prepared samples are mounted on sonically cleaned aluminium stubs with close contact between sample and stub being very important so that charge build-up, image distortion or loss of sample is minimised. A number of adhesives are available such as silver paint, silver pastes, conductive epoxies and double sided tape. However, the latter should be used with caution as it may out-gas into the instrument column and produce contamination. Again the importance of cleanliness must be stressed and prepared samples should always be stored in dust and moisture free containers prior to analysis.

Special care is needed to prepare clay samples for SEM analysis because of their hydrous nature. Whole stone samples can be air or oven dried, but this treatment causes certain clays to shrink. Other methods such as freeze drying in a cryogenic liquid such as liquid nitrogen or propane (Green-Kelly, 1973) may be used but this has drawbacks, in that formation of ice crystals may distort some surface structures and drying time may be long (Postek, et al., 1980). Critical point drying is used mainly for biological samples where water is exchanged for liquid carbon dioxide using a miscible fluid such as methanol or acetone (Koller and Bernard, 1964; Diamond, 1970; Parsons, et al, 1974; Newman and Thomasson, 1979; McHardy, et al., 1982; Boyd and Tamarin, 1984). However, disagreement persists concerning moisture removal from clays and in the former method organic liquids may cause swelling in some clays (Erol, et al., 1976).

Weathered stone samples that lack cohesion need to be impregnated in a resin of low toxicity and viscosity. The impregnated sample is cut using a diamond blade saw and the surface polished on a lapping machine using various grades of diamond paste (Smart and Tovey, 1981; McHardy and Birnie, 1987). For effective viewing, surfaces must be electrically conductive to remove surplus electrons and hence a build-up of negative charge. This is achieved by coating the surface with a layer of gold or carbon. The type of coating used will depend on the electron microscope and a number of coating methods exist including electrodeposition and anodisation (Echlin, 1978; DeNee and Walker, 1975; Postek, 1980).

CHEMICAL ANALYSIS

Chemical analysis of materials invariably depends on measuring interactions between a substance and some form of electromagnetic radiation. The energy of this radiation depends on its frequency which leads to the term spectroscopy where studies are carried out in the visible, ultraviolet, infrared, X-ray, microwave and radio-frequency regions of the electromagnetic spectrum. Popular spectroscopic techniques used in building stone analysis employ the visible, ultraviolet and X-ray regions which encompasses a wide range of wavelengths and energies. An X-Ray photon for example is 10,000 times more energetic than an ultraviolet or visible one. The theoretical background is expanded in Ingle and Crouch (1988) and Skoog (1985). What follows is a review of some of the techniques particularly applicable to building stone analysis.

Atomic emission (AES) and absorption spectroscopy (AAS)

When atoms or ions absorb energy from a hot source they are excited to a higher energy level. On relaxing to the ground state each gives off a photon of radiation and atomic emission spectra are produced. Radiation wavelength is a unique property to individual elements. Classification of atomic spectroscopic methods is based on how a sample solution is atomised. Sources used mainly for stone analysis include flame, electrothermal furnace, and inductively coupled plasma. Atomic emission spectroscopy (AES) uses flame and plasma sources, with the latter reaching temperatures that are two to three times higher than the hottest combustion flame. As the number of atoms in the excited state increase, sensitivity of the AES technique also increases. This is in contrast to AAS where sensitivity is directly proportional to the number of atoms in the ground state. Three types of plasma sources are used: inductively coupled, direct current and microwave induced plasmas (Thompson and Walsh, 1983; Ingle and Crouch, 1988; Lajunen, 1992; Vardecasteele and Block, 1993). In AAS atomisation can be achieved either by flame or electrothermal methods. Electrothermal heating methods have certain advantages over flame atomisation which include longer residence time of individual atoms in the optical path, small sample size and higher temperature (Price, 1983; Skoog, 1985; Fifield and Kealy, 1983; Lajunen, 1992; Vandecasteele and Block, 1993).

Inductively coupled plasma (ICP)–mass spectroscopy (MS)

This technique combines the analytical capabilities of mass spectroscopy with the convenience and efficiency of passing sample solutions into a plasma source. Sample solutions are pneumatically nebulised in a stream of argon into the plasma and ions are extracted into a vacuum system which is compatible with that used for operation of the mass spectrometer. This instrumental combination is used mainly for simultaneous multi-element and isotopic ratio determinations. Analytical limitations may be introduced by matrix induced changes in ion signal intensity and these effects are more problematic than when ICP–AES is used alone. Dissolved solids can cause matrix interference and solutions containing more than 10 g/l cause major problems. However the extent of matrix effects will depend on the analyte element, matrix operating conditions and the type of instrument used. Several techniques have been introduced to analyse solids without dissolution and these include, laser ablation, arc and slurry nebulisation and electrothermal vaporisation (Lajunen, 1992; Vandecasteele and Block, 1993).
This technique is very sensitive and detection limits for more than sixty elements are between 0.03–0.30 mg/l (ppb) and for the halogens, phosphate and sulphur, between 0.001–1.0 mg/l (ppm) (Date and Gray, 1989; Vandecasteele and Block, 1993).

X-ray fluorescence (XRF) and electron probe microanalysis (EPMA)

Concentrations of individual elements can be determined by the number of X-ray counts emitted from a prepared sample. X-ray emission is produced by bombarding the sample with high energy X-rays. The spectrum produced shows the relationship between wavelength and atomic number of the element and forms the basis of XRF spectroscopy (Moseley, 1913). Detailed explanations of the process are given by Norrish and Chappel (1977), Muller (1972), Price (1983) and Bain, et al., (1994). Two types of instrument are employed, wavelength dispersive (WDXRF) and energy dispersive (EDXRF) and instrumental comparisons have been made (Chandler, 1977; Potts, et al., 1985; Potts, 1987).
An EDXRF added to an SEM system can provide rapid qualitative analysis of a morphological feature. Quantitative analysis with the correct specimen conditions and an elemental distribution map are also available. Current EPMA systems may be equipped with four computer controlled crystal spectrometers (WDXRF) and an energy dispersive (EDXRF) system for preliminary qualitative analysis.
The number of characteristic X-ray counts emitted from the sample

over a fixed time interval (Nspec.) is compared with the number emitted from a standard of known composition over the same time interval (Nstd.). The concentration of individual elements (Cspec.) is given as Cspec. = Nspec./Nstd. × Cstd.

Complications may arise due to differences in sample and standard and corrections for atomic number effect (Z), absorption (A) and fluorescence (F) can be made. This is known as the ZAF technique and corrections are carried out by computer.

Ion chromatography (IC)

Ion chromatography (IC) is a liquid–solid chromatographic technique that has become more frequently used since simultaneous determinations of inorganic and organic ions became possible. This technique is unique for stone analysis as it allows selective and rapid determinations of ions in water and acid extractions (Vleugels, et al., 1992; Torfs, 1992). IC is capable of determining anions such as chloride, bromide and sulphate, cations such as calcium, magnesium, sodium and potassium, transition metals and rare earth ions, low molecular weight (water soluble) carboxylic acids, organic bases and organometallic compounds such as tributyltin. Various IC instruments are available and excellent reviews of the technique are given by Small, et al., (1975), Mulik and Sawick (1979), Smith and Chang (1983) and Haddad and Jackson (1990).

Sample preparation for chemical analysis

Preparation for AES, AAS and ICP–MS

Inevitably, the quality of any final analysis depends greatly on sample preparation regardless of how accurate and precise an analytical technique may be. Sample selection should be representative of total material bulk, but in the case of buildings this is usually difficult since small samples are either scraped or drilled from the stone surface. In addition, samples often require grinding which can cause contamination but this may be reduced by keeping grinding time to a minimum. Compositional changes may also occur and particle size should be reduced no more than is required for homogeneity and ready attack by reagents. Grinding mill lining material usually consists of tungsten carbide, nickel-chromium alloy or agate and proper choice is important for trace element analyses.

Methods for dealing with moisture depend on the information required. When total elements are analysed, samples are oven dried at 105°C and at 30–35°C prior to removal of extractable ions. Alternatively, water soluble chloride, sulphate, nitrate, potassium, sodium, calcium and magnesium can be removed by shaking samples for one hour using a ratio of 1:5 sample to deionised water and analysing the filtered extract. Total water soluble salts

180

can be determined by completely evaporating a measured aliquot of filtrate after the addition of 30% hydrogen peroxide. Weatherable Ca, K and P can be determined after heating a sample for 1 hour at 500°C in a porcelain crucible. After cooling, the residue is again heated in 30% HCl, filtered, made to volume and analysed (Kamp and Krist, 1988). Total elemental analysis involves attacking a sample with mineral acids or fusion with a suitable flux such as carbonates, peroxides and borates (Ingamells, 1966; Shapiro, 1967; Verbeek, *et al.*, 1982). Most substances will decompose at high temperature (300–1000°C) when mixed with a flux and production of a clear melt indicates that complete decomposition has occurred. A mixture of hydrofluoric acid and aqua regia is commonly used for stone analysis, where HF reacts with silicates to form tetrafluoride. Wet digestions may be carried out using either open or closed systems. Systematic errors can arise in open systems due to contamination by reagents and digestion vessel, loss of elements by volatilisation and by adsorption on vessel surfaces. These problems have led to development of pressurised closed systems using, for example, PFTE bombs. In these no volatilisation losses occur, decomposition is improved, reaction times are shortened and no contamination from external sources occurs (Bernas, 1968). Recent modifications have employed microwave ovens as a heat source for sample dissolution. The main advantages are speed of digestion, lower consumption of acids, no loss of volatile components and safety (Lamonthe, *et al.*, 1986; Papp and Fischer, 1987; Berman, 1988; Kemp and Brown, 1990). Sample decomposition methods are comprehensively reviewed by Dolezal, *et al.* (1968).

Contamination can become a major problem when amounts of < 1 mg are being measured. Contamination may arise during any stage and therefore sample preparation should be kept as simple as possible. Laboratory atmosphere for ICP–MS analysis should be under positive air pressure and have a filtration system for the removal of dust particles. All sample preparation steps should use ultra pure water and reagents and all glass and polyware should be washed, rinsed and then soaked in 10–20% (v/v) and 1–5% (v/v) nitric acid respectively in order to minimise the risk of contamination.

Preparation for XRF and EPMA

XRF spectroscopy requires uniform, homogeneous samples and fine grinding may produce this for those that contain different phases. However, long grinding times increase the risk of contamination. Pressed powder samples may be analysed for heavy elements where maximum sensitivity is required and depth of penetration is not important (Hutchison, 1974). This method is subject to matrix or interelement effects, where intensity of a particular fluorescence line is not directly proportional to the concentration of the relevant element. These can be corrected using different mathematical models. Samples may be fused into a borate glass and matrix effects are suppressed by addition of a heavy absorber (Potts, 1987; Alvarez, 1990).

Sample preparation for EPMA is similar to that described for the SEM imaging, except that carbon based conducting pastes are used. Samples may be fixed to aluminium stubs or double sided tape prior to analysis and they should have flat surfaces coated with a reproducible thickness of carbon film (Kerrick, *et al.*, 1973; Springer, 1974).

Preparation for IC

For analysis using ion chromatography (IC) solid and liquid samples are subject to the same requirements. Aqueous extraction of homogenised samples depends largely on solubility of the ionic species in water. Samples can be extracted either by shaking or ultrasonically dispersing in deionised water. The extract is then filtered and injected into the IC. Choice of extractant will depend on both sample matrix and nature of the solute to be extracted. Extraction with deionised water is preferred whenever possible since alternative solutions may introduce extraneous peaks. Acid digestion procedures used in AES and AAS techniques may be inappropriate as a large excess of anions are introduced which lowers solution pH and thus disrupts multiple equilibrium between eluent species and the column. Cation concentration can be determined after acid digestion but certain clean-up procedures may have to be employed, especially for monovalent cation analysis. These problems are not apparent in the analysis of transition metals or rare earths. Sample dissociation using fusion techniques offer a better alternative to acid digestion procedures for anion determination since some of the fluxing materials are identical to eluent components (Wilson and Gent, 1983). Samples may also be ashed in air or totally combusted in oxygen to convert some non-metallic elements into volatile gaseous compounds such as Hg, F, Cl, S, P and I. The gases are then collected in suitable absorber solutions and injected directly into the IC for analysis (Evans and Moore, 1980). Sample clean-up procedures may involve filtration, selective removal of analyte or removal of interfering matrix components. These procedures may be carried out prior to analysis or incorporated as an on-line process (Haddad and Jackson, 1990). Chemical modifications to sample solutions such as pH adjustment involves more than straightforward addition of an acid or base due to anion or cation contamination. Other methods include addition of cation or anion exchange resins, (Haddad and Jackson, 1990), dialysis (Cox and Twardowski, 1980; Cox, *et al.*, 1988), electrodialysis (Pettersen, *et al.*, 1988; Haddad and Jackson, 1990) and commercially available disposable cartridge columns (Haddad and Jackson, 1990).

Ultra trace analyses require high sensitivity and this will depend on the type of detector used. Conductivity and indirect spectrophotometric detectors have limits of approximately 100 ppb for a 100 ml injection. Preconcentration techniques may be used, but these are complex and should not be considered as a simple extension of direct sample injection (Haddad and Jackson, 1990).

182

OTHER MICROANALYTICAL TECHNIQUES

A number of less widely available analytical techniques exist and some of these alternative techniques are based on different excitation radiation and analytical signals. SEM/XM (X-ray microscopy) methods integrate a compositional measurement over a surface depth of approximately 1 mm or 10,000 atom layers and are regarded as bulk analysis. These techniques are restricted to elements of atomic number ≥ 5, H and He produce no X-rays and those for Li and Be are so long that they are absorbed in the specimen. Electron probe microanalysis gives a greater accuracy for quantitative work, but ZAF matrix correction limits analysis to those elements of atomic number 11 (Na) or higher.

Research into improving spatial resolution of analysis of bulk samples like building stone to below 1 mm involves, low energy beam and ion beam analysis (Newbury, et al., 1987). Those techniques that restrict analysis to approximately 1 nm depth are now being examined.

Auger microanalysis

The de-excitation process of ionised atoms in X-ray spectroscopy can follow a path that involves an electron transition to fill the primary inner shell vacancy. The excess energy produced is transferred to another outer shell electron that is subsequently emitted with a characteristic energy i.e. Auger electron. This electron represents a surface-sensitive signal and when characteristic X-ray yield is low, Auger yield is high and vice versa, making this technique suitable for the analysis of light elements. Also since the Auger signal is constrained both laterally and in depth, scanning Auger maps which are surface images can be obtained (Dawson, 1978).

Secondary ion mass spectrometry (SIMS)

This technique is based on a sputtering process whereby atoms of the sample are ejected due to impact of primary ions which have energy levels in the range of 1–25 KeV. Neutral and ionised atoms plus molecules are ejected and ionised particles (0.1–1% of total sputtered) are attracted by electrostatic fields into a mass analyser. The SIMS signal is derived from the first few atom layers and this provides surface-sensitive information. This surface technique is the only one that offers access to the whole periodic table, including all isotopes. However this method is destructive, visual quality is inferior and quantification is often a problem (Newbury, et al., 1987). SIMS is seldom used in cultural heritage fields and only a few references exist (Schreiner, et al., 1984; Schreiner, et al., 1988).

Laser probe microanalysis (LAMMA)

In this technique a pulsed photon beam is focused to a probe of sufficient power to evaporate a small volume of sample (Leysen, *et al.*, 1987). Ions are created essentially at the same instant since laser ionisation pulse time is short and as all ions are given the same kinetic energy, a velocity distribution occurs according to mass. Analysis is qualitative or semi-quantitative in the ppm range.

Particle induced and synchrotron induced X-ray emission analysis (PIXE)

In this method photons are focused to yield a spatial resolution of a few nanometers. Detection limits are lower than those for EPMA (Swann and Fleming, 1987).

X-ray photo-electron spectroscopy (XPS)

This technique is often referred to as electron spectroscopy for chemical analysis (ESCA). Photo-electrons induced by an X-ray beam carry information on the elemental composition and oxidation state in a surface layer of approximately 5 nm (Mossoti, *et al.*, 1987; Wilson and Burns, 1987).

Raman microprobe analysis (RLMP)

When a beam of monochromatic light of frequency (n) is directed at a substance that is transparent to that frequency a certain amount of the light is scattered and this results in a change of frequency. This results in Raman scattering due to interaction of the light with the sample molecules (Woodward, 1967; Griffith, 1974). Both inorganic and organic properties are studied, it is a non-destructive technique and micrometer size samples may be analysed (Guineau, 1984).

Fourier transform infrared spectroscopy (FTIR)

Fourier transform spectroscopy has become increasingly popular over the past decade since it provides infrared spectra more conveniently than a dispersive (grating) instrument. Most commercial instruments are designed around a Michelson interferometer where the optical system consists of two plane mirrors at right angles to each other and a beamsplitter at 45° to the mirrors. Reflected beams from the two mirrors recombine at the beamsplitter and emerge as one which is then passed into a detector. Displacement of

Table 14.1 Principal characteristics of a wide range of analytical techniques available for building stone analysis.

Technique	MINERALOGY			ELEMENT ANALYSIS		Grind Sample	Digest Sample	Size Fraction.	Grain Quantitative Analysis	Morphology	SURFACE	
	Salts	Clay Minerals	Primary Minerals	Major	Trace						Lateral	Depth
XRD	XXXX	XXXX	XXXX			Y		Y	XX			
DTA	XXXX	XXX	XXX			Y		Y	X			
DTG	XXX	XXX	XXX			Y		Y	XX			
TG	XX	XX	XX			Y		Y	XX			
IR	XXXX	XXXX	XXX			Y		Y	XX			
SEM	XXX	XXX	XXX	XXX	XXX	Y			XXX	XXXX	XX	X
XRF				XXXX	XXXX	Y			XXXX			
AAS				XXXX	XXXX	Y	Y		XXXX			
ICP/AES				XXXX	XXXX	Y			XXXX			
ICP/MS				XXXX	XXX	Y	Y		XXXX			
IC				XXXX	XXX	Y			XXXX			
EPMA				X	XX				X		XX	X
SIMS				X	XX				X	X	XXXX	XXXX
LAMMA					X	Y			X	X	X	X
FTIR				X	X				X		X	X
XPS				X	X				X		X	
RLMP				X	X							
Auger				XXX	XX				XX	XX	XXX	XXXX
PIXE											X	X

XXXX = Excellent   XXX = Very Good   XX = Good   X = Poor   Y = Yes the moving mirror by one quarter wavelength brings the two beams 180° out of phase and they will destructively interfere. An interferogram is obtained by plotting the detector signal as a function of mirror distance. This technique offers high sensitivity, speed and good resolution. Very small samples can be analysed and information on molecular structure can be obtained (Martin, 1980; Durig, 1980; Shearer, *et al.*, 1983; Roekens, *et al.*, 1988; Baker and Von Endt, 1988).

Table 14.1 shows a summary of all the analytical techniques mentioned. Instrumental comparisons are made with respect to their ability to carry out mineralogical, element, morphorlogic and surface analyses.

CONCLUSIONS

Only a very brief outline of the most widely available analytical techniques is presented here. Each of these has specific applications and limitations with regard to type of sample and analytical range. However, through the combined use of appropriate techniques, addressing different aspects of analysis, a clearer understanding of the nature of stone weathering and breakdown may be achieved.

Regardless of instrumental precision, analytical techniques should not be seen as an end in themselves but an essential component of the analytical process. The results obtained are only as meaningful as sample selection allows. More significantly, results can be greatly influenced by sample preparation. This includes factors such as size fractionation – particularly important in the identification of clay minerals, contamination during grinding, mounting and digestion and selection of appropriate extraction procedures. What is clear is that there now exist an enormous range of analytical techniques available to those interested in stone decay. Unfortunately, most of them still require destructive sampling of stone, are expensive and produce results that require careful interpretation. Nevertheless, availability and ease of use will no doubt improve with time and it is essential that as researchers we are fully aware of the analytical opportunities open to us – and their limitations.

References

Alvarez, M. (1990) Glass disk fusion method for the X-ray fluorescence analysis of rocks and silicates. *X-Ray Spectrometry* **19**: 203–206.

Bain, D.C. McHardy, W.J. and Lachowski, E.E. (1994) X-ray spectroscopy and microanalysis. In M.J. Wilson (ed.) *Clay Mineralogy: Spectroscopic and Chemical Determinative Methods.* Chapman & Hall, London, pp. 260–299.

Baker, M.T. and Von Endt, D.W. (1988) Use of FTIR microspectrometry in examinations of artistic and historic works, *Proceedings of the Materials Research Symposium* **123**: 71–76.

Berman, S.S. (1988) Acid digestion of marine samples for trace element analysis using microwave heating. *Analyst* **113**: 159–163.

Bernas, B. (1968) A new method for decomposition and comprehensive analysis of silicates by atomic spectrometry. *Analytical Chemistry* **40**: 1682–1686.

Bohor, B.F. and Hughes, R.E. (1971) Scanning electron microscope of clays and clay minerals. *Clay and Clay Minerals* **19**: 49–54.

Borst, R.L. and Keller, W.D. (1969) Scanning electron micrographs of API reference clay minerals and other selected samples, *Proceedings of the International Clay Conference, Tokyo*, **1**. Israel University Press, Jerusalem, pp. 871–901.

Boyd, A. and Tarmarin, A. (1984) Improvement to critical point drying technique for SEM. *Scanning* **6**: 30–35.

Brady, G.S. (1971) *Materials Handbook 10th edn.* McGraw-Hill, pp. 4–6.

Brindley, G.W. and Brown, G. (1980) *Crystal Structures of Clay Minerals and their X-ray Identification.* Mineralogical Society, London.

Brindley, G.W. and Kurtossy, S.S. (1961) Quantitative determination of kaolinite by Xray diffraction. *American Mineralogist* **46**: 1205–1215.

Brown, G. (1953) A semi-micro method for preparation of clays for X-ray study. *Journal of Soil Science* **4**: 229–232.

Chandler, J.A. (1977) X-ray microanalysis in electron microscopy. In A.M. Glavert (ed.) *Practical Methods in Electron Microscopy*, **5**. Amsterdam, Holland.

Cox, J.A. and Twardowski, Z. (1980) Donnan dialysis. Matrix normalization for the voltammetric determination of metal ions. *Analytica Chimica Acta* **119**: 39–45.

Cox, J.A., Dabex-Zlotorzynska, E., Saari, R. and Tanaka, N. (1988) Ion exchange treatment of complicated samples prior to ion chromatographic analysis. *Analyst, London* **113**: 1401.

Cullity, B.D. (1956) *Elements of X-ray Diffraction.* Addison-Wesley Publishing Co., Reading, Massachusetts, USA.

Daniels, T. (1973) *Thermal Analysis.* Kogan Page, Tiptree, Essex.

Date, A.R. and Gray, A.L. (1989) *Applications of Inductive Plasma Mass Spectrometry.* Blackie, Glasgow and London.

Dawson, P., Heavens, O. and Pollard, A. (1978). Glass surface analysis by Auger electron spectroscop, *Journal of Physics, C., Solid State Physics* **11**: 2183–2193.

DeNee, P.B. and Walker, E.R. (1975) *Specimen coating techniques for the SEM – a comparative study* SEM/1975, 11T Research Institute, Chicago, IL 60616, 225–232.

Diamond, S. (1970) Pore size distribution in clays. *Clays and Clay Mineralogy* **18**: 7–23.

Dolezal, J., Povondra, P. and Sulick, Z. (1968) Decomposition techniques. In *Inorganic Analysis*, Iliffe Books, London.

Durig, J.R. (1980) *Analytical applications of FTIR to molecular and biological systems*, NATO, Advanced Studies Institute, Series D. Reidel,

Dordrecht.

Echlin, P. (1978) *Coating techniques for scanning electron microscopy and X-ray microanalysis*, SEM/1978/1 SEM Inc. AMF O'Hare 1L, 60666, 109–132.

Erol, O., Lohnes, R.A. and Dernivel, T. (1976) Preparation of clay-type moisture containing samples for scanning electron microscopy. In *Proceedings of the Workshop on Techniques for Particulate Matter Studies*. Illinois Inst, of Technol. Press, Chicago pp. 769–776.

Evans, K.C. and Moore, C.B. (1980) Combustion-ion chromatographic determination of chlorine in silicate rocks. *Analytical Chemistry* **58**: 1908–1912.

Farmer, V.C. 1974) *The Infrared Spectra of Minerals*. Mineralogical Society London.

Farmer, V.C. and Mitchell, B.D. (1963) Occurrence of oxalates in soil clays following hydrogen peroxide treatment. *Soil Science* **96**: 221–229.

Fifield, F.W. and Kealy, D. (1983) *Principals and Practice of Analytical Chemistry*. International Text Book Co., London.

Gibbs, R.J. (1965) Error due to segregation in quantitative clay mineral X-ray diffraction mounting techniques. *American Mineralogist* **50**: 741–751.

Gillot, J.E. (1969) Study of the fabric of fine-grained sediments with scanning electron microscope. *Journal of Sedimentary Petrology* **39**: 90–105.

Goodhew, P.J. (1972) Specimen preparation in materials science. In, A.M. Glauent (ed), *Practical methods in electron microscopy*. N. Holland Publishing Co., New York and Oxford.

Goodhew, P.J. and Humphreys, F.J. (1988) *Electron microscopy and analysis*. Taylor & Francis, New York.

Green-Kelly, R. (1973) The preparation of clay soils for the determination of structure. *Journal of Soil Science* **24**: 277–283.

Griffith, W.P. (1974) Raman spectroscopy of minerals, In V.C. Farmer (ed.) *The Infrared Spectra of Minerals*. Mineralogical Society, Adlard and Son, Bartholomew Press, Dorking, Surrey, pp. 119–135.

Guineau, B. (1984) Microanalysis of painted manuscripts of coloured archaeological materials by Raman laser microprobe. *Journal of Forensic Science* **29**: 471–485.

Haddad, P.R. and Jackson, P.E. (1990) *Ion Chromatography. Principals and Applications*. Elsevier, Amsterdam.

Hadni, A. (1967) *Essentials of Modern Physics Applied to the Study of the Infrared*. Pergamon Press, Oxford.

Hutchison, C.S. (1974) *Laboratory Handbook of Petrographic Techniques*. J. Wiley & Sons, New York.

Ingle, J.D. and Crouch, S.R. (1988) *Analytical spectroscopy*. Prentice Hall, Englewood Cliffs, New Jersey.

Ingramells, C.O. (1966) Absorptiometric methods in rapid silicate analysis. *Analytical Chemistry* **38**: 1228–1234.

Kamp, H.H. and Krist, H. (1988) *Laboratory Manual for the Examination of Water, Wastewater and Soil.* V.C.H. Publishers, New York.

Kemp, A.J. and Brown, C.J. (1990) Microwave digestion of carbonate rock samples for chemical analysis. *Analyst* **115**: 1197–1199.

Kerrick, D.M., Eminpizer, L.B. and Villauine, I.F. (1973) The role of carbon film thickness in electron microprobe analysis. *American Mineralogist* **58**: 920–925

Klug, H.P. and Alexander, L.E. (1974) *X-ray diffraction procedures,* J. Wiley & Sons, New York.

Koller, T. and Bernhard, W. (1964) Séchage de tissues au protoxyde d'azote (N_2O) et coupe ultrafine sans matière d'inclusion. *Journal of Microscopie* **3**: 589–606.

Lajunen, L.H.T. (1992) *Spectrochemical Analysis by Atomic Absorption and Emission.* Royal Society of Chemistry, London.

Lamonthe, P.J., Fries, T.L. and Consul, J.J. (1986) Evaluation of a microwave oven for the digestion of geological samples. *Analytical Chemistry* **58**: 1881–1886.

Leysen, L., De Waele, J., Roekens, E. and Van Grieken, R. (1987) Electron probe micro analysis and laser microprobe mass analysis of material leached from a limestone cathedral. *Scanning Microscopy* **1**: 1617–1630.

MacEwan, D.W.C. (1946) The identification and estimation of the mont morillinite group of minerals with specific reference to soil clays. *Society of The Chemical Industry Journal* **65**: 298–305.

MacKenzie, R.C. (1970) *Differential Thermal Analysis, 1, Fundamental Aspects.* Academic Press, London.

MacKenzie, R.C. (1980). Differential thermal analysis and differential scanning calorimetry: similarities and differences. *Analytical Proceedings* **17**: 217–220.

MacKenzie, R.C. (1984a) De Calore: prelude to thermal analysis. *Thermochimica Acta* **73**: 251–306.

MacKenzie, R.C. (1984b) Origin and development of differential thermal analysis. *Thermochimica Acta* **73**: 307–367.

MacKenzie, R.C. and Mitchell, B.D. (1972) Soils. In R.C. MacKenzie (ed.) *Differential Thermal Analysis*, **2**. Academic Press, London, pp. 276–297.

Martin, A.E. (1980) Infrared interferometric spectrometers, In J.R. Durig (ed.) *Vibrational Spectra and Structures*, **8**. Elsevier, Amsterdam.

McAlister, J.J., Svehla, G. and Whalley, W.B. (1988) A Comparison of various pre-treatment and instrumental techniques for the mineral characterisation of chemically weathered basalt. *Microchemical Journal* **38**: 211–231.

McAlister, J.J. and Smith, B.J. (1995a) A pressure membrane technique to prepare clay samples for X-ray diffraction analysis. *Journal of Sedimentary Research* **A65**: 569–571.

McAlister, J.J. and Smith, B.J. (1995b) A rapid preparation technique for

X-ray diffraction analysis of clay minerals in weathered rock material. *Microchemical Journal* **52**: 53–61.

McHardy, W.J. and Birnie, A.C. (1987) Scanning electron microscopy. In M.J. Wilson (ed.) *A Handbook of Determinative Methods in Clay Mineralogy,* Chapman & Hall, New York, pp. 174–208.

McHardy, W.J., Wilson, M.J. and Tait, J.M. (1982) Electron microscope and X-ray diffraction studies in filamentous illitic clay from sandstones of the Magnus field. *Clay Mineralogy* **17**: 23–29.

Moseley, H.G.J. (1913) The high frequency spectra of the elements. *Philosophical Magazine* **26**: 1024.

Mossotti, V.G., Linday, J.R. and Hochella, M.F. Jr. (1987) Effect of acid rain environment on limestone surfaces. *Material Performance* **26**: 47–52.

Mulik, J.D. and Sawicki, E. (1979) Ion chromatograph., *Environmental Science and Technology* **15**: 804–809.

Muller, R.O. (1972) *Spectrochemical Analysis by X-ray Fluorescence.* Adam Hilger, London.

Nagelschmidt, G. (1941) Identification of clays by aggregate diffraction diagriams. *Journal of Science and Instrumentation* **18**: 100–101.

Newbury, D.E., David, C., Echlin, J.P., Fiori, C.E. and Goldstien, J.I. (1987) *Advanced Scanning Electron Microscopy and X-ray Microanalysis.* Plenum Press, New York, London.

Newman, A.C.D. and Thomasson, A.J. (1979) Rothamsted studies of soil structure 111: Pore size distributions and shrinkage processes. *Journal of Soil Science* **30**: 415–439.

Norrish, K. and Chappell, B.W. (1977) X-ray fluorescence spectrometry. In J. Zussmann (ed.) *Physical Methods in Determinative Mineralogy, 2nd edition.* Academic Press, London, pp. 201–272.

Norvich, B.E. and Martin, R.T. (1983) Solvation methods for expandable layer clays. *Clays and Clay Mineralogy* **31**: 235–238.

Nuffield, E.W. (1966) *X-ray Diffraction Methods,* J. Wiley & Sons Ltd, New York.

Papp, C.S.E. and Fischer, L.B. (1987) Application of microwave digestion to the analysis of peat. *Analyst* **112**: 337–338.

Parsons, E., Bole, B., Hall, D.J. and Thomas, W.D.E. (1974) A comparative study of techniques for preparing plant surfaces for the scanning electron microscope. *Journal of Microscopy* **101**: 59–75.

Paterson, E., Bunch, J.L. and Duthie, D.M.L. (1986) Preparation of randomly orientated samples for X-ray diffractometry. *Clay Mineralogy* **21**: 101–106.

Paterson, E. and Swaffield, R. (1987) Thermal analysis. In M.J. Wilson (ed.) *A Handbook of Determinative Methods in Clay Mineralogy.* Chapman & Hall, New York, pp. 99–152.

Petterson, J.M., Johnson, H.G. and Lund, W. (1988) The determination of nitrate and sulphate in 50% sodium hydroxide solution by ion chromatography. *Talanta* **35**: 245–247.

Postek, M.T., Howard, K.S., Johnson, A.H. and McMichael, K.L. (1980) *Scanning Electron Microscopy. A Students Handbook.* Ladd Research Industries Inc.

Potts, P.J. (1987) Principles and practice of wavelength dispersive spectrometry. In *A Handbook of Silicate Rock Analysis, X-ray Fluorescence Analysis.* Blackie, Glasgow, pp. 226–285.

Potts, P.J., Webb, P.C. and Watson, J.S. (1985) Energy dispersive X-ray fluorescence analysis of silicate rocks, comparison with wavelength dispersive performance. *Analyst, London* **110**: 507–573.

Price, W.J. (1983) *Spectrochemical Analysis by Atomic Absorption.* Heyden, London.

Redfern, J.P. (1970) Complementary methods. In R.C. MacKenzie (ed.) *Differential Thermal Analysis 1.* Academic Press, London, pp. 123–158.

Rhoton, F. E., Grissinger, E. H. and Bingham, J.M. (1993) An improved suction apparatus for placing clay suspensions onto ceramic tiles. *Journal of Sedimentary Research* **63**: 763–765.

Rich, C.I. (1975) Determination of the amount of clay needed for X-ray diffraction analysis. *Proeedings of the Soil Science Society of America* **39**: 161–162.

Roekens, E., Leysen, L., Stulens, E., Philippaerts, J. and Van Grieken, R. (1988) Weathering of Maastricht limestone used in construction of historical buildings in Limburg, Belgium, *Proceedings of the VI International Congress on Deterioration and Conservation of Stone*, Copernicus University Press Department, Torun, Poland, pp. 45–56.

Russell, J.D. (1987) Infrared Spectroscopy of Inorganic Compounds. In H. Willis (ed.) *Laboratory Methods in Infrared Spectroscopy.* J. Wiley & Sons, New York.

Russell, J.O. (1974) Instrumentation and techniques. In V.C. Farmer (ed.) *The Infrared Spectra of Minerals.* Mineralogical Society London, pp. 11–25.

Schreiner, M., Stingeder, G. and Grasserbauer, M. (1984) Quantitative characterization of surface layers on corroded medieval window glass with SIMS. *Fresenius Zeitschrift für Analytische Chemische* **319**: 60–605.

Schriener, M., Grasserbauer, M. and Marek, P. (1988) Quantitative NRA and SIMS depth profiling of hydrogen in naturally weathered medieval glass. *Fresenius Zeitschrift für Analytische Chemische* **331**: 428–432.

Shapiro, L. (1967) Rapid analysis of rock and minerals by a single – solution method, *US Geological Survey Professional Paper* **575B**: B187–B191.

Shearer, J.C., Peters, D.C., Hoepfner, C. and Newton, T. (1983) FTIR in the service of art conservation. *Analytical Chemistry* **55**: 874A–880A.

Skoog, D.A. (1985). *Principals of Instrumental Analysis.* Sanders College Publishing, New York.

Small, H., Stevens, T.S. and Bauman, W.C. (1975) Ion exchange chromatographic method using conductimetric detection. *Analytical Chemistry* **47**: 1801–1809.

Smart, P. and Tovey, N.K. (1981) *Electron Microscopy of Soils and Sediments: Examples*. Clarendon Press, Oxford.

Smith, F.C. and Chang, R.C. (1983) *The Practice of Ion Chromatography*. J. Wiley & Sons, New York and London.

Springer, G. (1974) The role of carbon film thickness in electron microprobe analysis: a comment. *American Mineralogist* **59**: 1121–1122.

Swan, C.P. and Fleming, S.J. (1987) PIXE spectrometry in archaeometry: The development of a system with high spatial resolution. *Nuclear Instrumental Methods for Physics Research* **B22**: 407–410.

Thompson, M. and Walsh, J.N. (1983) *Inductively Coupled Plasma Spectrometry*. Blackie, London.

Thompson, A.P., Duthie, D.M.L. and Wilson, M.J. (1972) Randomly orientated powders for quantitative determination of clay minerals. *Clay Mineralogy* **9**: 345–348.

Todor, D.N. (1976) *Thermal Analysis of Minerals*. Abacus Press, Kent.

Torfs, K. (1992) *Verwerring van zandsteen, marmer en graniet onder atmosferische omstandigheden*. Licenciaatsthesis, University of Antwerp.

Turrell, G. (1972) *Infrared and Raman Spectra of Crystals*. Academic Press, London.

Vandecasteele, C. and Block, C.B. (1993) *Modern Methods for Trace Element Determination*. J. Wiley & Sons Ltd, New York.

Verbeek, A.A., Mitchell, M.C. and Ure, A.M. (1982) The analysis of small samples of rocks and soil by atomic absorption and emission spectrometry after lithium metaborate fusion/nitric acid dissolution procedure. *Analytica Chimica Acta* **135**: 215–228.

Vleugels, G., Roekens, E., Van Put, A., Azevedo Alves, L. and Aries-Barros, L. (1992) Analytical study of the weathering of the Jeronimos Monastery in Lisbon. *Science of the Total Environment* **120**: 225–243.

Walker, G.F. (1957) On the differentiation of vermiculites and smectites in clays. *Clay Mineralogy Bulletin* **3**: 154–163.

Walker, G.G. (1961) Vermiculite minerals. In G. Brown (ed.) *The X-ray Identification and Crystal Structures of Clay Minerals*. Mineralogical Society London.

White, R.G. (1964) *Handbook of Industrial Infrared Analysis*. Plenum Press, New York.

Wilson, M.J. (1987) X-ray powder diffraction methods. In M.J. Wilson (ed.) *A handbook of Determinative Methods in Clay Mineralogy*. Chapman & Hall, New York, pp. 26–98.

Wilson, S.A. and Gent, C.A. (1983) Determination of chloride in geological samples by ion chromatography. *Analytica Chimica Acta* **148**: 299–303.

Wilson, Y.K.M. and Burns, G. (1987) X-ray photoelectron spectroscopy of ancient murals in tombs at Beni Hasan, Egypt. *Canadian Journal of*

Chemistry **65**: 1058–1064.

Woodward, L.A. (1967) General introduction. In L.A. Woodward (ed.) *Raman Spectroscopy Theory and Practice*. Plenum Press, New York, pp. 1–43.

Contact address
School of Geosciences
The Queen's University of Belfast
Belfast
BT7 1NN
United Kingdom

15 Predicting the weathering of Portland limestone buildings

T. YATES and R. BUTLIN

ABSTRACT

Limestone from the Isle of Portland has been used for the construction of major buildings in urban areas for more than 300 years. The stone has been extracted from many areas of the Isle but only from three main beds. The Building Research Establishment has been involved with the assessment of the durability of Portland limestone for more than 60 years and during this time a substantial record of the relationship between the petrography, physical properties and durability has been built up. In addition, a number of long-term weathering trials have been carried out covering a period of nearly 40 years. The results from these trials have been used as a basis for predicting the decay of Portland limestone in the UK and to establish some relationships between laboratory test results and observed weathering rates on buildings.

INTRODUCTION

The Isle of Portland lies between Weymouth Bay and Lyme Bay in Dorset. The island is linked to the mainland by a causeway that follows the eastern end of Chesil Beach. The extensive deposits of limestone that occur on the Isle of Portland have been used for many hundreds of years on the island. The stone was in use in London from the early seventeenth century when Inigo Jones selected it for the construction of the Banqueting House in Whitehall. However, it was the extensive rebuilding of the City of London after the Great Fire in 1666 by Sir Christopher Wren that took Portland limestone from being a good local stone to one of national and international

Processes of Urban Stone Decay. Edited by B.J. Smith and P.A. Warke. © 1996 Donhead Publishing Ltd.

importance. The stone used by Wren came from the landslip deposits on the eastern side of the island. Here the stone was not only exposed and easily extracted but could also be transported by sea to London. Wren is recorded as selecting his stone with great care and was reputed to label each block he required with his own mark.

The stone that outcrops in the landslip deposits is the southernmost exposure of the extensive Jurassic Portlandian deposits that extend south west from Yorkshire. The Portland Freestone, which forms part of this extensive geological series is exposed at a number of coastal locations in Dorset (including Portland and Worth Matravers) and also, to a lesser extent, in The Vale of Wardour, Wiltshire. The stone from the areas outside the Isle of Portland has traditionally been considered more difficult to work because of its higher silica content.

In petrographic terms the stone from Portland is an open structured oolitic limestone of late Jurassic age. The deposits are overlaid by the Lulworth Beds and underlain by the Portland Sands. The quarried stone comes from three beds, from the top of the sequence these are:

(a) Roach Bed – an open texture with extensive fossil shells and a large number of holes resulting from the dissolution of shells (termed a biosparite).
(b) Whit Bed – denser in texture than the Roach but still containing some fragments in a fine-grained oolitic structure (termed an oobiosparite).
(c) Base Bed – the structure is less clearly oolitic than is Whit Bed, it is largely free from shell fragments (termed oosparite).

The Base Bed was also known as the 'Best Bed' because it was easily worked but it is generally recognised as being less durable than the Whit Bed. The Base Bed is often stronger in compression than Whit Bed because of the greater amounts of cement between the ooliths but the structure of the cement results in a stone that weathers more easily. The Roach stone can be very durable but has been unpopular with architects as masonry because of the large number of fossils. There is one other bed in the sequence known as the Curf. This lies between the Whit and Base but its chalky structure has meant that it is not used as a building stone.

As demand for stone increased the quarries expanded in size and also to other areas of the island. By the early part of this century there were quarries over much of the eastern part of the island and as mechanisation increased so the quarries were able to excavate to greater depths and remove the extensive overburden that is found in the western part of the island. By the 1930s (see next section) there were more than 20 quarries on the island and a railway system to transport the stone to the mainland. As with so many industries, recent years have seen a considerable reduction in the number of quarries and presently only three – Coombefield, Independence and Bowers – are open for the production of building stone.

SURVEYS OF PORTLAND LIMESTONE

The Portland surveys in the 1930s

The Building Research Establishment's connections with Portland limestone began in the late 1920s when R.J. Schaffer was studying stone and its weathering. Much of Schaffer's early work was published in his book *The Weathering of Natural Stone* (Schaffer, 1932, reprinted as a facsimile, 1985). In 1930 the Building Research Station (as it was at that time) undertook a survey of all of the Portland quarries on the Isle and on the Dorset mainland. The survey was undertaken jointly with F.H. Edmunds of the Geological Survey. In 1933 a second survey was carried out at the request of the South-Western Stone Company which lead to the publication of a book on Portland limestone and its production (South Western Stone, 1933). The two surveys produced a substantial archive of maps and photographs which record the quarries and quarrymen of the time. Figure 15.1 was taken at Suckthumb Quarry in April 1930 and shows a general view of the beds following the removal of about 20 m of 'rubble' and 'cap'. The scale of the quarry is given by the size of the three men trimming a block of stone, shown within the black circle.

Figure 15.1 View of Suckthumb Quarry, Isle of Portland, April 1930. The scale of this quarry can be seen from the size of workmen inside the black circle. (Published with permission of the Building Research Establishment.)

In addition to the photographic records, every quarry and bed was sampled and the stones characterised using a range of tests including porosity, microporosity, water absorption, compressive strength and a sodium sulphate crystallisation test. Specimens were also exposed at the Building Research Station in 'open tray frost tests'. In this test half the specimens were placed upright in trays that filled with rainwater in the winter whilst the others were raised on a freely drained rack. The results from these tests were combined with those obtained from samples collected from buildings and with observation regarding the weathering of these buildings.

Studies between 1950 and 1985

Studies of Portland limestone continued in the post war years. In the 1960s there was concern over the rapid weathering of headstones in the care of the Commonwealth War Graves Commission. Research was undertaken by David Honeyborne (BRE, 1963; BRE, 1965) to look for links between measured properties of the stone and observed weathering patterns (see below).

The next large scale survey was in the early 1980s as part of the research for *The Building Limestones of the British Isles* (Leary, 1983). In this survey small samples of stone were collected from all of the quarries in production and subjected to porosity and sodium sulphate salt crystallisation tests (Ross and Butlin, 1989).

Studies in the 1990s

The 1990s have seen a considerable debate on the validity of the sodium sulphate crystallisation test. As part of BRE's response to this debate an extensive series of samples were collected from Bowers Quarry and Independence Quarry. Samples were collected from two or more places in each of the current beds in these quarries. Prior to testing, the blocks were marked so that the exact relationship of individual test specimens was known. The samples were then tested for porosity, microporosity, water absorption and sodium sulphate crystallisation tests. The results were used to assess within bed variations in results and also to reassess some of the earlier durability classification systems (see next section).

USING TEST RESULTS TO CLASSIFY PORTLAND LIMESTONE

It seems that much of the laboratory research on Portland limestone has been aimed towards classification in terms of weathering and durability of stone from different beds and quarries. The earlier classifications by Schaffer (Schaffer, 1937) and Honeyborne (BRE, 1963) were based on relationships between field observations of the weathering of Portland stone in buildings and the laboratory results obtained during the surveys described above. The classification devised by Schaffer was based on the porosity and water absorption characteristics, which Schaffer believed are keys to the way in which the stone would weather when subjected to frost, rain and pollution.

The classification was:

	Microporosity	Saturation coefficient	Suitability
Group 0	< 8.0%	< 0.65	Monumental quality
Group 1	< 11.0%	< 0.72	All general building purposes
Group 2	> 11.0% or	> 0.72	Interior only

Where the microporosity is defined as the total volume percentage of the stone of pore size less than 5 mm. The saturation coefficient is the ratio of the weight of water absorbed at atmospheric pressure to the weight absorbed under vacuum (Hirschwald, 1912).

The original concern that lead Schaffer to study Portland was the occasional use of blocks that weathered very badly over a 30–40 year period. However, the classification took a form that had the potential to classify all stones by their suitability for use.

In the early 1960s Honeyborne was asked to devise a simple system that would allow poor quality Portland stone to be detected prior to use in buildings and also prior to the carving of gravemarkers for the Commonwealth War Graves Commission. The classification was again based on the porosity and water absorption characteristics which Honeyborne had studied extensively in the preceding decade (Honeyborne and Harris, 1958). This classification took the form shown below and is illustrated graphically in Figure 15.2.

	Classification	Suitability
Class A	$(100 \times S) + (0.5 \times M) < 79$	Exceptionally good service in large towns or coastal districts
Class B	$(100 \times S) + (0.5 \times M) < 95$	Good service in large towns or coastal districts
Class C	$(100 \times S) + (0.5 \times M) < 115$	Good service in large inland towns but not very satisfactory in coastal districts
Class D	$(100 \times S) + (0.5 \times M) > 115$	Poor service everywhere except possibly in rural districts inland

Where S = the saturation coefficient as defined above and M = the microporosity expressed as percentage of the total porosity.

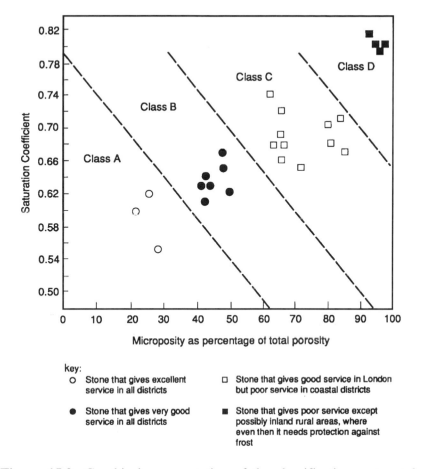

Figure 15.2 Graphical representation of the classification system taken from Honeyborne (1963).

In the 1970s a third classification system was devised and applied to all limestone in the UK. This system used results from the sodium sulphate crystallisation test which was originally devised in the early nineteenth century as a surrogate frost test. This test was applied extensively by Schaffer and Honeyborne in the course of their research though there does seem to have been some variation in the exact details of the test method during this time. In this method the stones were classified A–F based solely on the weight loss during the test (Leary, 1983). Their suitability was then determined by considering proposed geographical location and use, for example, as copings or paving. It seems likely that the classification was based on the observed weathering of different stones in the preceding 50 years and that it accurately represented the weathering of stones in locations where salt damage was the dominate decay process. It should be noted that the pollution climate was very different in the period 1930–1980 from that currently found in urban or rural areas (Table 15.1).

The results in Table 15.1 show that in some cases the classifications are consistent but in other cases, for example, the Whit Bed from the Independence Quarry the results give a complete range from Schaffer's 'monumental' to crystallisation 'Class D'.

Stone type	Schaffer class	Honeyborne class	Crystallisation class
Whit Bed (1) (Fancy Beach)	Class 0	Class A	Class A
Whit Bed (2) (Independence)	Class 0	Class B	Class D
Base Bed (2) (Bowers)	Class 2	Class D	Class E
Base Bed (2) (Independence)	Class 2	Class C	Class D

(1) Leary (1983).
(2) Research undertaken at BRE 1993–95.

Table 15.1 Results of applying the three classification systems to Portland limestone.

LONG-TERM EXPOSURE TRIALS

The results described briefly in the previous section demonstrate the importance of underpinning laboratory results with longer term exposure trials. BRE has collected a significant data set for Portland limestone from exposure trials that cover most of the period between 1955 and 1995. The first programme, known as the Garston–Westminster Study, began in 1955 and continued until 1965. The samples were $100 \times 50 \times 50$ mm blocks exposed on glass supports. The results are described in the report of the Buildings Effect Review Group (BERG, 1989).

The second series of samples were exposed in 1977 as control stone in a long-term trial on the effectiveness of stone preservation treatments at St Paul's Cathedral, London. The trial is still in progress with the samples (100 $\times 100 \times 75$ mm) being retrieved for measurement at approximately one year intervals. The results for the first 15 years were reported in Butlin, *et al.*, (1991).

The third part of the dataset comes from the National Materials Exposure Programme (NMEP). In this programme samples of a range of building materials were exposed at a wide range of locations in the UK, including central London. Samples of Portland limestone were included as one of three stone types. The samples ($50 \times 50 \times 8$ mm) were exposed on freely rotating carousels and retrieved after one, two, four and eight years. The results for the period 1987–91 are given in Butlin, *et al.*, (1993) and summarised in Massey, *et al.*, (1994).

It is possible to compare the rates of decay from these different trials if some corrections are made for the different shapes and sizes of sample involved. In the present research a correction based on the surface area/volume ratio derived from a comparison of samples from the stone preservative control samples and NMEP samples showed this to be suitable. Figure 15.3 shows the results combined together in a plot of the decay rate against measured atmospheric sulphur dioxide concentration. The graph shows the clear relationship between decay and the sulphur dioxide concentration and emphasises the importance of considering the pollution climate. Buildings used to 'calibrate' the classifications described above in the 1950s were exposed to much higher concentrations of sulphur dioxide with annual mean concentrations of around 300 μg m^{-3} being common compared to around 20 μg m^{-3} today.

It is also important to note that the NMEP contained samples of Monks Park limestone, which is traditionally classified as being of poor durability – that is Class E in the sodium sulphate crystallisation test compared to Class A for the Portland limestone used in the NMEP. However, the results from the first four year period of the NMEP show that the difference in the weathering rate is now only a factor of 1.6. In part this must be directly caused by the reduction in the concentrations of pollutants but it may also reflect a change in the dominant processes that cause decay in porous calcareous stones. In the past it has been stated that the main cause of stone decay in the UK is the crystallisation of soluble salts within the pores of stone (Price, 1975) and the emphasis on the use of the sodium sulphate crystallisation test largely reflects this. It seems now that the reduction in salts from deposition of sulphur dioxide and the changes in the use of stone from solid masonry walls to thin cladding panels could be leading to a dominance by other processes, for example, rainwater erosion. It may also be necessary to differentiate between the weathering of stone used in the restoration of an existing building, where salts are already present, and the weathering of new stone used in a new building where dissolution processes will predominate.

OBSERVED RATES OF WEATHERING ON BUILDINGS

Most of the laboratory studies and all of the exposure trials described above were carried out using new stone, but the question asked by most of the

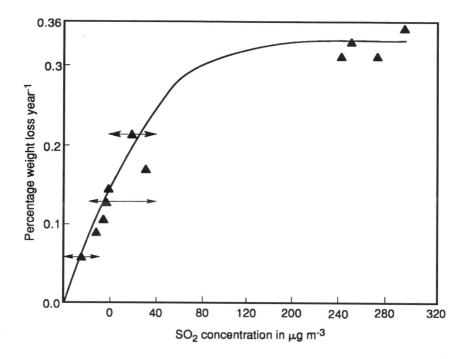

Figure 15.3 Collated data for exposure trials of Portland stone between 1955 and 1990 in London showing the clear relationship between sulphur dioxide concentrations and decay rates. The current sulphur dioxide concentration is around 20 μm m^{-3}.

those responsible for the construction and maintenance of buildings is how will the stone weather on actual buildings. The research undertaken by Schaffer and Honeyborne showed that they were using data from existing buildings to interpret laboratory results but, as the previous section has demonstrated, stone is now subjected to a much reduced rate of decay. However, there is evidence that old stone will weather at a faster rate than new stone because of the so-called 'memory' effect. This theory attributes the faster weathering of old stone to its past exposure history – that it was exposed to much greater concentrations of pollutants and its fabric or structure was effected in such a way as to make the stone more susceptible to decay processes. The only research that is relevant to both the study of decay rates on buildings and the 'memory' effect is the series of measurements made at St Paul's Cathedral, London and reported in Sharp, *et al.*, (1982), Trudgill, *et al.*, (1989) and Trudgill, *et al.*, (1990). This work shows the mean erosion rate for six locations to be 50μm year^{-1} between 1980–85 and around 100 μm for the period 1718–1987. The long-term values are similar to those for the 1955–65 exposure trial and reflect exposure through periods of high pollution. The results for 1980–85 are around twice those measured for samples of new stone at St Paul's in the same period and this difference can be attributed to the 'memory' effect. It is, therefore, difficult to establish if new stone will weather as predicted, but the results obtained indicate that predicted rates will be similar to those found on buildings.

CONCLUSIONS

The research carried out at BRE on Portland limestone during the last 60 years has shown that both laboratory studies and exposure trials have an important part to play in the assessment of stone. It is also clear that classification systems can be of great use if based on a series of site and laboratory measurements and that they can be used to identify stones that will weather more rapidly or that are unsuited for some particular locations. However, it is also very clear that any classification must reflect the pollution climate, the use of the stone and expected decay processes and that research into the selection of stone needs to continue if the optimum use is to be made of natural limestones in the UK.

Acknowledgements

This research project was funded by the Construction Directorate, Department of the Environment and the paper is published by permission of the Chief Executive, BRE. The paper is dedicated to R.J. Schaffer whose records of this work at BRE in the 1930s provided such a valuable archive of data and information.

References

BERG (1989) *The Effect of Acid Deposition on Buildings and Building Materials in the United Kingdom.* Report. HMSO, London.

Building Research Establishment (BRE) (1963) *The Selection of Portland Stone for Various Conditions of Severity of Exposure.* BRE Report A112.

Building Research Establishment (BRE) (1965) *An Investigation of the Failure of Portland Stone in the Belgian Memorial at Shorncliffe Military Cemetery.* BRE Report IC39/65.

Butlin, R.N., Yates, T.J.S., Ridal, J.P. and Bigland, D. (1991) Studies of the use of preservative treatments on historic buildings. In N.S. Baer, C. Sabbioni and A.I. Sors (eds) *Science, Technology and European Cultural Heritage.* Butterworth-Heinemann, Oxford, pp. 664–667.

Butlin, R.N., Yates, T.J.S., Coote, A.T., Lloyd, G.O. and Massey, S.W. (1993) *The First Phase of the National Materials Exposure Programme 1987–1991.* BRE Report CR253/93.

Hirshwald, J. (1912) *Handbuch der Bautechnischen Gesteinprüfung.* Borntraeger, Berlin.

Honeyborne, D.B. and Harris, P..B. (1958) The structure of porous building stone and its relation to weathering behaviour. In D.H. Everett and F.S. Stone (eds) *The Structure and Properties of Porous Materials. Proceedings of the 10th Symposium of the Colston Research Society.* Butterworths, London, pp. 343–365.

Leary, E. (1983) *The Building Limestones of the British Isles.* HMSO, London.

Massey, S.W., Butlin, R.N. and Yates, T.J.S. (1994) Monitoring the urban environment and its effects on masonry materials. In B. Dellow (ed.) *Proceedings of Conference on Improving the Environment,* London, June, pp. 31–47.

Price, C.A. (1975) Testing porous building stone. *The Architects' Journal* **162**: 337–339.

Ross, K.D. and Butlin, R.N. (1989) *Durability Tests for Building Stone.* BRE Report 141.

Schaffer, R.J. (1932) *The Weathering of Natural Building Stones.* HMSO, London, (BRE Fascimile, 1985).

Schaffer, R.J. (1937) *Portland Stone and the Estimation of its Weathering Quality by Means of Laboratory Tests.* Unpublished BRE Report.

Sharp, A.D., Trudgill, S.T., Cooke, R.U., Price, C.A., Crabtree, R.W., Pickles, A.M. and Smith, D.I. (1982) Weathering of the balustrade on St Paul's Cathedral, London. *Earth Surface Processes and Landforms* **7**: 387–389.

South Western Stone Company (1933) *Portland Stone.*

Trudgill, S.T., Viles, H.A., Inkpen, R.J. and Cooke, R.U. (1989) Remeasurement of weathering rates, St Paul's Cathedral, London. *Earth Surface Processes and Landforms* **14**: 175–196.

Trudgill, S.T. Viles, H.A., Cooke, R.U. and Inkpen, R.J. (1990) Rates of stone loss at St Paul's Cathedral, London. *Atmospheric Environment* **24B**: 361–363.

Contact address
Building Research Establishment
Garston
Watford
WD2 7JR
United Kingdom

16 The permeability testing of masonry materials

J. BEGGAN, A.E. LONG
and P.A.M. BASHEER

ABSTRACT

The Autoclam was developed for measuring the *in situ* permeation properties of concrete. It is a quick and effective method for establishing air/water
permeability and water absorption (sorptivity) of concrete. The existing
Autoclam and a modified version have been used to determine the permeation properties of seven common masonry cladding materials. Materials
tested were diorite, basalt, granite, shelly limestone, clay brick, manufactured facing stone and two fine-grained sandstones. Four samples of each
material were tested for air/water permeability and sorptivity. Results indicate that all the materials can be tested for sorptivity using the Autoclam
with the exception of the Scrabo sandstone and the shelly limestone. Air permeability of the other fine-grained sandstone and the brick could only be
quantified using a modified Autoclam. Air/water permeability of the Scrabo
sandstone and the shelly limestone could not be measured without further
modification of the Autoclam. Results indicate that further modification of
the Autoclam will allow measurement of permeation properties of the full
range of masonry cladding materials currently in use.

INTRODUCTION

The movement of water and gases through building materials has many
repercussions with respect to the durability of the material in an aggressive
environment. Concrete durability is heavily influenced by the movement of
water, carbon dioxide and chloride ions into the structure. Other materials
commonly used in the construction industry, such as brick and natural stone

Processes of Urban Stone Decay. Edited by B.J. Smith and P.A. Warke. © 1996 Donhead Publishing Ltd.

also depend on their permeation properties to resist degradation. Deterioration mechanisms such as freeze thaw and salt weathering depend largely on the ingress of water into the material for their destructive success.

It has been shown that the permeation properties of concrete can adequately be quantified using the Autoclam apparatus. Many procedures exist to quantify the permeation properties of concrete but the Autoclam has shown itself to have distinct advantages which justify its use. Among these advantages flexibility, adaptability, simplicity and robustness are the most important. The Indices measured by the Autoclam, viz water/air permeability and sorptivity, have been exhaustively correlated with the basic material properties inherent in concrete. It is hoped that with development the Autoclam could be utilised to test other building materials with the same efficiency as it does with concrete.

The materials were chosen to provide contrasting permeation properties that were reasonably representative of the variation which occurs in practice. The results would then provide benchmark values from which the merits of the clam could be judged. The igneous rock samples were included to provide information on the sensitivity of the Autoclam indices to subtle changes in pore structure and size. The Scrabo sandstone provides the extreme permeability case. The source of the other fine grained sandstone is unknown as it was obtained from the remains of a wrought iron railing constructed in the 1860s. Under microscopic examination the grain size of the building sandstone was seen to be smaller than the Scrabo sample and the structure denser and more compact. The limestone sample displayed very small shell fragments throughout its structure. The manufactured stone was a cast facing panel consisting of fine aggregate, cement and colouring agent.

PRINCIPLES OF OPERATION

Air permeability test

To carry out an air permeability test using the standard Autoclam, the piston is pushed down through the cylinder and is kept at the bottom. This is to ensure the volume of air used for the air permeability test is constant for the different cylinder sizes used. The pressure inside the apparatus is increased to slightly above 0.5 bar and the decay of it is monitored every minute from 0.5 bar for 15 minutes or until the pressure has diminished to zero. A plot of natural logarithm of pressure against time is linear, hence the slope of the linear regression curve between the 5th and 15th minute for tests lasting 15 minutes is used as an air permeability index, with units of Ln (pressure)/min.

Sorptivity test

The sorptivity test can be carried out at the same location shortly after the air permeability test. The piston is brought to the top of the cylinder. Water is admitted into the test area through the priming valve by means of a syringe, with the air escaping through the bleed valve at the top of the piston. For tests on vertical surfaces, air should be allowed to escape first through the bleed valve in the base of the unit then through the bleed valve at the top of the piston. When the system is completely filled with water, both the bleed valve and priming valve are closed. Normally these operations do not take longer than two minutes, which does not significantly influence the sorptivity index. As the bleed valve is completely open during the priming, the pressure is atmospheric. The piston is pushed down in order to raise the pressure to 0.02 bar above atmospheric pressure. At this pressure water is considered to be absorbed by capillary pores rather than by pressure induced flow. As water is absorbed by capillarity, the pressure inside would tend to decrease, hence it is maintained at a constant level by the movement of the piston down the cylinder. The movement of the piston is measured at one minute intervals for a period of 15 minutes and as the area of the cylinder is known the quantity of water absorbed during the test can be determined. Extensive testing has shown that a linear relationship exists between the quantity of water absorbed and the square root of time elapsed. This relationship depends to some extent on the material tested but for all practical purposes a square root time plot may be employed. The slope of this graph is reported as the sorptivity index with units Cu.m/√min. and if only the portion of the graph between the 5th and 15th minutes is used errors associated with initial stages of the procedure are avoided.

Water permeability test

The water permeability test is conducted elsewhere on the sample using the same test procedure as that for the water absorption test. In this case, after priming the system, the pressure inside is increased to 0.5 bar by means of a syringe, in comparison with the 0.02 bar used for the sorptivity test. Again, when the quantity of water absorped is plotted against the square root of time, it is also found to be linear with the slope of the square root time plot between the 5th and 15th minute used to specify the water permeability index with units Cu. m/√min. The major difference between the sorptivity test and the water permeability test is that, in the former case, capillary absorption causes the penetration of water whereas in the latter the applied pressure also contributes to the rate of flow.

APPARATUS

The Autoclam apparatus consists of two parts, the Autoclam 'head' and the controller unit. The head (Figure 16.1) contains all the mechanical parts including the pressure transducer, the cylinder and the piston. The Autoclam controller contains the electronic controls for the operation of the Autoclam and for recording test results.

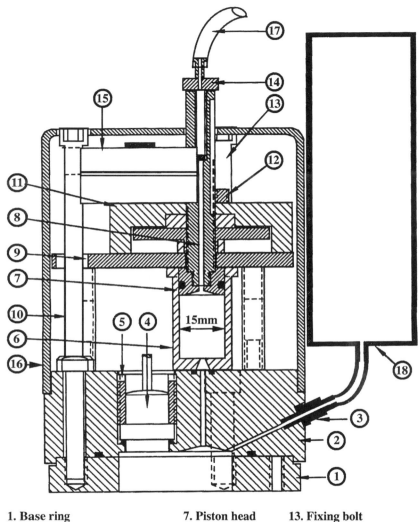

Figure 16.1 Modified Autoclam body (sectional elevation).

1. Base ring	7. Piston head	13. Fixing bolt
2. Base unit	8. Stem of piston	14. Bleed valve
3. Bleed valve for vertical test	9. Middle plate	15. Motor
4. Pressure transducer	10. Pillars	16. Case
5. Transducer retaining ring	11. Gear assembly	17. Bleed tube
6. Cylinder	12. Key	18. Air reservoir

The modified Autoclam section is shown in Figure 16.1, the addition being the cylinder attached to the side of the head which provides an increase to the air system during the air permeability index test. The cylinder was attached to the Autoclam system through the side bleed valve which is normally used to allow air to escape when carrying out a water permeability or sorptivity test on vertical surfaces. With this modification the Autoclam can only be used for air permeability tests with an unmodified Autoclam required for the water permeability and sorptivity tests. With the modified Autoclam the air system has been increased by a factor of 18 primarily to accommodate the testing of clay brick specimens.

TEST PROCEDURE

The first stage in the preparation of the sample for an Autoclam test is the fixing of an Autoclam ring to the surface of the sample. The base ring to which the Autoclam head is attached may be held in place by two methods (1) clamping or (2) adhesive. The ring can be clamped to the sample surface, with non-absorbent foam providing the seal between the ring and the sample. It is always desirable to clamp the clam rings as it is more accurate because no adhesive is present to influence the test area either by increasing or decreasing the size of it. However in this test programme many of the samples had uneven surfaces and it was impractical to clamp the rings in place. The Autoclam rings were, therefore, bonded to the sample surface using an epoxy resin adhesive. Care must be taken to ensure that sealant exuded from under the Autoclam ring does not encroach into the test area.

The standard Autoclam ring isolates an area of 50 mm diameter. The brick samples tested have special rings with an elongated hole designed to maximise the test area and minimise the edge effects due to the proximity of the brick edge to the test area. The Autoclam indices measured using the non-standard brick ring must be adjusted to reflect the decreased test area.

PRESENTATION AND DISCUSSION OF RESULTS

It can be seen from the results presented in Table 16.1 that the Autoclam or the modified Autoclam could not obtain air permeability indices for Scrabo sandstone or the shelly limestone. The missing values reflect the limits of the Autoclam and the modified Autoclam as a means of testing permeation properties of masonry materials. Attempts to test the Scrabo sandstone and the shelly limestone for air permeability failed because on starting a test the pressure within the system dissipated before the first minute had elapsed. The present Autoclam, therefore, requires a large increase in capacity before it can cope with the permeation properties of materials such as Scrabo sandstone.

Current modifications do, however, increase the range of materials which can be measured for air permeability but it is estimated that the air

Material	Air permeability Ln (pressure)/min	Water permeability Cu.m × E-7/min	Sorptivity Cu.m × E-7/min
Shelly limestone	--------	---------	---------
Manufactured stone	4.626[A]	116.84	38.042
Scrabo sandstone	--------	---------	---------
Granite	0.042	41.86	29.770
Diorite	0.004	2.02	3.970
Basalt	0.033	1.19	2.310
Clay brick	8.963[AB]	13.16[B]	6.010[B]
Fine grained sandstone	3.330[A]	-105.95	52.400

A Measurement adjusted to take account of the use of the modified Autoclam.
B Measurement adjusted to allow for the use of non-standard 'brick' Autoclam rings.

Table 16.1 Autoclam indices for various materials.

system would have to be increased by a factor of approximately 600 to obtain sustained pressure dissipation for 15 minutes. To increase the air permeability system by a factor of 600 would require major modifications to the Autoclam. An annular tank which surrounds the Autoclam head may prove to be a more efficient and manageable way of providing increased air capacity than the present solid cylindrical tank. However, provision of a large cylinder connected by means of an incompressible tube which may be removed when not required might provide a more convenient alternative. This addition would not be an integral part of the Autoclam head, as in the present modified Autoclam, but would be an effective way of allowing highly permeable materials to be tested for air permeability by means of a relatively simple modification.

Neither water permeability nor sorptivity measurements could be made on Scrabo sandstone or shelly limestone due to the piston attaining its full displacement after only five minutes and the pressure not being constant during the test. The maximum cylinder size which can be used at present is 30 mm but this is not sufficient to sustain water flow for more than 10 minutes. The Autoclam cannot deal with the increased water permeability and sorptivity because it runs out of piston travel before the end of the test. Normally when a test does not last the full 15 minutes the indices can be calculated from the data obtained during the test run. However, in this instance, indices cannot be calculated using the available test data because the Autoclam piston speed is insufficient to maintain constant pressure within the cylinder. The pressure variation within the cylinder then becomes a variable which cannot be controlled and thus effects the repeatability of the Autoclam index.

The Autoclam indices obtained for igneous rock samples are extremely low. These samples may have given more revealing results had the tests been extended to a period of 1 hour or 24 hours. This can be achieved with some simple reprogramming within the Autoclam control unit, but an alternative to an extended test would be to increase the size of the area exposed to water/air during a test run. For the water permeability and sorptivity tests a decrease in the piston diameter used would increase the sensitivity of measurements made by the Autoclam.

CONCLUSIONS

(1) Provision must be made to increase the volume of air available during the air permeability test if the Autoclam is to be used to test very permeable material such as the Scrabo sandstone used in this study.
(2) A larger internal piston and cylinder is needed to allow water permeability and sorptivity measurements to be made on very absorbent material.
(3) The Autoclam can easily be used to measure the permeation properties of low permeability materials (igneous rocks) at present although a longer test, larger test area or smaller piston and cylinder may provide more detailed information on the index in question.
(4) Correlations between Autoclam indices and inherent material properties similar to those carried out for concrete must be conducted for other materials. Autoclam indices may then be related to parameters such as freeze–thaw durability and used to predict process response characteristics.

References

Basheer, P.A.M., Montgomery, F.R., Long, A.E. (1993) The'Autoclam' permeability system for measuring the *in situ* permeation properties of concrete. *Proceedings of the International Conference on Non Destructive Testing in Civil Engineering,* Liverpool. 14–16 April, pp. 235–260.

The Concrete Society (1988) *Permeability testing of site concrete – A review of methods and experience.* Report of a concrete society working party. Concrete Society Technical Report No. 31, London.

Basheer, P.A.M. (1991) *Clam permeability tests for assessing the durability of concrete.* Unpub. Ph.D. Thesis, Queen's University of Belfast.

Contact address
Department of Civil Engineering
The Queen's University Belfast
Belfast
BT7 1NN
United Kingdom

17 Methods for investigating stone decay mechanisms in polluted and 'clean' environments, Northern Ireland

C. A. MOSES

ABSTRACT

Exposure trials were conducted to study decay mechanisms on Portland limestone surfaces. Detailed spatial and temporal changes in surface textural characteristics are investigated using small discs, tablets and large blocks exposed at urban, rural and coastal sites. Samples are characterised using weight loss indices, optical and scanning electron microscopy (SEM) and surface roughness profiling. Weight loss indices clearly illustrate the relative weathering aggressiveness of different environments. SEM examination shows how initial decay mechanisms operate and can be used to quantify the impact of acid deposition. For example, on urban samples surface calcite dust acts as a reactive surface upon which salts form from acid deposition, while on rural samples this dust is removed by solution. Surface roughness profiling reveals changes in rock surface texture through time as a function of decay. Large block exposures allow surface particulate deposition and biological colonisation to take place.

The techniques employed can be used to examine and quantify rock surface textural characteristics on a range of scales over a relatively short time period.

INTRODUCTION

In the late 1980s the Building Effects Review Group (BERG) reviewed the state of knowledge on acid deposition on buildings and building materials in the United Kingdom. It identified that weathering rates on urban historical buildings are higher than those on both natural outcrops and on rural

Processes of Urban Stone Decay. Edited by B. J. Smith and P. A. Warke. © 1996 Donhead Publishing Ltd.

buildings (BERG 1989, Cooke, 1989, Inkpen, *et al.*, 1994). This continued disparity in weathering rates occurs despite the fact that smoke and sulphur dioxide concentrations in UK urban areas have decreased by factors of 10 and 5 respectively since the early 1950s (BERG 1989). To address this problem BERG identified areas which required further research and/or better data. These include the need for a better understanding of damage mechanisms and improved methods of predicting damage at site specific, regional and national scales.

In the context of these needs this chapter reports on how exposure trials can be used to investigate variations in weathering aggressiveness at a regional scale between urban, rural and coastal environments, and at a local scale between exposed and sheltered micro-environments. Weathering aggressiveness is characterised using surface texture identified by optical and scanning electron microscopy (SEM) in combination with surface roughness profiling and percentage dry weight loss as a weathering index. The techniques allow not just a characterisation of weathering environments but also a detailed investigation of decay mechanisms.

LOCATION

Three sites were chosen in Northern Ireland to reflect the distinctive characteristics of natural, or 'clean', and polluted environments (Figure 17.1).

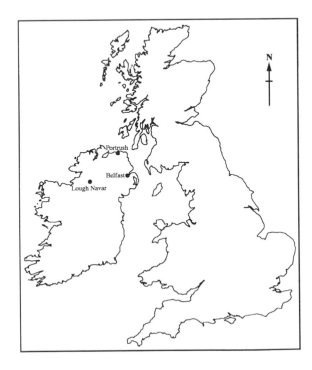

Figure 17.1 Exposure site locations.

213

Smith, *et al.* (1992) recognised that despite Northern Ireland's location to the northwest of mainland Europe, urban areas such as Belfast can experience high localised pollutant levels. In the 1960s and 1970s Belfast experienced falling smoke levels and sulphur dioxide concentrations, but during the 1980s sulphur dioxide concentrations increased again, while smoke levels continued to fall. Mean annual sulphur dioxide concentrations in urban and suburban Belfast can exceed those found in other UK cities (Smith, *et al.*, 1992). At the Belfast site, samples were located in the city centre at the City Hall and reflect the higher levels of gaseous and particulate pollution associated with urban environments.

Pollutant levels are low to the west of the Province, an area which is dominated by weather systems that originate over the Atlantic (Betts, 1982; Jordan, 1983) and the Lough Navar site, therefore, represents 'clean' rural conditions. To the east of the Province up to 20% of sulphate in bulk precipitation is derived from sea salts (Jordan, 1983). At the Portrush site, samples were exposed at approximately 100 m beyond high water level to reflect coastal conditions of high salt aerosol concentration.

METHODOLOGY

Three exposure trials were conducted at each site between April 1990 and January 1993 using disc, tablet and large block samples of Portland limestone, an oolitic limestone of Jurassic age.

Small disc samples

Discs of rock, 1.5 cm in diameter, and 0.5 cm thick, were attached to SEM stubs and held in a metal rack. They were exposed for 18 months (April 1990 to October 1991) and because of their small size could be placed directly in a scanning electron microscope (cf. Viles, 1990). Two racks, each with two vertical samples, were placed at each site, one exposed to rainfall and the other sheltered from the rain but exposed to the atmosphere and open to direct precipitation of dew, frost, airborne particulates and wind-driven rain.

Weight loss tablets

The method, originally used to expose metal samples for atmospheric corrosion testing and subsequently modified to study the weathering of building stones (Jaynes, 1985), involves attaching stone tablets ($50 \times 50 \times 10$ mm) to a rotating carousel. The carousel prevents samples from resting in standing water on wet days and rotates in the wind so that all samples receive equal exposure. Consequently samples are not influenced by orientation at the site with respect to the prevailing wind or the particular expo-

214

sure conditions of the site itself (Jaynes, 1985).

At each site a carousel was attached to the upper surface of a metal framed table. Each carousel has 12 arms and tablets of Portland limestone were attached to four of these. The remaining eight arms were used for two other limestones, results from which are not reported here. Over a period of 2 years the 4 tablets were collected singly at 6 monthly intervals, their percentage dry weight loss measured and their surface texture characterised.

Large blocks

Blocks, $25 \times 25 \times 10$ cm, were chosen as representative of building blocks (cf. Cooper, 1986; Reddy, 1987). They were encased on five sides with 5 cm thick expanded polystyrene and placed in a tight fitting wooden tray. Silica sealant at the join with the polystyrene prevents ingress of water down the sides and along the base of the blocks. At each location a block was placed on the top of the table and another beneath the table to shelter it from direct rainwash. The blocks were tilted at an angle of 5° to prevent water pooling on the surface.

ANALYSIS

SEM examination of small stone discs

After collection samples were coated with gold and placed in a Jeol 6400 scanning electron microscope (SEM) equipped with qualitative energy dispersive X-ray facility (EDX). To identify and quantify surface characteristics eight profiles were tracked across each exposed sample and control samples of fresh stone. The length occupied by, for example, etched calcite and gypsum salts was measured and used to calculate percentage cover values (cf. Viles, 1990).

Surface roughness of carousel tablets

Surface profiling is used widely within manufacturing industries to measure the surface characteristics of machine components (Dagnall, 1980). It has also been used to assess the surface textural characteristics of building stones (Grimm, 1983; Guidobaldi and Mecchi, 1985). Jaynes (1985) used surface roughness profile traces and roughness average (R_a) values in association with weight loss measurements to identify spatial variations in weathering intensity.

In this study a Talysurf plotter with a diamond tipped stylus, radius 3 µm, was used. Four initial measurements were taken to establish appropriate vertical and horizontal magnifications and to ensure that results were reproducible for each surface type. Measurements were taken along 5 mm transects at four different points on the sample surface so that damage caused by the stylus tip did not affect results. Horizontal magnification in all cases was $\times 5$ and vertical magnification $\times 100$. Visual comparison of roughness profiles is informative but the interpretation is subjective. In order to quantify surface characteristics roughness average values (R_a) were measured at 12 points on each sample. Six measurements were taken at different points on each side of the tablet and an average R_a value calculated.

Surface change of large blocks

The large blocks underwent visual examination using a hand lens and optical microscope to identify any surface alteration.

RESULTS

SEM examination of stone discs

Samples of fresh stone at low magnification show relatively even and smooth surfaces. Individual ooliths were obscured by a surface layer of calcite dust (Figures 17.2a and 17.2b) which also filled pore spaces and is presumably derived from the sawing of samples during preparation.

Exposed samples from Lough Navar were etched over the entire surface. Individual ooliths were clearly visible and etch features were noted on micritic oolith surfaces as well as on sparite cement material. On the sheltered samples individual ooliths were clearly visible and at high magnifications micrite etching was evident (Figure 17.2c).

Exposed samples from the Belfast City Hall showed severe etching across most of their surface. Although sulphation was not evident on the surface, carbonaceous particles were found trapped within pore spaces. Surface sulphation was almost complete on the sheltered samples with 75% of the sample surface covered with gypsum crystals (Figures 17.2d and 17.2e).

Exposed samples from Portrush exhibited etch features on more than 60% of the exposed sample surface, while halite salts constituted 30% cover. Halite was present as discrete crystals or aggregates of crystals blocking pore spaces between ooliths. Sheltered samples showed both gypsum and halite salt crystallisation (Figure 17.2f).

Surface roughness of stone tablets

Within site variations are shown in Figure 17.3. The main trend is that surface roughness values increase through time and roughness profiles become more irregular. The increase in roughness values was most evident after the first six months of exposure.

216

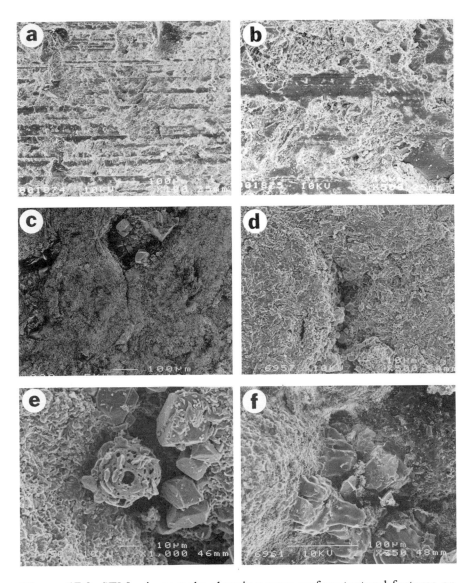

Figure 17.2 SEM micrographs showing some surface textural features on stone disc samples. (a) Relatively even surface cover of calcite dust – control sample (picture width 1 mm). (b) Fine-grained micritic nature of calcite dust – control sample (picture width 200 µm). (c) Etched ooliths typical of exposed samples (picture width 860 µm). (d) Gypsum crystals on surface of sheltered sample from Belfast (picture width 200 µm). (e) Gypsum nucleated from carbonaceous particle – sheltered sample, City Hall, Belfast (picture width 100 µm). (f) Halite in pore spaces – sheltered sample, Portrush (picture width 320 µm).

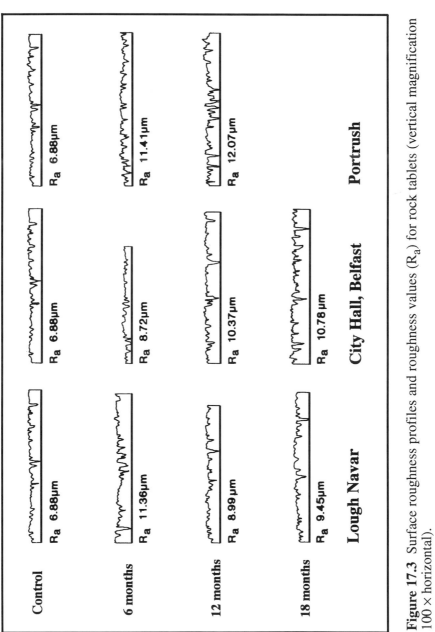

Figure 17.3 Surface roughness profiles and roughness values (R_a) for rock tablets (vertical magnification 100 × horizontal).

Weight loss index of stone tablets

Percentage weight loss figures for samples at each location for each six month period are shown in Table 17.1.

Site location	% weight loss through time (months)			
	6	12	18	24
Lough Navar (rural)	0.23	0.40	0.39	0.70
Portrush (coastal)	0.27	0.70	-----	-----
Belfast (urban)	0.45	0.63	0.84	1.17

Table 17.1 Dry weight loss values for stone tablets used in this study.

Surface alteration on large blocks

Particulate deposition was evident on both exposed and sheltered blocks from Belfast. Visual examination, by hand lens, showed the exposed block to have a fairly even, dull grey surface colouration due to carbonaceous particulates in pores between ooliths. In contrast, the sheltered block exhibited well developed patches of black crust on the lower half of the block. Optical microscope examination confirmed that this was a crust of 2–3 mm thickness growing out from the block surface.

The exposed block from Lough Navar had a clean surface with individual ooliths and upstanding fossil fragments visible by optical microscope. The sheltered block from the same location, however, was colonised by red algae. Algae was particularly evident on the lower half of the block and around edges adjacent to the waterproof sealant where a moist rock surface is conducive to biological colonisation. Optical microscope examination showed that the algae were present in pores between ooliths.

Both blocks from Portrush were colonised by green algae, but the sheltered block had a much more visible and even distribution which resulted in a green colouration of the lower half of the block. The exposed block surface had a patchy distribution with concentrations around the wetted perimeter adjacent to the sealed edges.

DISCUSSION

Stone discs

As expected, both exposed and sheltered samples at Lough Navar exhibited severe etching. In comparison, the exposed Belfast sample showed marginally lower amounts of etching but on the basis of amount of etching alone it is not possible to differentiate the two sites. Clear differences are evident, however, between sheltered samples. The Belfast sample experienced sulphation over 75% of its surface (Figure 17.4). It is probable that the calcite dust from sample preparation has acted as a reactive surface for gypsum transformation (Viles, 1990).

Evidence for an external source of gypsum was also found on the sheltered Belfast sample where carbonaceous particles had nucleated gypsum crystals (Figure 17.2e) under the influence of fluctuating moisture conditions characteristic of a sheltered position. This has important implications for the rapid build-up of black crusts on limestone surfaces and goes some way to explaining how gypsum crusts (black crusts) accumulate on non-carbonate rocks such as granite and sandstone (Smith and Magee, 1990; Smith, et al., 1994). The gypsum crystals nucleated in this study under natural conditions are not needle shaped like those produced in the laboratory (Del Monte and Sabbioni, 1984), but are more tabular in form and protrude at right angles to the particulate surface. It is not clear whether the gypsum was nucleated before or after deposition. Nonetheless such deposition would accelerate black crust build up on carbonate surfaces and provide a source of gypsum for black crusts on non-carbonate surfaces.

At the coastal site (Portrush), sheltered samples differed from the two exposed samples in that etch features were evident on calcite crystals and more than 75% of their surface was covered in crystals of both gypsum and halite salts. Halite and gypsum present within pore spaces may ultimately contribute to granular disintegration and disruption of the surface. A short distance away on the same stretch of coast granular disintegration by salt weathering is responsible for deterioration of a sandstone sea wall (McGreevy, 1984).

Exposed samples at all three sites were subject to considerable dissolution with calcite dust entirely removed to expose individual ooliths. Cement material had been dissolved away from between ooliths and etching was evident on both micrite and sparite crystals. This was particularly evident at Lough Navar where samples appeared to have been subject to more aggressive dissolution than the other sites. It might have been expected that the Belfast samples would be subject to more aggressive dissolution because of its higher pollutant levels. Rainfall at Lough Navar is, however, higher because of its location in the west of Northern Ireland.

The sheltered samples from Lough Navar were only subject to dissolution and had a similar surface roughness value to those from Belfast. The Belfast sample however, was subject to sulphation over 75% of its surface area. Sulphation was expected but a more significant outcome was the

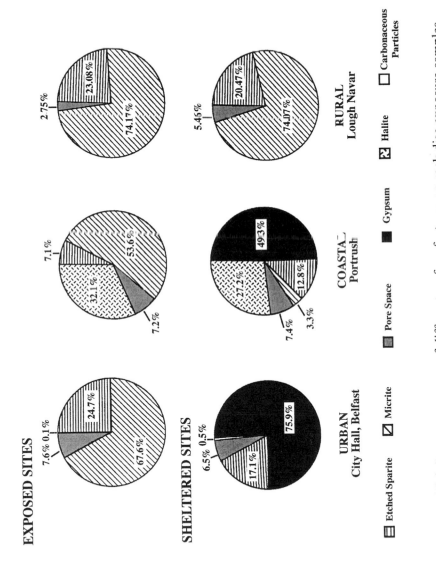

Figure 17.4 Percentage cover of different surface features on rock disc exposure samples.

deposition of pollution particles which act as external sources of gypsum for black crust formation.

These results accord well with those of Viles (1990). After only two months of sample exposure in a polluted environment she noted extensive etching on exposed samples and gypsum formation on sheltered samples and suggested that some calcite dust may remain on sheltered samples to act as a reactive surface for sulphation. Retention of calcite dust on the sheltered samples from Belfast contributed to the 75% surface cover of gypsum.

Stone tablets

The overall trend was one where weight loss increased steadily over the first twelve months of exposure with little change evident between 12 and 18 months. Over the entire two year period values compare well with those of Jaynes (1985) for mainland UK (Table 17.2). Central Belfast values are only marginally greater than those of the industrial/commercial centre of London while a much smaller difference is evident between the rural sites (0.685%, Jaynes, 1985; Lough Navar 0.70% – Tables 17.1 and 17.2).

After 18 months weight loss increased quite dramatically until the end of the trial. Initial weight losses may be related simply to removal of calcite dust from tablet surfaces. Although care was taken to ensure that all calcite sludge and dust from sample preparation was washed off some may have remained and inflated readings for the first 6 to 12 months of exposure. The slight increase in weight loss between 12 and 18 months, and sudden increase up to 24 months is a little more problematic. It has been suggested that polished rock surfaces create a threshold which must be breached before

Site location	% weight loss
London industrial/commercial	1.006
London residential	0.860
All London residential sites	0.924
Provincial centres	0.813
Rural centres	0.685

Table 17.2 Dry weight values for stone tablets used by Jaynes (1985).

weathering processes can be effective (Klein, 1984). Once this artificially smoothed surface is breached weathering should be more effective over the greater surface area and may explain the increased weight loss between 18 and 24 months.

After 6 months exposure the Belfast tablet showed greatest weight loss, Lough Navar least and Portrush just slightly more than Lough Navar. After 12 months however, the Portrush tablet was subject to a slightly greater weight loss than either the City Hall or Lough Navar samples (Table 17.1). Calcite dust may have initially blocked pore spaces and prevented salt crystallisation within them. This could explain the relatively low weight loss after 6 months exposure. Removal of the calcite dust would allow salts access to the pore system and thus facilitate salt weathering. Unfortunately this cannot be confirmed since only the first two tablets were recovered from the coastal site. Other workers have noted localised higher weight loss values for tablets exposed at coastal sites and attribute this to more aggressive salt weathering (Jaynes and Cooke, 1987).

At all sites it is likely that weathering over the first 6 months primarily involved removal of superficial calcite dust. After this, changes in surface texture and roughness were probably due to weathering of a fully exposed rock surface. In most cases a slight increase in roughness value was noted between 6 and 12 months. Between 12 and 18 months the change in roughness was negligible. It has been suggested that stone surfaces reach an 'equilibrium' roughness in the first year or so of exposure (Grimm, 1983; Jaynes, 1985). In this study differences in roughness values between the rock discs and 12 and 18 month tablets is negligible. This may represent some kind of 'equilibrium' roughness. To test this, however, the exposure period would have to be extended beyond two years.

Between-site comparisons show that tablets at Portrush experienced most surface disruption, possibly related to salt-induced disaggregation. City Hall values are similar to those of Portrush, and may reflect sulphation and associated salt weathering (Figure 17.2d and 17.2e). This agrees with Jaynes (1985) findings that salt weathering was responsible for most surface disruption.

Large blocks

The exposed block from Belfast was the most discoloured due to deposition of carbonaceous particles. Both the exposed Lough Navar and Portrush blocks appeared, from visual assessment at least, to have clean surfaces free from discolouration and affected only by dissolution. The presence of a salt efflorescence on the Portrush block suggested that granular disintegration by salt weathering may be active. Optical microscope examination showed the Portrush block to have a much more porous open structure than the Lough Navar block. Some cement removal by dissolution was evident on the Lough Navar block but on the Portrush block cement and ooliths had also been lost. Optical microscope examination showed the Belfast block to have a similar open porous surface morphology to that of the Portrush block. Although a salt efflorescence was not visible on the City Hall block it is likely that salt weathering associated with deposition of carbonaceous particles may have occurred. Salt crystallisation occurred on algal coated surfaces at Portrush, suggesting that biological and salt weathering processes may act in conjunction. A salt efflorescence formed on the surface of exposed and sheltered blocks during transport to the laboratory. This indicates that although the exposed block was rainwashed this was not sufficient to remove all salts from its surface but may have washed them into the fabric of the stone possibly resulting in damage at depth.

Unlike the exposed samples, surface discolouration was evident on all three sheltered blocks. On both the Lough Navar and Portrush blocks this was the result of biological colonisation. Dissolution and biological weathering may have been responsible for removing ooliths from the surface of the sheltered Lough Navar block, although it is difficult to assess the extent of their interaction. Salt weathering was an additional process which may have contributed to surface disruption of the Portrush block. Protection from direct rainfall whilst still allowing moisture penetration may account for extensive biological colonisation of the sheltered block while exposure to direct rainfall may have a limiting effect on biological growth.

The sheltered Belfast block showed completely different characteristics including the initial stages of black crust development on the lower half of the block. At this city centre site moisture contained within the lower half of the block will be acidic due to the presence of pollutants. Not only is the block subject to some rainwash blown in around the sides of the exposure table but more importantly to occult and dry deposition of pollutants. Protection from washing by rainfall and run-off allows deposited pollutants to react with the limestone to form gypsum salts (Figure 17.2e). Microscope examination showed that, on the surface at least, more damage had been caused to the sheltered Belfast block than to the exposed one. On the exposed block individual ooliths were clearly visible and no surface disruption was evident. Individual ooliths on the sheltered block were generally obscured by the black crust. Where this was absent oolith details were obscured by rock meal suggesting that salt weathering is more dominant on the sheltered block and dissolution on the exposed. Even if salts were not seen on the exposed block surface it may simply be because they have been washed into the stone.

SUMMARY

Weight loss trials

Weight loss trials clearly illustrate the spatial variability of weathering with the coastal site being the most aggressive environment while the rural location appears to be the least aggressive and the urban environment to be intermediate. These findings are in accordance with Jaynes (1985) who found that coastal sites disturb what is thought of as an 'ideal' increase in weathering rates from rural to urban environments.

Stone discs

Both salt weathering and dissolution were effective at the coastal and urban sites, but only dissolution was noted at the rural site. At the coastal site salt weathering was more effective on discs sheltered from direct rainwash but at the rural site shelter resulted in less effective dissolution and incomplete removal of calcite dust. Exposed urban samples were free from salts with only etching evident. Adjacent sheltered samples showed extensive sulphation and incipient gypsum crust development, possibly aided by the presence of calcite dust which may have acted as a reactive surface. Combustion particles, including flyash, were seen to be trapped within these crusts and also provided nucleii for gypsum growth.

Large blocks

After 33 months exposure significant changes in surface characteristics were noted between and within sites. The exposed urban block exhibited dissolution and sulphation while the sheltered block developed a partial black crust. Dissolution was dominant on the exposed rural block but biological colonisation was extensive on the sheltered block. Active dissolution and salt weathering characterised both coastal blocks, but extensive biological colonisation was restricted to the sheltered block. Large blocks provide valuable information on alteration features of larger stone surfaces as often the dimensions of many decay features are greater than those of small stone discs and tablets.

CONCLUSION

The results of this study, in combination with those of previous work (e.g. Jaynes and Cooke, 1987; Viles, 1990) illustrate the potential of exposure trials to provide damage functions for construction materials over relatively short time periods in polluted and 'clean' environments. SEM examination of stone discs provides detailed and quantifiable evidence of the mechanisms involved in the initial stages of stone decay. Surface changes observable at the micron scale (μm) are, however, difficult to translate into visible decay features using information gleaned from small stone discs alone. Weight loss indices combined with surface roughness profiles facilitate the quantification of small-scale change while the use of large exposure blocks allows these to be related to larger-scale features. Integrated exposure trials of this type provide useful information on the response of stone to a range of decay mechanisms at various scales.

Acknowledgements

The author would like to thank Bernard Smith and Patricia Warke for their constructive comments on this paper and the cartographic staff of the School of Geosciences and staff of the Electron Microscope Unit at Queen's University for their technical assistance. Thanks must also be extended to E. and B. Moses for invaluable assistance in the field and to Belfast City Council for access to Belfast City Hall. This work was funded by a studentship from the Department of Education for Northern Ireland.

References

Betts, N.L. (1982) Climate. In J.G. Cruickshank andD.N. Willcock (eds) *Northern Ireland – Environment and Natural Resources*. The Queen's University of Belfast and the New University of Ulster, Belfast, pp. 9–42.

BERG (1989) *The Effects of Acid Deposition on Buildings and Building Materials in the United Kingdom*. Building Effects Review Group Report, HMSO, London.

Cooper, T.P. (1986) Saving the buildings from the weather. *Technology Ireland*, June: 32–33.

Del Monte, M. and Sabbioni, C. (1984) Morphology and mineralogy of fly ash from a coal-fired power plant. *Archives for Meteorology, Geophysics and Bioclimatology* **35 Ser. B**: 93–104.

Grimm, W.D. (1983) Measurements of surface roughness to characterise the degree of deterioration of natural stones. *Conference on Material Science and Restoration*, Esslingen, September, pp. 321–324.

Guidobaldi, F. and Mecchi, A..M. (1985) Corrosion of marble by rain. The influence of surface roughness, rain intensity and additional washing. *Proceedings of the 5th International Congress on Deterioration and Conservation of Stone*. Presses Polytechniques Romandes, Lausanne, pp. 467–474.

Inkpen, R., Cooke, R.U. and Viles, H.A. (1994) Processes and rates of urban limestone weathering. In D.A. Robinson and R.B.G. Williams (eds) *Rock Weathering and Landform Evolution*. J. Wiley & Sons, Chichester, pp. 119–130.

Jaynes, S. (1985) *Studies of building stone weathering in south-east England*. Unpublished Ph.D. Thesis, University of London.

Jaynes, S. and Cooke, R.U. (1987) Stone weathering in southeast England. *Atmospheric Environment* **21**: 1601–1622.

Jordan, C. (1983) The precipitation chemistry of a rural site in Co. Antrim, Northern Ireland. *Record of Agricultural Research* **31**: 89–98.

Klein, M. (1984) Weathering rates of limestone tombstones measured in Haifi, Israel. *Zeitschrift für Geomorphologie N.F.* **28**: 105–111.

McGreevy, J.P. (1984) A preliminary Scanning Electron Microscope study of honeycomb weathering of sandstone in a coastal environment.

Earth Surface Processes and Landforms **10**: 509–518.

Moses, C.A. (1994) *The origin and implications of microsolutional features on the surface of limestones.* Unpublished Ph.D. Thesis, The Queen's University Belfast.

Reddy, M. (1987) *Acid rain damage to carbonate stone: a preliminary quantitative assessment based on the aqueous geochemistry of rainfall runoff.* US Geolological Survey, Water Resources Investigations Report 87, 4016.

Smith, B.J. and Magee, R.W. (1990) Granite weathering in an urban environment: an example from Rio de Janeiro. *Singapore Journal of Tropical Geography* **II**: 143–153.

Smith, B.J., Whalley, W.B. and Magee, R. (1992) Background and local contributions to acidic deposition and their relative impact on building stone decay. In J.W.S. Longhurst (ed.) *Acid Deposition: Origins, Impacts and Abatement Strategies.* Springer-Verlag, Heidelberg, pp. 241–266.

Smith, B.J., Magee, R.W. and Whalley, W.B. (1994) Breakdown patterns of quartz sandstone in a polluted urban environment, Belfast, Northern Ireland. In D. Robinson and R.B.G. Williams (eds) *Rock Weathering and Landform Evolution.* J. Wiley & Sons, Chichester, pp. 131–150.

Trudgill, S.T., Viles, H.A., Cooke, R.U. and Inkpen, R.J. (1990) Rates of stone loss at St Paul's Cathedral, London. *Atmospheric Environment* **24B**: 361–363.

Viles, H.A. (1990) The early stages of building stone decay in an urban environment. *Atmospheric Environment* **24A**: 229–232.

Contact address
The Geography Laboratory
Arts Building
University of Sussex
Falmer
Brighton
BN1 9QN
United Kingdom

18 Errors associated with determining P and S acoustic wave velocities for stone weathering studies

W. MURPHY, J.D. SMITH
and R.J. INKPEN

ABSTRACT

Direct measurement of P and S acoustic wave velocities from samples of Portland limestone are repeatable. Moisture content, coupling pressure and sample geometry can act as potential sources of error and may be important considerations when using the technique for determining rock degradation. The importance of moisture content on transmission of seismic waves, could be seen in two separate groups of measurements of S waves, whereas, there appears to be no linear variation with moisture content for P waves over a range from 0.02% to 5.4% (saturated moisture content, under atmospheric conditions). The effects of increasing pressure on the transducer to give a better acoustic couple resulted in increased signal amplitude, but no increase in velocity. Subsequent increases in wave amplitude introduced errors in the automatic detection systems. Finally, the effects of sample geometry indicate that anomalous acoustic wave reflections from the free sample surface give erroneous results between manual measurements on the CRO and the automatic detection systems. Results indicate that automatic detection systems, such as the PUNDIT (Portable Ultrasonic Non-destructive Digital Indicating Tester), can give highly repeatable results under controlled stress conditions and carefully chosen sample geometries, but can produce anomalous results when these parameters are not tightly constrained.

INTRODUCTION

Geophysical techniques have been used for the non-destructive testing of stone materials for some time. The International Society of Rock Mechanics

Processes of Urban Stone Decay. Edited by B.J. Smith and P.A. Warke. © 1996 Donhead Publishing Ltd.

(Rummel and Van Jeerden, 1977) outlined a suggested method for the collection of geomechanical moduli using such small strain geophysical techniques. One of the most common methods, however, examines relationships between material properties and the time taken for seismic waves to pass through the material. Two different types of seismic waves have been used in these studies; primary (P, or compressional) waves and secondary (S, or shear) waves. P waves exhibit the highest velocities and propagate from the source by a series of compressions and dilations, with particle motion parallel to the direction of wave travel. S waves are somewhat slower, and have particle vibrations perpendicular to the direction of wave propagation. The speed of wave travel is controlled by fundamental material properties shown in equations 1 and 2.

$$\mathbf{V_p} = \sqrt{\frac{k \mid 4/3\mu}{\rho}}$$

(1)

and,

$$\mathbf{V_s} = \sqrt{\frac{\mu}{\rho}}$$

(2)

where V_p and V_s are the P and S wave velocities respectively, k is the compressibility, μ is the shear modulus and ρ is the material density. As these waves travel through the body of the stone, the direction of wave travel can be altered as a result of refraction, but more importantly in this case, by reflection from subsurface micro-cracks, fractures, grain boundaries and the sample free surface. Further details of seismic wave propagation can be found in any standard text on seismology (e.g. Bullen and Bolt, 1985).

Whilst the use of ultrasonic techniques has existed in the fields of engineering geology, rock mechanics and seismology for some time, application of such techniques to studies of weathering did not occur until the late 1980s. Allison (1988, 1990) used acoustic velocity measurements to monitor weathering during environmental cabinet experiments and, more recently, Esbert, et al., (1994) used ultrasonic methods to investigate the decay of granite in Spain. The theory behind these techniques is simple; since weathering results in the degradation of the material properties which control P and S wave velocity, increased weathering will reduce the acoustic velocity of the stone. This is especially true of limestones where solution changes pore characteristics.

VARIATION OF ACOUSTIC VELOCITY IN WEATHERED STONE

Stone degradation involves alteration of the structure of the stone, the magnitude and nature of which depends on the agents of weathering. Where weathering agents, such as salt, migrate into the pore structure and cracks in the stone and cause disruption, the internal coherence of the stone is altered. Acoustic waves travel through and along this internal framework and any alteration influences the manner and rate at which the waves pass through the stone. Breakdown of the pore structure or replacement of the stone with a less dense material such as salt, decreases the velocity of V_p, increasing the frequency with which relatively high travel times are recorded. Similarly, the velocity of V_s increases because these waves are transmitted more effectively across pore spaces filled with a crystalline material. A detailed study of the detection of stone alteration under simulated salt weathering (0.5M NaCl and 0.25M Na_2SO_4) and dissolution by acid rainfall simulations using acoustic velocity measurements suggests that such changes occur upon weathering (Inkpen and Murphy, 1995). Detecting such changes, however, is limited by the accuracy of measurements and the elimination of possible sources of error.

TEST PROCEDURE AND VARIATION IN RESULTS

To monitor changes in building stones which result from weathering it is necessary to eliminate possible sources of error which could mask weathering effects. To eliminate error and hence to guarantee that variations in V_p and V_s are only influenced by weathering effects, five main parameters were investigated.

(1) Variability in P and S wave velocity in the same sample.
(2) Variability in P and S wave velocity in different samples from the same block of rock.
(3) Effects of coupling pressure on the precision of velocity determinations.
(4) Effects of sample length:height ratio in determination of instrumental error.
(5) Effects of changing moisture content on P and S wave velocities.

The equipment used to measure P and S wave velocities is shown in Figure 18.1. This consists of a load frame, two 200 MHz P and S wave transducers, a Portable Ultrasonic Non-destructive Digital Indicating Tester (PUNDIT) and a Cathode Ray Oscilloscope (CRO). Occasional use was made of 250 kHz P and S wave transducers, but repeatability of results was better using the higher frequency equipment.

Intra-sample variation

The variability of measurements on the same sample is a fundamental check on the repeatability of the test. Table 18.1 shows the mean, standard deviation, coefficient of variation and the sample size for tests carried out on the

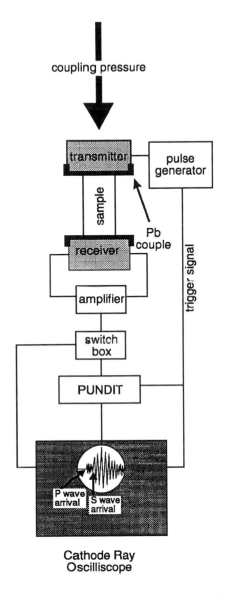

coupling pressure

transmitter

pulse generator

sample

Pb couple

receiver

trigger signal

amplifier

switch box

PUNDIT

P wave arrival   S wave arrival

Cathode Ray
Oscilliscope

Figure 18.1 Equipment used for measurement of P and S wave velocities.

same sample. The sample was loaded into the frame, coupling pressure applied and four readings taken, i.e. V_s CRO, V_s PUNDIT, V_p CRO and V_p PUNDIT. The sample was loaded and then unloaded from the test frame after testing and this procedure was repeated 40 times to determine the extent of intra-sample variations.

	S wave velocity (kms^{-1})		P wave velocity (kms^{-1})	
PARAMETER	CRO	PUNDIT	CRO	PUNDIT
Maximum	2.49	2.31	4.36	4.36
Minimum	2.37	1.98	4.21	4.32
Range	0.12	0.33	0.15	0.04
Mean	2.45	2.05	4.28	4.32
Standard deviation	0.02	0.01	0.06	0.01
N	40	40	40	40
C of V	0.82%	0.49%	1.40%	0.23%

Table 18.1 Statistical variation from multiple tests on the same sample.

Figures 18.2–18.5 show histograms for V_p and V_s as determined by the CRO and PUNDIT respectively. The range over which variation occurs in Figures 18.2, 18.3 and 18.5 is relatively small by comparison to that shown in Figure 18.4. This plot clearly shows a bimodal distribution within a range of S wave velocities clustered around 2.0 kms^{-1} with another set of data separated from the first by approximately 0.22 kms^{-1} and accounting for 10–15% of the measured results.

An outlier of data can also be seen on measurements of V_p made using the PUNDIT (Figure 18.4). The data collected using the CRO showed a much sharper and narrower distribution especially for P wave values (Figure 18.3) with a larger scatter for S wave values (Figure 18.5). The larger scatter of V_s measurements using the CRO are attributed to difficulties in determining the S wave arrival. Results indicate that determination of V_s by automatic detection systems showed the greatest error.

The coefficients of variation are all below 1.5% of the mean suggesting a very peaked distribution of the data which indicates that most readings are close to the mean value. The data does suggest, however, that repeatability of readings from the same sample is enhanced if operator judgement is exercised rather than just using the automated reading.

Inter-sample variation

Inter-sample variability was assessed by comparing all types of readings from samples cut from the same sample block of Portland limestone. Figures 18.6–18.9 and Table 18.2 show the histograms of frequency of read-

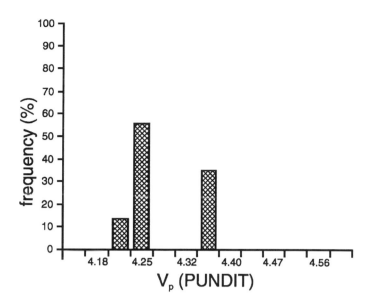

Figure 18.2 Frequency distribution of V_p determined from the PUNDIT.

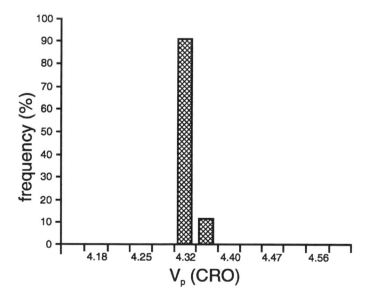

Figure 18.3 Frequency distribution of V_p determined from the CRO.

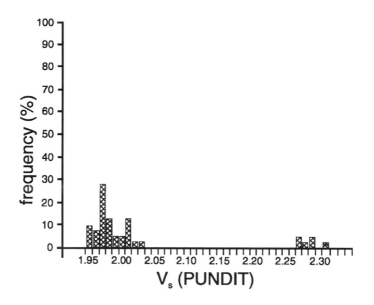

Figure 18.4 Frequency distribution of V_S determined from the PUNDIT.

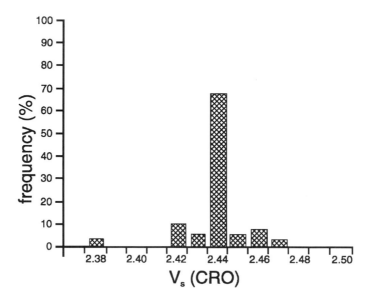

Figure 18.5 Frequency distribution of V_S determined from the CRO.

ings between the samples and statistical analysis of these data respectively. Most of the values are clustered close to the mean with the coefficient of variation being highest for PUNDIT as opposed to CRO readings. Although the data are slightly more variable than for repeated readings made on an individual sample their coefficients of variation are only 0.5 to 1.0% higher implying a relatively low scatter of values. These data suggest that different samples tend to give similar readings but that the degree of variability changes with the method of velocity measurement used.

	S wave velocity (kms^{-1})		P wave velocity (kms^{-1})	
PARAMETER	CRO	PUNDIT	CRO	PUNDIT
Maximum	2.57	2.33	4.43	4.55
Minimum	2.46	1.93	4.22	4.18
Range	0.11	0.39	0.21	0.37
Mean	2.53	2.03	4.32	4.31
Standard deviation	0.02	0.05	0.04	0.06
N	63	63	63	63
C of V	0.79%	2.46%	0.93%	1.39%

Table 18.2 Descriptive statistics for acoustic velocity measurements on multiple samples.

Sample geometry

One of the main aims of this study is to assess whether V_p and V_s can be used to predict the durability and strength of stone. However, the sample geometry for rock mechanics testing (in this case triaxial testing) is tightly constrained due to edge and end effects (Vogler and Kovari, 1977). The suggested method for determining the compressive strength of rocks under triaxial stress conditions recommended that sample geometry should be 2:1 (length:breadth). Hence, given that a clear advantage of this group of techniques is to remove inter-sample variability, triaxial tests should be carried out on samples upon which V_p and V_s have been measured. Figure 18.10 shows that for P waves, at sample lengths greater than 48 mm (keeping a 25 mm diameter core breadth) the P wave arrival should be measured using the CRO. However, this is further complicated by the increased attenuation of

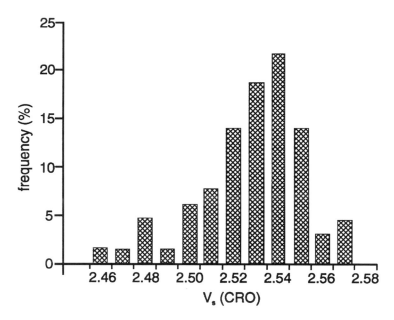

Figure 18.6 Distribution of V_S measurements made using the CRO.

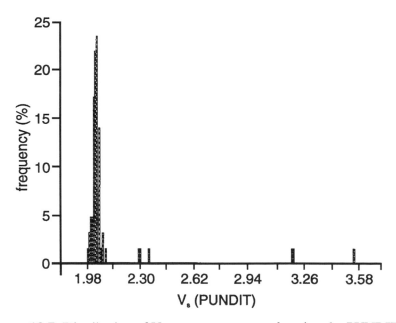

Figure 18.7 Distribution of V_S measurements made using the PUNDIT.

236

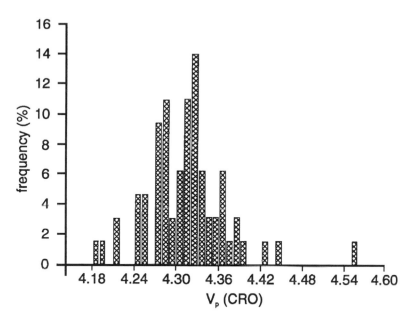

Figure 18.8 Distribution of V_p measurements made using the CRO.

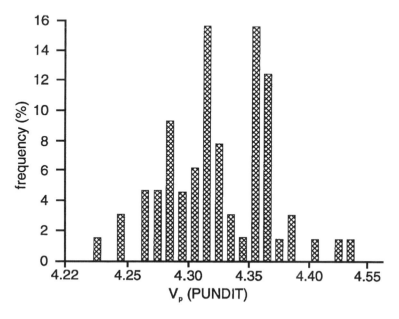

Figure 18.9 Distribution of V_p measurements made using the PUNDIT.

the signal at longer core lengths for these high frequency waveforms and in practice the P wave arrival determined by the PUNDIT was always used since the core lengths were normally within the range of 49.5–50.5 mm. The S wave arrival times shown in Figure 18.10, suggest that above sample lengths of the order of 24 mm the CRO should be used in order to differentiate between the S wave arrival, and the P wave reflected from the free surface of the sample (Pp) wave arrival time.

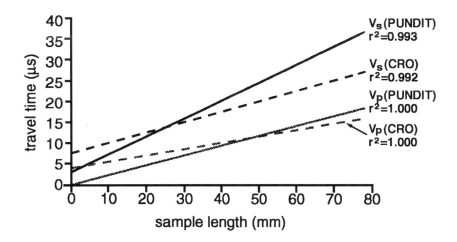

Figure 18.10 The effect of sample length (with a standard diameter) on P and S wave travel times.

Moisture content

In order to investigate the effects of moisture content on V_p and V_s, samples were saturated for 24 hours. One sample was placed between the transducers and readings of V_s and V_p were taken at half-hourly intervals. Additional saturated samples were stored alongside the compression frame and allowed to dry under the same ambient conditions. Every time a reading was taken, the moisture content was determined from one of the adjacent samples. It was found that samples dried very quickly under laboratory conditions. Even though the ends of the sample may not dry out during the experiment this will not dramatically influence acoustic velocities as these waves pass through the whole body of the rock rather than just the ends. It is the moisture condition of the whole sample rather than any small portion of it that determines travel time.

The results of this investigation are summarised in Figure 18.11. Visual analysis of the data (Figures 18.12 and 18.13) suggest that V_p is not influenced by moisture content in any simple linear fashion. The relationship between moisture content and V_p and V_s was investigated using linear regression analysis (Table 18.3). Whilst moisture content appears to affect the velocity of V_s (as moisture content increases V_s decreases), V_p does not appear to be influenced. Figure 18.12, however, suggests that a curvilinear relationship may exist between the two variables.

The results shown in Table 18.3 have implications for the investigation of weathered rocks under field conditions, namely that monitoring of

Regression output	P wave (PUNDIT)	S wave (PUNDIT)	P wave (CRO)	S wave (CRO)
X coefficient	-0.00	-0.01	0.00	-0.01
Constant	4.12	1.97	4.24	2.42
r^2	0.02	0.74	0.06	0.76
N	19	19	19	19
Standard errors:				
Coefficient	0.01	0.00	0.00	0.00
Y estimate	0.10	0.01	0.01	0.01

Table 18.3 Results of regression analysis using moisture content as the independent variable against P and S wave velocities measured on both the PUNDIT and the CRO.

acoustic velocities should be performed under standardised moisture conditions where possible to reduce the influence on V_s. This specification was incorporated into the experimental design used by Inkpen and Murphy (1995). The magnitudes of the changes in velocities of 0.1 kms^{-1} for both V_p and V_s are not as great as the changes exhibited by samples upon weathering, which were up to 65% of the original velocities. This implies that the technique could be used in the field to determine degradation although errors due to differences in moisture content would have to be considered in any analysis. The relationship between moisture content and V_p, however,

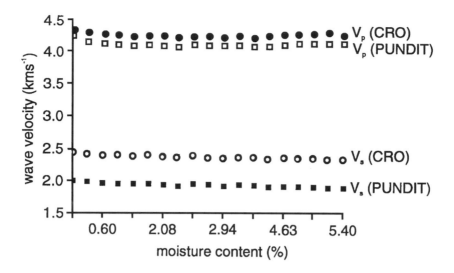

Figure 18.11 V_p and V_s measured at different moisture contents.

requires more detailed analysis before any comprehensive field requirements can be made.

Pressure

If it is necessary to load a sample in order to achieve an effective acoustic
couple between the transducer and the material under investigation, a sample which has been intensely weathered may fail at low pressures (e.g. 5–10
MPa). In order to determine an optimal range of pressures for obtaining
readings of sonic velocity in weathered stone, readings were taken under
several pressure conditions as shown in Figure 18.14. Two broad observations can be made;

(1) P and S wave readings made from the CRO were insensitive to coupling pressure.

(2) A marked increase occurred in both P and S wave travel times as determined by the automatic detection system on the PUNDIT. For the P
wave, this increase is most marked between 1 and 1.5 MPa, with a
gradual increase thereafter until a pressure of 4 MPa is reached at
which point V_p measurements stabilise. For the S wave, a generally
linear relationship between coupling pressure and V_s is separated by a
marked jump between 3 and 4 MPa.

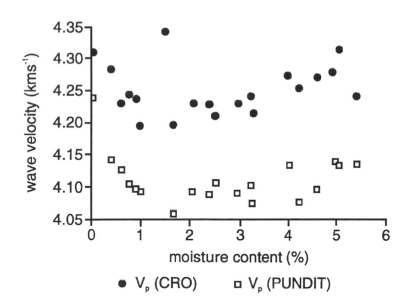

Figure 18.12 V_p measured at different moisture contents (no regression line is shown because r^2 was so low (0.0–0.1).

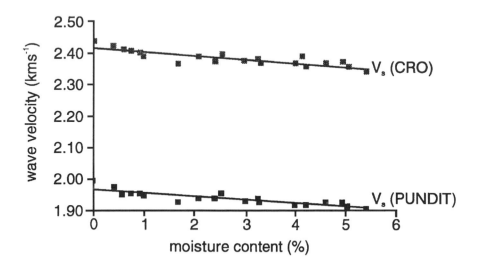

Figure 18.13 V_s measured at different moisture contents with regression lines (for fit details see text).

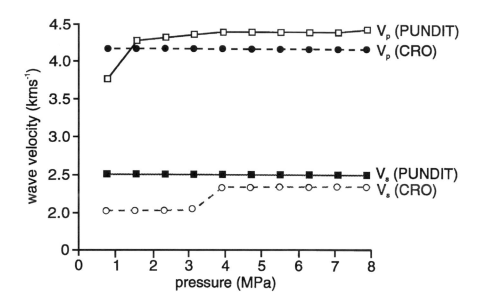

Figure 18.14 The effect of coupling pressure on the measurement of V_p and V_s.

It is unlikely that the low pressures used in testing these unweathered samples were causing non-recoverable strain. Such an hypothesis is supported by the absence of a similar discrepancy in the travel times determined using the CRO. A closer consideration of the waveform on the CRO suggests one possible explanation. There is an increase in wave amplitude with increasing coupling pressure. Therefore it seems likely that a reflected wave phase (most likely the Pp reflected wave) is arriving at the detector before the slower S wave. Calculations of P wave arrival times, based on a point source with an origin in the centre of the top of a sample, with reflection of the wave from the middle of the free surface then to the middle of the sample base, tends to support this hypothesis with the reflected P wave arriving approximately 0.93 µs before the direct S wave. Hence with high amplitude waves, the Pp reflection may trigger automatic detection systems before the S wave. In more weathered rocks, the initiation of large (on a single sample scale) fractures are likely to provide a reflector, or potentially a number of reflectors, which may produce a complex pattern of particle motions resulting in an anomalous estimate of V_s from an automatic detection system. This observation also accounts for the anomalous outlier of data shown in Figure 18.4.

DISCUSSION AND CONCLUSIONS

The use of P and S wave velocities and travel times is a useful technique for the non-destructive assessment of stone. However, the technique needs to be clarified so that inherent errors are not generated in the measurement of V_p and V_s, which may mask the effects of weathering at low intensities. Of the parameters investigated in this paper the most important to control are pressure, sample geometry and, in the case of V_s, moisture content. These conclusions can be summarised as shown below:

(1) The pressure used to ensure an effective acoustic couple does not influence V_p and V_s. Variation will alter the amplitude of the seismic waves arriving at the detector. This has the effect of making the interpretation of S wave train difficult, and may fool automatic detection systems into recording an incorrect S wave arrival.

(2) Moisture content appears to have no effect on V_p, but V_s decreases as moisture content increases.

(3) Sample length:width ratio affects automatic detection systems due to reflected waves from the free sample surface.

Therefore, on the basis of these findings it is recommended that;

(1) Measurements of P and S wave velocities should be carried out at a constant pressure to ensure consistent interpretation of results.

(2) Interpretation of V_s is aided by using samples which are wider than they are long. This ensures that the S wave arrives at the detector in advance of the reflected P (Pp) wave. If this is not possible a CRO should be used to constrain the results.

In summary, the direct measurement of P and S wave velocities is a useful method of determining the geomechanical characteristics of rock materials. Initial research shows that this technique can discriminate between different degrees of weathering. The advantage of the technique is that it allows the repeated testing of the same sample thereby reducing the effects of inter-sample variability which, even within the space of a single block of stone, shows significant variations in V_p and V_s.

Acknowledgements

This research was carried out with the financial support of Her Majesty's Inspectorate of Pollution (research contract: HMIP/CPR2/41/1/134). The technical assistance of Geoff Long and Wes Hart of The University of Portsmouth is gratefully acknowledged. We would also like to acknowledge the assistance of Independent Quarries in the selection and provision of Portland stone samples.

References

Allison, R.J. (1988) A non-destructive method of determining rock strength. *Earth Surface Processes and Landforms* **13**: 729–736.

Allison, R.J. (1990) Developments in a non-destructive method of determining rock strength. *Earth Surface Processes and Landforms* **15**: 571–577.

Bullen, K.E. and Bolt, B. (1985) *An Introduction to the Theory of Seismology* (4th Edn). Cambridge University Press, Cambridge.

Esbert, R.M., Perez-Ortiz, A., Ordaz, A. and Alonso, F.J. (1994) Intrinsic factors influencing the decay of granite as a building stone. In R. Oliveira, L.F. Rodrigues, A.G. Coehlo and A.P. Cunha, (eds) *Proceedings of the 7th International Congress of the International Association of Engineering Geologists*, 5–9, September, Lisbon, pp. 3659–3665.

Inkpen, R.J. and Murphy, W. (1995) *Stone weathering: the alteration of geotechnical properties and the memory effect.* Unpublished report to Her Majesty's Inspectorate of Pollution, Department of the Environment.

Rummel, F. and Van Jeerden, W. L. (1977) Suggested method for determining sound velocity. In E.T. Brown, (ed.) *Rock Characterization, Testing and Monitoring* (Commission on testing methods, International Society of Rock Mechanics). Pergammon Press, Oxford, pp. 105–110.

Vogler, U.W. and Kovari, K. (1977) Suggested methods for determining the strength of rock materials in triaxial compression. In E.T. Brown, (ed.) *Rock Characterization, Testing and Monitoring* (Commission on testing methods, International Society of Rock Mechanics). Pergammon Press, Oxford, pp. 123–127.

Contact address
Department of Geology
The University of Portsmouth
The Burnaby Building
Burnaby Road
Portsmouth PO1 3QL
United Kingdom

SECTION THREE

ANALYSIS AND APPLICATION

(B) Conservation Practice

19 English Heritage's current building conservation research

J. FIDLER

INTRODUCTION

Research into the decay and treatment of historic building materials is the province of the Archaeological Conservation Branch within English Heritage. Currently within the organisation's Science and Conservation Services Division, Research and Professional Services Group, the team of fourteen staff are soon to move to the external programmes side of the establishment, in Conservation Group's Policy and Research Division upon re-organisation of all central technical services.

Its extensive programme of scientific testing and development, now worth more than £0.5 million per year, is organised through agreements and contracts with over fifteen national and international groups of collaborators consultants and contractors and indirectly employs more than thirty specialists on eighteen projects in the service of better building conservation.

Most of the projects are of two to five years duration and involve substantial programmes of monitoring and testing to establish scientific facts. A short description of current work is set out below and a longer report has recently been published in a special supplement to the winter/spring edition of English Heritage's Conservation Bulletin. Unless stated specifically in the text, there are no official published outputs available from research yet. But all the work will be published when tests are complete and the results are finalised.

AC1 Mortars (Smeaton Project)

This research is investigating factors affecting the properties of lime-based mortars used in conservation and the results of the first of three phases of the

Processes of Urban Stone Decay. Edited by B.J. Smith and P.A. Warke. © 1996 Donhead Publishing Ltd.

project have just been published (1). The initial work was designed by collaboration between English Heritage, ICCROM in Rome and Bournemouth University's Department of Conservation Sciences, with all the testing executed by the Building Research Establishment (BRE).

AC2 Masonry consolidants

We are currently writing the conclusions of a unique long-term field review of the 'Brethane' alkoxysilane consolidant trials on English Heritage's and other historic estates. We are also now attempting to establish innovative laboratory-based methods for provoking exactly *where* and *in what* condition residual consolidating material remains in weathering subject stone to tackle the question of retreatment. Again the consultant is the Building Research Establishment.

AC3 Floor wear and tile pavement decay

This work, again by BRE, seeks to find ways of measuring the rate of wear and decay in historic floors, especially of medieval encaustic tile pavements. It is also concerned to define decay mechanisms and find ways of ameliorating their effects: externally on ruin sites and internally in heavily trafficked buildings. With this in mind, we have appointed a ceramics conservator, Sandra Davison, to work with BRE on several aspects of the project.

AC5 Polishable limestone decay

Decay in Purbeck marble and other stones is being monitored by us and the BRE at several cathedral sites and laboratory testing is also helping us to understand the causes and processes involved.

AC6 Sandstone decay

This programme is seeking to define and explain the decay systems in sandstones with a view to preparing appropriate treaments. A literature review and decay survey mapping system will be published as a culmination to the first phase of the work.

AC7 Anti-graffiti barriers

This research by BRE is assessing whether wax-based anti-graffiti barriers, and their regular removal and re-application, can be recommended for use to protect friable historic masonry.

AC8 Structural fire protection

In Phase 1, Warrington Fire Research Consultancy has established the performance of historic panelled timber doors and their upgrading in fire and the results will be published later in 1995. Other outputs will include advice on fire engineering principles and a model fire safety manual.

AC9 Lime and lime treatments

This project commissioned from the Department of Conservation Science at Bournemouth University is seeking to characterise all currently available building limes for publication in a directory. The second stage will look at lime treatments (lime watering, lime repairs and lime shelter coating) and their effectiveness, following on the work of Dr C. Price when he was at the Building Research Establishment (2).

AC10 Underside lead corrosion

We have a long-term programme to determine the key parameters affecting underside lead sheet corrosion in historic roofing, with scientific activities marshalled by Dr Bill Bordass and Rowan Technology Ltd as consultant corrosion engineers. We are collaborating with other researchers from the Lead Sheet Roofing Association, with the zinc roofing industry and with BRE Scotlab and the National Trust (that has been running a CASE studentship at the Interface Analysis Centre at Bristol University) and are about to publish a state-of-the-art summary of progress. We are also heading towards the patenting of one particular solution to lead corrosion.

AC11 Timber decay and moisture ingress

This project completed its third and final stage in 1993/4, assessing the inter-relationships between environment, fungi and beetles in cathedral roof spaces with special respect to moisture ingress. The results are to be assembled in a book to be launched in the winter of 1995 by SPONS Publishers and we have arranged a partnership with Historic Scotland to sponsor the programme and a supporting campaign of public awareness.

AC11/12 Woodcare project

In 1994/5, English Heritage was fortunate to be awarded a significant grant from the European Commission DGXII to study the inter-relationships connected with Deathwatch beetles and timber decay in cathedral roofs.

Running over three years in collaboration with University College, Dublin, Birkbeck College, London, the Royal Botanical Gardens at Kew and with TNO–Bouw, Delft, the project is led by Dr Brian Ridout, English Heritage's consultant entomologist. We are already well on the way to understanding as never before the susceptibilities of this supposedly well-known insect.

AC12 Masonry cleaning

This project updates our assessments of currently available masonry cleaning systems so that we can establish policies and guidelines towards them. Our consultant, Nicola Ashurst of Adriel Consultancy, is redrafting the British Standard Code of Practice for the Cleaning and Surface Repair of Buildings (BS CP 6270 Pt. 1: 1982) and has commenced work on a priority list of cleaning problems where additional research might assist in making recommendations to specifiers and practitioners.

AC13 Fire safety in cathedrals

Our consultants from the Warrington Fire Research Consultancy recently completed a two year study of the fire safety provisions in cathedrals, measured in the light of the recommendations in the Bailey Inquiry Report following the fire at Windsor Castle. Their report has been submitted to peer review and final revisions of the text are now being made before publication.

AC14 Terracotta decay and conservation

This project runs over two years and seeks to understand the special sensitivities of architectural terracotta to soiling, decay and treatment; thereby to devise better care for the material. The first phase involves testing methods to assess the cleaning sensitivities of terracotta surfaces and substrates and includes a general literature review on terracotta decay and conservation. The work follows a protocol designed and trialled by Frank Matero at the Architectural Conservation Laboratory at the University of Pennsylvania (3).

AC17 Stained glass

This two and a half year project in three phases seeks to discover the factors affecting the durability of mastics, lead cames and Paraloid B72 adhesive in stained glass repair and conservation.

AC21 Mosaic clad concrete

This project, in the early development stage, will bring together a team of building pathologists from Bickerdike Allen and Partners of London and mosaic conservators from the Victoria and Albert Museum to elucidate how and why glass mosaic cladding decays on modern concrete buildings. The work brings into the public domain much work done in the 1970s and 80s.

AC23 Stone slate roofing

Our work here is concerned with the technical and economic issues surrounding the decline in the production of non-metamorphic fissile stone roofing tiles and flags, e.g. Cotswold and Collyweston tiles, etc. and the northern sandstone/gritstone flags. The first part, attempting to establish durability and appearance criterion for non-metamorphic slates/tiles is being undertaken by BRE, whilst the latter socio-economic exercise is co-sponsored by Derbyshire County Council and the Peak Park Planning Board and is being executed by Terry Hughes, a quarrying specialist.

AC204 National sand and aggregates library

Undertaken originally as a student intern's exercise, this project has developed a national reference collection of sands and aggregates for building mortars for English Heritage.

AC207 Earthen structures

This study has fostered research and other technical studies in the decay and conservation of earthen architecture. We helped to set up the Earth Structures Committee of the International Council on Monuments and Sites. We also encouraged the establishment of the National Centre for Earthen Architecture at the School of Architecture at Plymouth University and, through advice with others to the University's architecture and material science departments, enabled the centre to win several university research fellowships (4).

CONCLUSION

Because of limitations on our resources, we are unfortunately not able to discuss our current findings in detail on a one to one basis until the work is complete. Technical advice to local authorities and to historic building owners and their professional advisers remains the responsibility of the regional teams in our Conservation Group and their technical policy stance to material recipes and practice remains unchanged until research findings are ultimately debated and corporate advice is announced.

NOTES TO THE TEXT

(1)   See Tentonico, J.M., McCraig, I., Burns, C. and Ashurst, J. (1994) 'The Smeaton Project: factors affecting the properties of lime-based mortars'. *Bulletin of the Association for Preservation Technology* (ATP). Albany, NY, USA. September 1994. Offprints are available from English Heritage, [Architectural Conservation Branch, Room 528, 429 Oxford Street, London] price £10.00 including post and packing.

(2)   No scientific proof has been found for the evidence of surface consolidation of friable stonework often reported by experienced conservators. See Price, C., Ross, K. and White, O. (1988) 'Further Appraisal of the Lime technique for Limestone Consolidation, Using a Radio-active Tract'. *Studies in Conservation* **33**: 178–186.

(3)   The work was presented at a national Architectural Ceramics Conference, set up by English Heritage and the United Kingdom Institute for Conservation held at the Ironbridge Institute at Telford, Shropshire in September. Proceedings from this event will be published shortly.

(4)   Outputs include published proceedings from a conference on the Conservation of Earthern Architecture at Dartington Hall, Devon [available from Plymouth University] and the creation of a national travelling exhibition called 'OUT OF EARTH', held at English Heritage.

Contact address
English Heritage
429 Oxford Street
London
W1R 2HD
United Kingdom

20 A basis for evaluating the durability of new building stone

A.P. DUFFY and P.F. O'BRIEN

ABSTRACT

There is currently considerable controversy surrounding stone durability tests which have now lost much credibility in the building industry; these tests are questionable in their applicability and usefulness. This paper proposes a new approach to assessing the durability of stone which is based on laboratory testing and design methodology. It stresses that stone durability is not an absolute property, but depends on the conditions to which a stone is exposed. A design methodology based on inferring the surface environments which exist on a building is outlined; laboratory tests are then used to measure the durability of a stone in different surface environments. Such a combined methodology allows a designer to choose stone types which are most suitable for different areas of a building, or to redetail a façade to minimize the incidence of adverse surface environments.

INTRODUCTION

Stone, as a building material, has undergone a renaissance in use since the late 1970s. For a period of twenty years or so before this, concrete was the standard external building finish. To some extent the rebirth is linked to a disillusionment with concrete as an external cladding material, both on aesthetic and durability grounds. Indeed, the return to stone is partially the result of its lasting and dependable image and metaphors such as 'carved in stone' attest to this general perception of durability. Stone has not, however, entirely lived up to this reputation. Designers have become concerned due

Processes of Urban Stone Decay. Edited by B.J. Smith and P.A. Warke. © 1996 Donhead Publishing Ltd.

to reports of physical failure, such as the bowing of cladding and aesthetic problems, such as iron staining or biological colonisation. Some of these problems are closely linked to modern design practices – the use of thin cladding being a prime example. Related to this is the fact that stone, as an external cladding material, seems to have missed out on much of the durability and design research conferred on other, more modern, materials.

Because of these problems, there is currently a degree of concern in the building industry regarding stone durability and, in particular, the validity of current stone durability and characterisation tests. Accelerated weathering tests, such as the salt crystallisation test (which was developed as a substitute for freeze/thaw testing – Evans, 1970) are regarded as having no bearing on real-life situations and tests which characterise a stone, such as those which determine pore size distribution or flexural strength, are not seen to be related in any obvious way to the material's future performance. Although there are some tests and parameters which are useful in assessing stone durability, such as the solubility and saturation coefficient, their usefulness is diminished because there is often little confidence in the tests within the industry. The fact is that designers either distrust tests or do not know how to apply their results.

For these reasons, a new approach to the assessment of stone durability is required which is practical, related to real-life conditions and which has the backing of those in the construction industry who deal with stone. This paper attempts to summarise the requirements of such a system for evaluating stone durability and proposes a combined laboratory- and design-based approach to the problem.

WHAT IS STONE DURABILITY?

For the purposes of this paper, the concept of stone durability is based on the requirements of the material as perceived by the building industry, designers (primarily architects and engineers, to a lesser extent quantity surveyors and specialist contractors) and stone suppliers. The fundamental requirement of any designer or supplier is that they can be confident that the material they specify or supply will perform adequately. Therefore, durability should, in some way, be based on predicting the future 'performance' of a stone.

The concept of 'performance' is different for architects, engineers and the other groups mentioned above; however, one common definition is that the stone sufficiently maintain its physical, mechanical and aesthetic integrity for a reasonable period of time – say at least for the design life of the building, approximately fifty years. Therefore, stone durability evaluation should be concerned with assessing how resistant a stone is to changes of its physical, mechanical and aesthetic properties over time. But before developing an acceptable evaluation system we must first understand what factors lead to changes in physical, mechanical or aesthetic properties; these changes are referred to as stone 'decay'.

THE CAUSES OF STONE DECAY

The fundamental causes of building stone decay can be deduced by observing decay patterns on buildings. By examining a variety of stone buildings, it can be seen that different stone types exhibit different visual forms of decay. For example, calcareous sandstones often exhibit granulation and irregular flaking, whereas oolitic limestones might display uniform delamination of a perfectly intact surface two millimetres or so in depth. Hence, it can be postulated that stone decay is in some way caused by an adverse environment acting on the different material properties of different stone types.

However, it can also be seen that façades constructed of the same stone type throughout are subject to various decay forms. Thus, because the material properties of the building stone can be assumed to be more or less uniform over the façade, the existence of different visual decay types must be attributed to the presence of spatially variable environmental stresses. These different stresses are often referred to as 'micro-environments'; this term, however, implies a discrete environment which exists outside or above the surface of the stone where the decay occurs. The term 'surface environment' is more appropriate for describing a stress which is related to surface and sub-surface decay phenomena. 'Surface environments' thus refers to the conditions on and below a stone's surface which influence the manner in which it decays. These conditions include: moisture content, chemistry and movement (these being the most important as water drives almost all decay processes); dry gaseous and particulate chemistry and temperature.

In summary, stone decay is a product both of the material properties of the stone and of the surface environment to which it is exposed. For example, the dissolution of Portland limestone is the result of large amounts of water movement in a surface environment and the relatively high solubility of the component minerals (sparite, micrite, calcite). The salt-induced decay of granite is conversely related to the quantities of calcium and sulphate ions deposited in the surface water film and the degree of microporosity of the stone.

Thus, the evaluation of the durability of stone in any building should be based on predicting what future surface environments will be present and how the physical, mechanical and aesthetic properties of the stone will be affected by these conditions.

THE BASIS FOR STONE DURABILITY TESTING

The durability of any stone is not, as traditionally viewed, an absolute or inherent property, but is rather a function of the material characteristics of the stone and the surface environment to which it is exposed. So for any particular stone there might exist a variety of durabilities, these depending on the surface environment to which it is subject. For example, granite is extremely durable in situations of high surface water flow, but can decay severely in areas subject to high salt concentrations and low moisture content. Conversely, oolitic limestones are not durable in heavily wetted areas but are relatively resistant to damage by salt crystallisation in dry surface environments.

Thus, the evaluation of the durability of a building stone must first be based on determining the surface environments which the stone will encounter; information about the durability of different building stones in each surface environment can then be used to choose the most durable stone or stones for the task. This system requires both the development of a methodology for determining surface environments on buildings and a system of durability tests which simulate accelerated weathering due to these environments. Two possible design- and laboratory-based methodologies are briefly developed below.

PREDICTING SURFACE ENVIRONMENTS

It might seem strange to suggest that surface environments on new buildings can be determined at the design stage, given that the measurement of surface environments on existing buildings is generally held to be difficult, if not impossible. It is possible, however, to determine many aspects of a building's surface environment in a qualitative sense; for example surface moisture content might be measured as high, medium or low, each division having an upper and lower quantitative threshold.

The most important characteristics of a surface environment with regard to stone decay are: the amount of water present, water movement, water chemistry, dry deposition of gases, dry deposition of particulate material and temperature. Of these, it is possible to qualitatively determine surface moisture and temperature characteristics. The types and concentrations of dry deposited gases and particles are difficult to determine and, in any event, are not important unless activated by the presence of water (in which case they are covered by the surface environment moisture chemistry parameter).

Surface environment moisture content and movement can be resolved with a knowledge of prevailing wind directions, the geometry (or architecture) of the building and the porosity of the building material, in a manner similar to that developed for concrete (Beijer, 1977). Surface environment salt content can also be qualitatively determined with a knowledge of water movement and the solubility of the substrate so that areas where salt deposition and damage might be a problem can be identified. Finally, the acidity of the surface water film can be inferred from whether it is static or dynamic – thin, static water films can become highly acidic.

The temperature of different areas of a façade can be broadly categorized from information on ambient temperatures, radiant energy and the orientation and geometry of the exterior of the building.

Such a surface environment prediction methodology would allow the designer to determine the conditions encountered by different areas of a building. The durability of the proposed stone in these inferred qualitative

surface environments can then be assessed with the aid of laboratory tests
(for less well known stone types), or standard data sheets (for commonly
used stone). Figures 20.1–20.3 depict typical surface environments on a
façade.

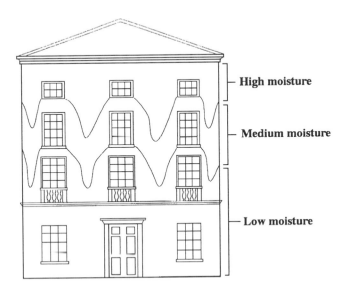

Figure 20.1 Inferred moisture regime on a typical historic building façade.
The upper 25% of the façade receives 60% of the driving rain (Beijer, 1977),
and therefore this area has the greatest washing. The effect of projections
such as window sills is superimposed on this.

ASSESSING STONE DURABILITY

The assessment of the durability of a building stone is based on predicting
how its physical, mechanical and aesthetic properties are affected in each of
the surface environments identified using the prediction methodology outlined above. Thus, the designer requires data on stone behaviour in each
surface environment. To generate this information, stone needs to be subjected to a series of laboratory tests which simulate different surface
environments. As each new stone type is tested, the designer's data bank
grows and a greater range of stone types and characteristics can be chosen
to meet his or her aesthetic and durability requirements.

Some laboratory tests which could be used to determine the behaviour
of a stone in various surface environments are outlined in Table 20.1. For
example, stone likely to be subjected to flowing water should be resistant to
dissolution. This can be determined by solubility tests in the laboratory or
by exposure under real conditions in a micro-catchment unit (O'Brien, *et al.*,

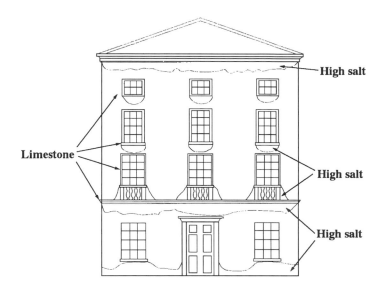

Figure 20.2 Inferred salt regime on the same façade as depicted in Figure 20.1 composed of granite ashlar with soluble limestone window surrounds and decorative features such as string courses.

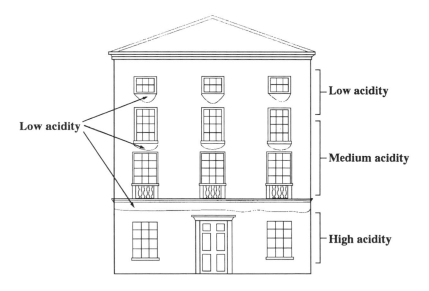

Figure 20.3 Inferred surface acidity on the same façade.

1992, 1995; Cooper, *et al.*, 1992). This list is by no means exhaustive and the selection of appropriate tests for assessing durability in different surface environments is a task that requires concerted research effort.

Surface environment	Decay process	Parameter	Measurement method
Flow	Dissolution	Solubility	Micro-catchments
Low/high			Laboratory tests
Water content	Freeze/thaw	Susceptibility to freeze/thaw	Freeze/thaw tests
High/low			Saturation coefficient
Salt loading	Salt crystallisation	Salt crystallisation disruption	BRE crystallisation test
High/low	Salt hydration/ dehydration		Saturation coefficient
	Differential thermal expansion		Pore structure
			Water absorption
			Water uptake
Acidity	Dissolution	Acid solubility	Laboratory tests
High/low			
Temperature	Differential thermal expansion	Susceptibility to differential thermal expansion	Thermal cycling
High/low	Freeze/thaw		Freeze/thaw cycling

Table 20.1 Laboratory and field tests which can be employed to measure durability of a stone exposed to different surface environments.

CONCLUSIONS

The current concept of stone durability, which is based on a fragmented and outdated set of laboratory tests, is at best unhelpful and at worst misleading. The durability of any stone is not an absolute measure based on a laboratory test which has no bearing on reality, but depends on the surface environment to which the material is exposed; thus, different stone types have different durabilities when exposed to different surface conditions. This fact must be incorporated both into a new set of durability tests as well as into current design practice.

The fact that stone decays because of the effects of a surface environment on its material properties should be the fundamental premise of any new durability assessment methodology. In this paper, a combined design- and laboratory-based solution to the problem is proposed where designers determine what conditions their building will encounter, and laboratory tests are based on assessing the durability of the stone types under these conditions.

This approach has a number of advantages: designers can confidently choose appropriate stone types for their façade, they can choose different stone types which are more suitable for different areas of each façade (for example, a granite for well-washed areas and a macroporous limestone for an area subject to large amounts of salt crystallisation) and they can redetail façades in such a way that more desirable surface environments are created for the stone type to be used. Such a methodology, if successful and widely accepted within the industry, could be easily extended to the choice, design and detailing of a wide variety of external building materials.

References

Beijer, O. (1977) Concrete Walls and Weathering. In *Symposium on the 'Evaluation of the Performance of External Vertical Surfaces of Buildings'*, RILEM/ASTM/CIB, Otanieme, Espoo, Finland, 28 Aug– 2 September, Volume 1.

Cooper, T.P., O'Brien, P.F. and Jeffrey, D. (1992) Rates of deterioration of Portland limestone in an urban environment. *Studies in Conservation* **37**: 228–238.

Evans I.S. (1970) Salt crystallization and rock weathering: a review. *Révue de Géomorphologie dynamique* **19**: 153–177.

O'Brien, P.F., Bell, E.M., Orr, T.L. and Cooper, T.P. (1995) Stone loss rates at sites around Europe. *The Science of the Total Environment* **167**: 111–121.

O'Brien, P.F., Cooper, T.P. and Jeffery, D. (1992) Measurement of stone decay rates at remote locations using ion exchange resins. *Environmental Technology* **13**: 485–491.

Contact address
Carrig Conservation Engineering Ltd
32 Westland Square
Pearse Street
Dublin 2
Ireland

21 Retreatment of consolidated stone

A. NANDIWADA and C. A. PRICE

ABSTRACT

Attention is drawn to some of the problems that may be encountered when stone is given multiple applications of a consolidant. These problems may be physical, chemical or biological in origin. Current research at the Institute of Archaeology, UCL into the problems associated with consolidants is outlined.

INTRODUCTION

Stone weathering is an all too familiar problem. Cracking, spalling, flaking, powdering, eroding can all cause so much deterioration that eventually some action has to be taken. Usually the answer is straightforward: take the stone out and replace it. Problems arise, however, when the stone is of particular historical importance, or when it has been carved and cannot readily be copied. The sculpture which decorates the exterior of many historic buildings provides a good example. In such cases, it may be preferable to retain the original stone, whilst treating it in some way in order to extend its life.

The search for an effective stone preservative has gone on for more than 2000 years, with little success. However, a significant shift in strategy occurred in the early 1970s, when researchers started to investigate the use of consolidants which penetrated deeply into the stone. Previously, the emphasis had been very much on protective surface coatings, but now the search was on for treatments which would penetrate deeply into the stone, strengthening the decayed stone and binding it firmly to the sound stone beneath.

Processes of Urban Stone Decay. Edited by B.J. Smith and P.A. Warke. © 1996 Donhead Publishing Ltd.

The most promising materials included low-viscosity monomers which would polymerise once they were inside the stone, and of these, the two which have attracted the most attention are methyltrimethoxysilane, $CH_3Si(OCH_3)_3$ (MTMOS) and tetraethoxysilane, $Si(OC_2H_5)_4$ (TEOS). They react with water, which is either added to the formulation or picked up from the surroundings, to form a network polymer within the pore structure of the stone. This serves to strengthen the stone and, maybe, to protect it from further deterioration

The use of MTMOS and TEOS as stone consolidants is sometimes criticised because the process is not reversible. Reversibility is one of the fundamental principles of conservation: nothing should be done to an object unless it can be undone at some future date, if need demands. However, it has become generally recognised that few processes are genuinely reversible in the context of buildings, as opposed to museum objects. Retreatability has come to be accepted as a more realistic goal. In other words, no treatment should be carried out that will bar retreatment at some future date, either with the same material or any other.

It is important to recognise that retreatment may one day become necessary, for no treatment can be expected to last forever. Few would disagree, yet surprisingly little research has been carried out in this area. We therefore face the prospect of treatment upon treatment building up over the years in stonework of unique historical importance, with very little idea of how the treatments may interact with one another.

Two early studies raised the spectre of problems associated with the retreatment of stone that had been consolidated with MTMOS. Price (1981) observed that the second treatment caused temporary softening and swelling, but no detrimental effects in the long-term. Larson (1982) also reported swelling of the first treatment, with consequent disruption of the stone, when using catalysed MTMOS, but reported that no such problems occurred if the catalyst were omitted.

No further work appears to have been reported for some years. Recently, however, two teams have independently announced work in this area. The first is a project funded by the European Union and co-ordinated by Gifford and Partners, Southampton. A major component of the project is the development of procedures that provide an objective assessment of when retreatment is necessary. New materials for retreatment are also being developed (Tilly 1995, pers. comm.). The second team is at the Institute of Archaeology, University College London, whose work is outlined below.

PROBLEMS OF RETREATMENT

The problems that might be encountered in retreatment can be divided into three categories: physical, chemical and biological. Physical problems could include the solvent-induced swelling of the first treatment, or pore-blocking by the first treatment which prevented penetration by the second. Chemical effects could include disruption of the bond between the first treatment and the stone, or undesirable interactions between the two treatments (degradation of the first by the second, or interference by the first with the polymerisation of the second). Biological problems might include attack of the second treatment by micro-organisms which have found a suitable habitat in the treated stone, and which may indeed have brought about the need for retreatment.

RESEARCH AT THE INSTITUTE OF ARCHAEOLOGY

Research is under way to investigate some of the problems associated with consolidant treatments;

Polymer swelling

Attempts are being made to investigate the effects of water, silanes, methanol and ethanol in both liquid and vapour phases. Because of the difficulty of looking inside stone, a film of consolidant is deposited onto a glass slide, which is then exposed to the vapour or immersed in the liquid for a period of three weeks. The consolidants under investigation are MTMOS, TEOS, Wacker H and Wacker OH, the latter two being commercial consolidants supplied by Wacker Chemie, and which are based on MTMOS and TEOS respectively. The behaviour of the film is monitored by weighing and by visual examination.

The procedure is not without criticism, for it is probable that the nature of the polymer and of its bonding to the substrate will be influenced by the nature of the substrate itself. Nonetheless, the experiments do provide a preliminary indication of the susceptibility of the consolidants under one particular set of conditions. Experiments have also been carried out in which lumps of the polymerised silanes are immersed in water and monitored by weighing at regular intervals.

Surprisingly, none of these experiments has so far indicated any effect on the polymer film. However, the lumps of polymerised TEOS and Wacker OH crumbled into small fragments after 7–10 days immersion in water, whereas the lumps of polymerised MTMOS and Wacker H remained intact – due perhaps to their hydrophobicity.

Porosity, depth of penetration and polymer yield

Cubes of limestone and sandstone ($50 \times 50 \times 50$ mm) are being treated with each of the four consolidants by dipping one face into 2 mm of consolidant for a period of two hours. The extent of penetration is observed by the demarcation between wet and dry areas. In case there are spurious edge effects, the specimen is subsequently cut open and an attempt is made to detect the location of the consolidant, using electron-probe micro-analysis.

(Attempts to determine its location by measuring the absorption rate of water droplets proved unsuccessful, due to water repellency induced in the non-consolidated areas by the silane vapour). The porosity of the consolidated stone is determined by vacuum saturation with water, to which a small quantity of surfactant is added to overcome the hydrophobicity of some of the polymers. The polymer yield is calculated as the final weight of the polymer, expressed as a percentage of the initial uptake of liquid.

The whole sequence is then repeated, in order to see whether the first treatment has any influence on the penetration or polymerisation of the second. Preliminary results (Nandiwada, in press) show a significant decrease in porosity following both first and second treatments, and no evidence that the first treatment is inhibiting the penetration of the second.

Effect of ageing

Each of the previous tests has been undertaken as soon as the first treatment reached constant weight. It is possible, however, that the effect of the second treatment will be influenced by ageing of the first. A series of experiments has therefore been planned to investigate this effect. Cubes of sandstone and limestone ($50 \times 50 \times 50$ mm) have been treated with each of the four consolidants. Half have been left indoors, whilst the other half are exposed on the roof of the Institute of Archaeology. Cubes are brought in at six monthly intervals, and retreated. The retreated stone is then examined by optical and scanning electron microscopy, by colour meter, and by measurement of porosity, depth of penetration, abrasion resistance and modulus of rupture. The experiment is also designed to investigate the effect of catalysts in the consolidants: both catalysed and uncatalysed consolidants are being used for the first treatment, and each is being retreated with both uncatalysed and catalysed consolidants.

Depending on the outcome of these experiments, it is hoped to investigate the effect of second treatments on stone removed from monuments that were treated with silanes some fifteen to twenty years ago.

Acknowledgements

The support of the Commonwealth Scholarships Association is gratefully acknowledged.

References

Larson, J.L. (1982) A museum approach to the techniques of stone conservation. In K.L. Gauri and J.A. Gwinn (eds) *Proceedings of the Fourth International Congress on the Deterioration and Preservation of Stone Objects*. The University of Louisville, Louisville, Kentucky, pp.

219–237.

Nandiwada, A. (In press) Retreatment of consolidated stone – a preliminary investigation. *Proceedings of Conference on Conservation Science in the UK,* 18–20 September 1995, Glasgow.

Price, C.A. (1981) *Brethane Stone Preservative.* Current Paper CP1/81. Building Research Establishment, Watford.

Contact address
Institute of Archaeology
University College London
31–34 Gordon Square
London
WC1H 0PY
United Kingdom

22 Defensive conservation: a phased strategy for protecting outdoor stone carvings in the north of Ireland

M.F. FRY and A. MARTIN

ABSTRACT

Properly looking after outdoor stone carvings does not stop with preventing accident, vandalism or theft. Each remains a serious threat, of course, but not the overriding one, which nowadays comes from weathering. The effects of atmospheric stresses have accumulated insidiously over a long period of time, but have accelerated sharply within the last 150 years or so through increased anthropogenic inputs and must be squarely addressed. Protection needs broadening in scope, to confront decay with practical measures for ameliorating its impact upon irreplaceable parts of our heritage; if not on site then off it. This paper examines a radical programme whereby cherished local landmarks (High Crosses) are put into safekeeping and replaced with durable copies. An interim proposal is discussed whereby moulds create three-dimensional records of artefacts illustrating both the speed and seriousness of stone deterioration as a result of weathering.

INTRODUCTION

No matter how much is known about mechanisms of stone decay, and their consequences for vulnerable outdoor carvings (CCHSBM, 1982; Lazzarini and Pieper, 1988), people are poorly prepared for some of the remedies that must follow. The kind of action needed in the foreseeable future to protect field monuments from further weathering is likely to come as a shock, and may seem too radical for many to accept at first. Careful public relations management will be called for in order not to alienate communities, a number of which may find themselves under pressure to allow familiar local

Processes of Urban Stone Decay. Edited by B.J. Smith and P.A. Warke. © 1996 Donhead Publishing Ltd.

landmarks to be taken to places of proper safekeeping and replaced with durable copies.

In the meantime, a less controversial measure might be to make precise full-scale copies of those pieces, particularly High Crosses, which are most at risk. If nothing else, this will at least ensure that a tangible record exists of their present state, before weathering proceeds further. Comparing them with similar copies made in Ireland nearly a century ago will enable some determination of the degree and extent of deterioration since then and perhaps serve to hasten the day when more appropriate steps for preservation could be taken.

BACKGROUND

Field monuments are crucial weapons in the cultural armoury of a country like Ireland, relying heavily upon its past for much of its present income. In Europe and mainland Britain, for example, the ecclesiastically-minded visitor can be guided from one vast medieval cathedral to another. Ireland lacks similar attractions and therefore, relies far more on smaller scale artefacts of its religious history to engender the same interest.

Among the better and more interesting of these artefacts are the carved stone High Crosses (Harbison, 1992, 1994; Richardson and Scarry, 1990), many of which are almost 1000 years old. Some years ago concern was expressed about the current state of preservation of some of these High Crosses (Bourke and Fry, 1989) with consideration given to the possible efficacy of available intervention procedures and suggestions for future treatments.

There is still no magic substance to paint over their surfaces to stop them weathering away, although temporary palliative measures such as the application of a renewable coating to limestone statuary, do exist (Marsh, 1977; Caroe, 1979; Price, 1988; Odgers, 1992; Nimbus Conservation Ltd, 1993). Impregnating them with consolidant remains neither cheap nor foolproof and may, occasionally, create favourable conditions for further deterioration (Warscheid, et al., 1990; Elfving, et al., 1994), although it may be appropriate treatment in selected instances. Brethane (Price, 1981), for example, has been used on a nineteenth Century sandstone coat-of-arms on Scrabo Tower, County Down though it has not as yet been used on older stone carvings in Northern Ireland. Provision of on site shelter may provide another solution to the problem in certain instances, but often the mere suggestion of this raises a whole litany of objections, some quite reasonable, from the above-ground appearance to below-ground disturbance of historic landscapes and graveyards – graveyards being the sites of many High Crosses (Bruno, 1987; Camuffo, 1989). In addition, arguing for removal of the original to a protected site and its replacement with a solid wind- and sun-resistant reproduction, is generally not well received.

Since the article by Bourke and Fry (1989), perhaps the most notable steps towards some form of rational solution have been demonstrated by three separate undertakings. First, and most significant is that in County Offaly where the three Clonmacnois Crosses were moved indoors and replaced in two instances with weather-resistant copies (King, 1992; Harbison, 1994). Second, in County Galway, where the so-called Market Cross at Tuam, a composite structure, has also been moved indoors to a neighbouring cathedral but was not replaced with a copy on the original site (Harbison, 1994). Third, in County Armagh, where three fibre glass copies of the Kilnasaggart Pillar Stone were made for indoor displays in Belfast and Dundalk (Fry and Martin, 1994) (Figures 22.1 and 22.2).

The Kilnasaggart Pillar Stone remains where it has always stood. Meanwhile, for it and those like it that are still exposed, deterioration from

Figure 22.1 The Kilnasaggart Pillar Stone, County Armagh. (Photograph Crown Copyright.)

weathering and associated causes continues and in some cases their survival is threatened. In Northern Ireland during the last decade a cleaning programme aimed at removing lichen from badly affected sandstone monuments, including most of the High Crosses and headless Cross shafts, showed the extent of biological damage (Fry, 1985; Del Monte, 1992). This damage does not include that also related to the effects of gaseous and par-

268

Figure 22.2 The
Kilnasaggart Pillar Stone,
fibreglass copy.

ticulate atmospheric pollutants on limestone (Delopoulou and Sikiotis,
1991; Sikiotis, *et al.*, 1992) and calcareous sandstone (Sabbioni, 1991,
1994).

Despite difficulties in relating identifiable instances of atmosphere-
induced stone damage to specific chemical or physical origins (Livingston,
1991) local air quality, both past and present, is clearly an important factor
in stone decay (Bowler, 1991; Butlin, 1991; Cooper, 1994). Ireland lies well
away from the main industrial zones of Europe and is therefore, relatively
unaffected by their pollutant emissions. However, despite the relatively
good air quality currently experienced in Northern Ireland this has not
always been the case. Government data show that as recently as the mid-
1970s some of the highest smoke concentrations (and hence particulates)
recorded in Britain occurred over Northern Ireland (HMSO, 1980). There is
nothing to suggest that current cleaner air conditions have ameliorated the
deleterious effects of historic air pollution on stone, effects which accumulated over many decades.

THE INTERIM

Time will be needed to reach a final and appropriate solution to the problem, but there is good reason to proceed with interim measures, in particular the taking of moulds of structures under threat. Taking moulds, although not at present affording actual protection for carvings at risk, does offer two benefits. The first is an up-to-date three-dimensional record of the present state of the High Crosses. The second, arising directly from the first, is a base from which to create the best possible outdoor replacements in the future. Taking moulds now, before weathering gets any worse, and from these moulds making casts, is also a practical and relatively inexpensive way forward, even if the use of latex rubber is avoided in preference to more expensive silicone rubber (Watkinson, 1982; Bryce, *et al.*, 1991). Currently, moulding can be accomplished with very little risk to delicate stone surfaces, either from plucking or staining (Maish, 1994), provided that suitable release agents are applied.

One major advantage of the proposal to copy anew is that it will provide a means of comparing the current state of carvings with that recorded during an earlier programme carried out by the Irish Board of Works around the turn of the present century. Unfortunately, at that time, the Commissioners did not comprehensively document their work in any formal publication. Nevertheless, this programme produced a number of extremely impressive plaster casts of High Crosses, many of which were exhibited in the Rotunda at the National Museum in Dublin. The main objective then was to satisfy a remote audience, enthusiastic after reading groundbreaking studies on the ornamentation of the country's High Crosses (Allen, 1887; Stokes, 1898, 1901), but unable to visit the sites of the originals. These plaster copies have, however, provided invaluable evidence of the condition of individual pieces, allowing comparison with their current state. Information from recorded site visits, drawings and photographs taken during the intervening years as well as from a number of more advanced techniques for measuring surface regression, have also been useful in assessing surface change over time. However, many of these sources of information benefit from having a datable baseline provided by the now, rather elderly plaster casts (Carelli, *et al.*, 1990; Conti, 1991).

Generally speaking, the picture that emerges from comparing old casts with latter-day records, particularly photographs, is not good. A case exists, therefore, for giving the highest priority to making a further series of copies of the northern Crosses and Cross shafts. Modern moulding would be done using high quality synthetic rubber with good long-term dimensional stability. Each rubber mould, by way of an intermediate cast, could be converted into an additional plaster mould for a more permanent record. Stored correctly, plaster is the best medium to use when the desired result is clarity of fine detail. Plaster casts may be made from the plaster mould at any time providing a long-term record of surface condition, but the correct separating agent must be applied to the plaster mould when casting from it in the same material.

For ordinary study or display purposes, perhaps in more than one place at the same time, and certainly for outdoor replacements, further casts from the original rubber mould are possible in a wide variety of casting materials including fibre glass reinforced polyester resin, as long as the substance used does not damage the rubber mould. Casting with an artificial stone mix, for example, would appreciably shorten the useful life of any rubber because of its abrasive nature.

COST

One cannot place an absolute figure on the expenditure needed to accomplish a large-scale programme involving perhaps thirty-five pieces of varying complexity, spread over several field seasons and inevitably subject to inflationary pressures. However, the copy of the Kilnasaggart Pillar Stone (Fry and Martin, 1994) cost relatively little but this is one of Northern Ireland's smaller crosses. A true High Cross like the one at Arboe in County Tyrone which is 5.7 metres tall (Figure 22.3) would cost much more to copy.

Figure 22.3 The Arboe High Cross, County Tyrone. (Photograph Crown Copyright.)

Despite the cost, the goodwill likely to accrue from such a public demonstration of care may well reap a long-term dividend in the form of later more effective steps aimed at tackling the underlying problem by moving the Crosses indoors.

CONCLUSION

Taking fresh moulds of High Crosses, sometime after the first such undertaking in Ireland, will put in place a better structure for monitoring future change in the condition of copied stone while it remains outdoors. While taking non-interventionist conservation almost to its theoretical limit this method does not address the source of the problem, solutions to which remain pressing – not only in Ireland but also internationally (Rosvall and Aleby, 1988; Last and Watling, 1991). However, making copies of High Crosses and stone carvings at risk is probably as good a defence as any against the charge of failing to act at all.

Omnia mutantur, nos et al mutamur in illis

Acknowledgements

The authors would like to thank Mr Cormac Bourke of the Ulster Museum's Antiquities Department for many exchanges of ideas on the subjects discussed. This paper is published by permission of the Environment Service, Department of the Environment for Northern Ireland.

References

Allen, R.J. (1887) *Early Christian Symbolism in Great Britain and Ireland.* Whiting, London.

Bourke, C. and Fry, M.F. (1989) Outdoors or in? The future of Ireland's stone Crosses. *Archaeology Ireland* **3**: 68–71.

Bowler, C. and Brimblecombe, P. (1991) Long-term stone decay at York Minster. *European Cultural Heritage Newsletter on Research* **5**: 47–57.

Bruno, A. (1987) Protecting and preserving the column of Marcus Aurelius. *Museum* (Paris, UNESCO) **39**: 3–7.

Bryce, T., Quinn, A., Hogg, D. and Skinner, T. (1991) Moulding and casting of large scale stone monuments. *The Conservator* **15**: 57–64.

Butlin, R.N. (1991) Effects of air pollutants on building materials. *Proceedings of the Royal Society Edinburgh* **97B**: 255–272.

Camuffo, D. (1989) The Aurelian Column: can individual solutions resolve the general problems? *European Cultural Heritage Newsletter on Research* **3**: 5–8.

Carelli, P., Paoletti, D. and Schirripa Spagnolo, G. (1990) Multiple-source holography for artwork erosion measurements. *Studies in Conservation* **35**: 64–68.

Caroe, M.B. (1979) Wells Cathedral, the West Front: policy and techniques. *Association for Studies in the Conservation of Historic Buildings, Transactions* **4**: 43–44.

Committee on Conservation of Historic Stone Buildings and Monuments (1982) *Conservation of Historic Stone Buildings and Monuments.* National Academy Press, Washington DC.

Conti, W. (1991) A method for the evaluation of material loss from bas-reliefs due to air pollution. *Materiali e Strutture*, **1**: 12–26. Also abstracted in *European Cultural Heritage Newsletter on Research* (1991) **5**: 21–22.

Cooper, T.P. (1994) Effects of air pollution on historic buildings and monuments. Scientific basis for conservation: air pollution levels, stone decay rates and their interrelation at historic monuments. *European Cultural Heritage Newsletter on Research* **8**: 13–21.

Del Monte, M. (1992) Stone monuments and air pollution: magnification of damage caused by previous biodegradation phenomena. *European Cultural Heritage Newsletter on Research* **6**: 23–30.

Delopoulou, P. and Sikiotis, D. (1991) Dry deposition of nitrates on the Parthenon. *The Science of the Total Environment* **106**: 263–268.

Elfving, P., Johansson, L.–G. and Lindqvist, O. (1994) A study of the sulphation of silane-treated sandstone and limestone in a sulphur dioxide atmosphere. *Studies in Conservation* **39**: 199–209.

Fry, M.F. (1985) The problem of ornamental stonework – lichen. *Stone Industries* **20**: 22–25.

Fry, M.F. and Martin, A. (1994) Preserving by copying. *Archaeology Ireland* **8**: 13.

Harbison, P. (1992) *The High Crosses of Ireland.* (3 Vols). Bonn, Habelt.

HMSO (1980) *Facts in focus.* Central Statistical Office, HMSO/Penguin.

King, H. (1992) Moving Crosses. *Archaeology Ireland*, **6**: 22–23.

Last, F.T. and Watling, R. (eds) (1991) Acid deposition: its nature and impacts. *Proceedings of the Royal Society of Edinburgh* **97B**.

Lazzarini, L. and Pieper, R. (eds) (1988) The deterioration and conservation of stone. *Studies and Documents on the Cultural Heritage* **16**. UNESCO, Paris.

Livingston, R.A. (1991) Dose-response functions versus damage functions for materials effects studies. *European Cultural Heritage Newsletter on Research* **5**: 9–12.

Maish, J.P. (1994) Silicone rubber staining of terracotta surfaces. *Studies in Conservation* **39**: 250–256.

Marsh, P. (1977) Breathing new life into the statues of Wells. *New Scientist* **76** (1083): 754–756.

Nimbus Conservation Ltd. (1993) Conservation of the West Front, Bath Abbey. *Conservation News* **51**: 13–14.

Odgers, D. (1992) Limewatering. *Conservation News*, **48**: 23–24.

Price, C.A. (1981) *Brethane Stone Preservative.* Current Paper CP1/81. Building Research Establishment, Watford.

Price, C. A. (1988) A further appraisal of the lime technique for limestone consolidation, using a radioactive tracer. *Studies in Conservation* **33**: 178–186.

Richardson, H. and Scarry, J. (1990) *An Introduction to Irish High Crosses.* Mercier, Cork and Dublin.

Rosvall, J. and Aleby, S. (eds) (1988) *Air pollution and Conservation: Safeguarding our Architectural Heritage.* Elsevier, Amsterdam.

Sabbioni, C. (1991) The weathering of sandstone monuments in urban areas. *European Cultural Heritage Newsletter on Research* **5**: 10–16.

Sabbioni, C. (1994) Effects of air pollution on historic buildings and monuments. Scientific basis for conservation: physical, chemical and biological weathering. *European Cultural Heritage Newsletter on Research* **8**: 2–6.

Sikiotis, D., Delopoulou, Ph. and Kirkitsos, Ph. (1992) Effects of air pollution on historical buildings and monuments, and the scientific basis for conservation. (Dry deposition of air pollutants on Athenian monuments.) *European Cultural Heritage Newsletter on Research* **6**: 7–9.

Stokes, M. (1898) *The High Crosses of Castledermot and Durrow.* Dublin.

Stokes, M. (1901) Notes on the High Crosses of Moone, Drumcliff, Termonfechin and Killamery. *Transactions of the Royal Irish Academy* **31**: 541–578.

Warscheid, T., Petersen, K and Krumbein, W. E. (1990) A rapid method to demonstrate and evaluate microbial activity on decaying sandstone. *Studies in Conservation* **35**: 137–147.

Watkinson, D. (1982) Making a large-scale replica: the Pillar of Elise. *The Conservator* **6**: 6–11.

Contact address
Environment Service
Historic Monuments and Buildings
Department of the Environment (NI)
5–33 Hill Street
Belfast
BT1 2LA
United Kingdom